Mapping the Fiction of Cristina Fernández Cubas

Mapping the Fiction of Cristina Fernández Cubas

Edited by
Kathleen M. Glenn and Janet Pérez

DELAWARE

Newark: University of Delaware Press

*566 14378

Associated University Presses
2010 Eastpark Boulevard
Cranbury, NJ 08512

The paper used in this publication meets the requirements of the American National Standard for Permanence of Paper for Printed Library Materials Z39.48-1984.

Library of Congress Cataloging-in-Publication Data

Mapping the fiction of Cristina Fernández Cubas / edited by Kathleen M. Glenn and Janet Pérez.
    p.   cm.
    Includes bibliographical references and index.
    ISBN 0-87413-905-8 (alk. paper)
    1. Fernández Cubas, Cristina, 1945—Criticism and interpretation.   I. Glenn, Kathleen Mary.   II. Pérez, Janet.
    PQ6656.E72138Z73   2005
    863'.64—dc22   2004059836

Contents

Acknowledgment

EXCERPTS FROM "OMAR, AMOR," *MI HERMANA ELBA Y LOS ALTILLOS DE Brumal, El año de Gracia, El ángulo del horror, Con Agatha en Estambul, El columpio, Hermanas de sangre* and *Cosas que ya no existen* are reprinted with the generous permission of Cristina Fernández Cubas and Mercedes Casanovas, her literary agent.

Mapping the Fiction
of Cristina Fernández
Cubas

Introduction: Of Kitchens and Attics, Journeys and Quests

Kathleen M. Glenn and Janet Pérez

CRISTINA FERNÁNDEZ CUBAS IS, WITHOUT QUESTION, ONE OF THE MOST important of the Spanish writers who have begun to publish since the end of the Franco dictatorship. She is credited with playing a major role in the renaissance of the short story in Spain, winning national and international acclaim for her fiction. Works by her have been translated into eight languages and have become a staple of university courses on contemporary Peninsular literature. Fernández Cubas has created a remarkably coherent narrative world, nourished by a core of fundamental concerns. Mario Vargas Llosa recently compared writers to striptease artists and commented that the two differ primarily in that the former exhibit not their secret charms but the demons that torment and obsess them. The present volume exposes both the obsessions and the literary attractions of Fernández Cubas.

If we were to select one text as the perfect introduction to her fiction, that text might well be "Los altillos de Brumal" [The Attics of Brumal]. The toponym Brumal, based on the word *bruma* [mist, fog], evokes images of the confusion that swirls through her stories and novels, and the word *altillo* [attic] has special resonance for Fernández Cubas, who lives in an *ático* or top-floor apartment in Barcelona and has acknowledged a lifelong interest in *altillos*, which she describes as closed, rather mysterious spaces. Adriana, the narrator and protagonist of "Los altillos de Brumal," studies to achieve a degree in history to please her mother but is irresistibly drawn to cooking and kitchens. An exceptionally imaginative and adventurous cook, she creates vegetable soups without vegetables and fish fillets without fish, and her call for ancient recipes leads to the arrival of a wonderfully aromatic jar of strawberry jam that, she is convinced, contains neither berries nor sugar. Like a Proustian madeleine, it

11

triggers a flood of memories of the village where she spent the first seven years of her life and prompts the decision to journey back to Brumal, where she was known as Anairda and shared with her playmates a secret language based on the principle of inversion. Her brief stay in the village abounds in occurrences that defy all logic. Locked in an attic filled with strange equipment that is suggestive of alchemy or witchcraft, she hears voices calling for Anairda and experiences a vision of herself as a child. At the story's end Adriana decides to abandon her study of history, silence the voices of reason, and return to Brumal, whose name appears on no map. This rich and paradigmatic tale, with its literal and metaphoric journeys and insistence on *juego,* meaning both "game" and "play," foregrounds difference and absence. Problems of identity formation and the vagaries of memory lie just beneath the story's surface.

Issues of identity are paramount in Fernández Cubas's fiction. Doubles and reflecting surfaces proliferate as characters struggle to construct and maintain a sense of identity in a world that is fundamentally confusing and resists comprehension. Indecipherability and unreliability are leitmotifs of her writing, and she highlights both by means of untrustworthy narrators or limited narrative consciousnesses, narrative erasure, temporal and/or spatial vagueness, inclusion of Gothic elements and events, as well as a rhetoric of ambiguity. Character after character wrestles with linguistic and cultural signs, and national identity proves as elusive as personal identity and as much in need of constant renegotiation. Whereas a sense of place used to be perceived as an essential component of self, in the world of Fernández Cubas it does not fulfill that role. The settings of her narratives are frequently unspecified or foreign, and characters find themselves at sea (in her ironical version of *Robinson Crusoe*) or confronted with otherness (in tales set in Arab countries or in Scandinavia). The voyage motif, fundamental in this writer's fiction, not only evokes the conventional symbolism of life as a journey, but also repeatedly functions as a means to intensify the strangeness and indecipherability of the contexts in which her characters find themselves. Careful readers will note numerous works of Fernández Cubas that begin and end with a journey or for which the journey provides a framing device. Moreover, the journey often spurs the decision of the narrative consciousness to write. Given the slipperiness of language, Fernández Cubas's fictive writers and storytellers are unsurprisingly frustrated in their narrative endeavors.

Fernández Cubas also explores the nature of memory and history, an area of special concern in present-day Spain now that Franco is dead and many Spaniards recognize the need to recuperate a past long swept under a figurative rug. Indeed, this urgently felt need to understand the recent past and to revise the warped versions of twentieth-century Spanish history purveyed by official historiography of the Franco regime has given rise to one of the major narrative trends of Spain's era of democracy: the *nueva novela histórica* [new historical novel]. This phenomenon subverts official historiography, mocks its discourse, and often rehabilitates villains of the past or rescues marginalized characters from oblivion. Fernández Cubas shares a similar point of departure in her preoccupation with history and memory, but her plots generally depend less upon the collective or national and delve more deeply into the individual and subjective. Acquaintance with the coeval production of the new historical novel helps to illuminate aspects of *El año de Gracia* [The Year of Grace], for example, although its reference is more to international than national historiography.

A host of women writers began their literary careers after the dictator's demise in 1975: Carme Riera, Esther Tusquets, Lourdes Ortiz, Soledad Puértolas, Marina Mayoral, Rosa Montero, Paloma Díaz-Mas, Adelaida García Morales, Mercedes Abad, Almudena Grandes, Isabel-Clara Simó, Rosa Regàs, Nuria Amat, Clara Sánchez, Dulce Chacón, Olga Guirao, Belén Gopegui, Juana Salabert, Luisa Castro, Lucía Etxebarria, Angela Vallvey, Espido Freire, as well as a number of younger novelists. "Feminist" is a problematic term in Spain and, like many of the above-mentioned authors, Fernández Cubas insists that she is not a feminist writer. During a May 1991 conversation that took place in conjunction with the symposium "Female Discourses," held at the University of California, Los Angeles, Abad affirmed that she is not a spokesperson for her sex, and Puértolas rejected the idea that as a female author she should shed light on the world of women. Fernández Cubas was more categorical, asserting that "ninguno de nuestros libros se puede considerar feminista. . . . Y es que literatura y feminismo no tienen nada que ver" [none of our books can be considered feminist. . . . The fact is that literature and feminism have nothing to do with each other].[1] The three authors alleged that critics try to force writing by women into a specific framework or straitjacket, and Fernández Cubas used the feminine image of a corset to describe this situation: "Hay un corsé e intenta[n] que nuestro texto encaje en el corsé. Es como un corsé de talla única y que, sea una señora oronda o una señora delgadísima, pues a todas nos tiene que ir" [There is a corset and people try to make our text fit within it. The corset comes in only one size and has to fit all of us, fat or thin].[2] These attacks must be understood in the context of the history of feminism in Spain where for much of the post-Franco era, feminism was essentially synonymous with a certain political party and a specific political agenda, both more regimented and radical than the majority of women writers. Behind the protests voiced by Abad, Puértolas, and Fernández Cubas lie the identification of feminist writing with advocacy and the assumption that it lacks literary merit. Fernández Cubas wants her work to be taken seriously and valued for its artistic quality, which is exceptionally high.

Fernández Cubas's fascination with storytelling and the mysterious stems from her childhood. Born in 1945 in Arenys de Mar, a seaside town north of Barcelona, Cristina was the fourth of five children of a prosperous family. She spent her first fifteen years in a three-story, book-filled house which lacked an attic but did have strange rooms filled with useless objects that evoked images of other eras. Attention to language and narration have always been important parts of her life. Her father, a notary public by profession, devoted himself to the ambitious project of preparing a dictionary in all the languages of the world and thus foreshadowed his daughter's persistent search, as a writer, for the appropriate word. Cristina was fortunate to have as her nursemaid Antonia García Pagès, a woman who was blessed with a seemingly inexhaustible supply of stories and capable of captivating her listeners for hours on end. This consummate teller of tales served as the model for the character Olvido in "El reloj de Bagdad" [The Clock from Baghdad]. Cristina's brother Pedro, with his retelling of stories by Poe, awakened her interest in the American writer and the art of suggestion. Years later, after she read "The Fall of the House of Usher," Fernández Cubas wryly confessed to being struck by Poe's "omission" of several details that were present in her brother's version. She has often professed her admiration for oral narration.[3] Her *Cosas que ya no existen* [Things That No Longer Exist] celebrates the act and art of storytelling, and she uses the image of a game of table tennis to describe a wonderful afternoon in Palma de Mallorca when stories flew back and forth, following one another at a dizzying pace as one narrator stimulated another.[4] In this fascination with the storyteller's art and especially the oral act, Fernández Cubas echoes an abiding preoccupation of the late Carmen Martín Gaite who before her recent death had become the dean of living Spanish women writers. Martín Gaite's essay *El cuento de nunca acabar* [Never-Ending Story] relates her lifelong quest for the essence of narrative and links with another essay collection, *La búsqueda de interlocutor y otras búsquedas* [The Search for an Interlocutor and Other Searches], which expounds her theory of the key role of the listener or reader. Fernández Cubas explores these same issues in several tales which revolve around storytellers and/or would-be writers: "La noche de Jezabel" [The Night of Jezebel], "En el hemisferio sur" [In the Southern Hemisphere], and "Lúnula y Violeta" [Lunula and Violet], among others.

Fernández Cubas's early education was at a Catholic school, where she was a day student. She has given lasting form to one of her memorable experiences there in *Cosas que ya no existen*, which is composed of a series of *historias. Historia*, like *juego*, can be translated in more than one way, as "history" and as "story." The Spanish word can refer to what has happened or what might have happened, to truth or to invention. "Truth," however, is a slippery concept and the line between reality and fiction, memory and imagination, is indeed tenuous, as Fernández Cubas acknowledges. Concerning the first *historia* of the book, she declares that "a ratos tenía el aspecto de un cuento, aunque no lo fuera" [at times it resembled a story, even if it wasn't] (12). It is a fine example of Fernández Cubas's skillful use of first-person narration, creation of sharply defined characters, and effective use of humor. The opening sentences call attention to the search for the right term: "Pongamos que se llamase Luisa. Sor Luisa. Y que ella, Sor Luisa, me hubiera cogido tirria desde los primeros días. O quizás ojeriza, manía, odio... O tal vez otra palabra que todavía no se ha inventado" [Let's assume that her name was Luisa. Sister Luisa. And that she, Sister Luisa, had taken an instant dislike to me. Or perhaps a grudge, antipathy, hatred... Or perhaps another word not yet invented] (17). Sor Luisa, a name chosen to spare the guilty party, delights in humiliating and frightening the eleven-year-olds in her charge. The antithesis of Christian humility and charity, she boasts of being the daughter of a diplomat, which she is not, and cultivates an air of superiority. On an extremely flimsy pretext she shuts Cristina up in a freezing room and orders her to remain there while the nuns decide if she is to be expelled. Once she is liberated, the child turns the tables on the adult who has committed such an outrage against her, questioning everything Sor Luisa says and looking at her with a half-smile on her lips, making clear that she won't let the nun best her. Especially well drawn is the portrait of the small girl, trembling with cold and fear, horrified by the thought of how her father will react to being disturbed during office hours by the news of the expulsion she believes to be imminent. She never informs her parents of the episode, because she wants to keep the worlds of home and school separate, but the adult Fernández Cubas relishes imagining how her mother, a firm believer in proper nutrition and hygiene, would have responded had she known that her daughter had been confined to a figurative icebox and deprived of lunch and bathroom breaks.

Fernández Cubas attended secondary school in Barcelona, living with her older sister Pilar and brother Pedro in the family's flat in the city. At the University she followed the example of her father and brother and enrolled in law school, not because she ever intended to be a lawyer but because she thought law would provide a good mental discipline. Like Adriana, her real interests lay elsewhere and she devoted much of her time to a theater group. While still a child Cristina had begun to write as a form of entertainment, and she proudly signed her detective novels as "La gata Cristi" [Cristi the Cat], a punning tribute to Agatha Christie. During her late teens and early twenties, however, she stopped writing because shutting herself up in a room, cut off from the outside world, would have been too great a sacrifice. She preferred to open herself to stimulating contact with other people. Acting was now the medium in which she chose to express herself, and her interest in drama would lead years later to the play *Hermanas de sangre* [Blood Sisters]. She also studied journalism and pursued it as a career until she decided that it was incompatible with her literary writing. As she puts it, her typewriter finally rebelled and after transcribing factual material by day it refused to venture into the realms of imagination by night.[5] It is not merely "typewriter rebellion," however, but also a certain reticence on the author's part that strictly limits the amount of material available on her life. For one who has published a book of memoirs and given several interviews, she has told remarkably little about certain aspects of her adult life, successfully guarding her right to privacy. Fortunately, she has revealed much that helps to understand the genesis and meaning of her fiction.

Fernández Cubas's love of travel, perhaps first awakened by the trains that passed close by the family house in Arenys de Mar and the model ships in the family library, led to extensive travel in Latin America in 1974 and 1975. Stays in Cairo at the decade's end, in Berlin in the late eighties, where she spent a year on a fellowship, and in Athens in 1994 afforded the opportunity to study Arabic, German, and Greek. Many fictions of Fernández Cubas evince her abiding interest in languages, spurred at an early age by her father's undertaking of the quixotic, impossible enterprise of the universal dictionary. The quest for meaning (of a hermetic word, sign, or gesture) constitutes another recurring feature of her writing traceable to childhood. Unlike many writers who have some experience with other languages, Fernández Cubas does not pepper her fiction with foreign words; instead, her stories communicate the sense of mystery and fascination generated by unknown signs and symbols, alien systems of writing and thought. Repeatedly in her fiction, a perceived message is an enigma, as in "Los altillos de Brumal," "Lúnula y Violeta," "En el hemisferio sur," "Con Agatha en Estambul" [With Agatha in Istanbul], "La ventana del jardín" [The Garden Window], and "La Flor de España" [The Flower of Spain].

Interviewers frequently ask authors about the creative process. Fernández Cubas declares that when she begins to write she has a general idea about what she will narrate, but that idea changes. It is the unforeseen discoveries and the way characters grow or diminish in importance or a story veers off in a new direction that make writing an exciting adventure for her. Narratives, she emphasizes, are governed by secret norms, norms that writers themselves are unaware of, and what literary critics may have to say on the subject should be taken with the proverbial grain of salt.[6]

Fernández Cubas enjoys moving between the concision of the short story, in which every word is measured, and the greater amplitude of the novel, which allows her the freedom to digress. She suggests that the coherence of her fiction may be due in part to the fact that she did not begin to publish until she was in her thirties and had a clear idea of the kind of narrative world she wished to explore. Above all, she affirms, she is intrigued by human emotions (envy, jealousy, despair, fear), the working of the mind, especially in limit situations, and dreams.[7] What is not seen, not named, looms large in her fiction, and she deals preferentially less with the tangible world than with "una zona de límites imprecisos. Una zona de grises y claroscuros" [an area whose limits are imprecise. An area of various shades of gray and chiaroscuros].[8] Fernández Cubas is a firm believer in dreams. On more than one occasion the initial impulse for a story or even its nucleus and title, as in the case of "El ángulo del horror" [The Angle of Horror], have come to her in a dream.

In an interview published in 1991, she commented on the frequency with which she has treated the theme of childhood, not just because of her conviction that it is an exceedingly important period but also because of her belief that the prism through which children see the world and their code of values, so different from that of adults, can be used to great effect.[9] Several Spanish women writers from the Franco era are known especially for their sensitive and insightful characterizations of children and adolescents, among them Carmen Laforet, Elena Quiroga, Martín Gaite, and Mercè Rodoreda. But it is Ana María Matute whose peculiar, lyric vision of the special world of the child most clearly forecasts the manner in which Fernández Cubas views the child's perspective and values: both authors accord a crucial role to innocence, a lack of knowledge of the adult world and of developmental experiences that strip away the veil. In several of Matute's stories, loss of innocence means the end of childhood, often symbolized by death, and several parallels can be found in Fernández Cubas. Her stories "Mi hermana Elba" [My Sister Elba] and "El legado del abuelo" [Grandfather's Legacy], in particular, attest to the literary effectiveness of the "innocent" eye.

The contributors to *Mapping the Fiction of Cristina Fernández Cubas* are distinguished Hispanists, most of whom have published previously on Fernández Cubas. In their essays they employ a variety of critical and theoretical approaches, including reader-oriented, poststructural, and postcolonial, as well as a cultural studies perspective and various forms of psychoanalytical and feminist readings. Despite Fernández Cubas's vehement rejection of the label "feminist," feminist criticism illuminates certain facets of her work. While some of the essays that follow look at a single text, others examine several. As a group, the essays contribute to the current lively debate on issues of gender, the construction of subjectivity, language, nationality, and memory. The initial studies of our book deal with Fernández Cubas's stories, which have been published in four volumes: *Mi hermana Elba* [My Sister Elba] (1980) and *Los altillos de Brumal* [The Attics of Brumal] (1983), reissued together in 1988, *El ángulo del horror* [The Angle of Horror] (1990), and *Con Agatha en Estambul* [With Agatha in Istanbul] (1994). The remaining essays concentrate on the novels *El año de Gracia* [The Year of Grace] (1985) and *El columpio* [The Swing] (1995), the drama *Hermanas de sangre* [Blood Sisters] (1998), and the book of memoirs *Cosas que ya no existen* [Things That No Longer Exist] (2001).

Ana Rueda, drawing on psychological theory as well as literary history and criticism, investigates the figure of the double in "Lúnula y

Violeta" and "Helicón" [Helicon]. Rueda's arguments here concerning the uses and effects of the literary double update her earlier discussions of the subject and align with historical and critical insights that link doubling with the literary Gothic. Rueda centers on four concerns to which Fernández Cubas gives literary figuration through her use of the double: 1) the contradictory origins of writing, 2) practices of artistic imitation and rivalry, 3) the insuperable mismatch between oral and written discourse, and 4) the comical effects of artistic redoubling or what one may call doubling the double. Finally, she considers how, as self-conscious works, the two narratives studied duplicate (double) and exemplify the thematics of doubleness in their very structure. As short stories that are for, against, and about short stories, they adopt a "Siamese discourse" with competing story lines that split in two. They point, therefore, to the impossibility of their producing a "single, unifying effect," a formula previously invoked by authors and critics of the short story to describe the genre's presumptive "essence."

National identity, as Maryellen Bieder observes, is a recurrent preoccupation in Spanish fiction in the last decades of the twentieth century. Bieder elucidates how Fernández Cubas dramatizes the postmodern interplay of geography, nationality, and identity in two extraordinary stories, "La Flor de España" and "Con Agatha en Estambul." The first-person narrators of both tales are women who negotiate their Spanishness from outside Spain. Isolation from a familiar culture and a common language shapes their ongoing process of identity construction, destabilizes their reading of cultural signs, and calls into question the portability of national identity. Bieder points out that in these works, as in others, Fernández Cubas builds on the postmodern awareness that representations, including artifacts and performances, are politically and culturally constructed, although the unreliable narrators of her fictions are frequently oblivious to this constructedness. In "La Flor de España" and "Con Agatha en Estambul" nationality, language, and gender are performances—sustained at times, at others transitory—that produce a possible if constantly shifting construction of Spanishness as an other of the foreign culture in which the stories take place. The flickering ñ in the sign outside the store, La Flor de España, that sells the products of Spain in Scandinavia and the mutable fish in the hotel fish tank in Istanbul figure the "category crisis" of women that are—and are not—Spanish, are—and are not—other, as they continuously renegotiate their relationship to nation, language, and gender.

Place is again prominent in the next essay, in which Nancy Vosburg examines all the stories of *Con Agatha en Estambul* and inquires how Fernández Cubas exploits the paradoxical nature of the uncanny to create unsettling worlds for her narrators and her readers. These uncanny worlds fill the fictional characters with dread as they cross boundaries into "foreign" terrains. Yet as the stories progress, a gradual movement away from the uncanny occurs as the characters come to recognize or accept a certain familiarity within these new worlds. Sigmund Freud's 1919 exploration of the uncanny, or *unheimlich*, proves a useful tool for understanding the shift in these narratives from a situation of initial horror or apprehension to a recognition of the new place as something "long-known and familiar," spaces that the characters make or accept as "home-like," or *heimlich*. As a result, a common unifying theme of the desire to be other, or in another's place, initially configured as a crossing into an alien, or "other," world, eventually leads the characters to "home." According to Vosburg, this underlying theme can be found in many of Fernández Cubas's earlier narratives as well, situating the author's oeuvre in the realm of the uncanny, rather than the fantastic.

Elizabeth Scarlett affords further insights into a particular kind of milieu. Her essay seeks an understanding of the meaning of Islam and of Arabic and Near Eastern cultures in Fernández Cubas's works by returning to each of the texts in which Near Eastern or Islamic settings or characters play an important role. Scarlett interprets "Omar, amor" [Omar, My Love] as the extension of Egyptian cultural and religious syncretism to the handling of narrative time and space, and she probes the sexual and postcolonial significance of this enigmatic love story. She then investigates the multiplicity of belief systems in "Mi hermana Elba," the role of the Iraqi-made timepiece in "El reloj de Bagdad," and the significance of the sailor Naguib in *El año de Gracia*. Lastly, Scarlett discusses the title story of *Con Agatha en Estambul*, whose Western European protagonist uses the Eastern city as an escape from her usual holiday routines and discovers a new sense of self-direction through contact with Agatha Christie and a local family. Scarlett concludes that in all instances Islamic and Arabic figures and settings provide an encouragement to the Fantastic, destabilizing the assumptions of Western civilization and calling attention to the deforming influence of the Orientalizing gaze.

The problem of subjectivity and its representation in/through language engages Akiko Tsuchiya. Fernández Cubas's characters typically find themselves living "on the boundary," struggling with psychic issues of self and otherness, unconscious fears and desires, repressed memories, and uncanny events that defy rational explanation. Consequently, her works have lent themselves to a variety of psychoanalytic approaches. Concentrating on "En el hemisferio sur" and *El columpio*, Tsuchiya explores the way in which Fernández Cubas appropriates the psychoanalytic paradigm to comment on the nature of representation itself, particularly in relation to the formation of subjectivities. In this context, the author's use of repetition proves noteworthy, as does the literary reenactment of similar scenarios from work to work, beginning with her early short stories and continuing through *Cosas que ya no existen*. Narrative becomes a form of repetition-compulsion through which the narrating subject seeks to recapture the past symbolically. In the end, however, the repetitive gestures of language can lead only to a consciousness of the impossibility of return, of recuperating that which has been lost forever: innocence, integrity, and the satisfaction of desire. In Fernández Cubas's works, the construction of subjectivities seems inseparable from the literary process: fiction brings to light what is inherently literary in the narrative of subject-formation, by reflecting self-consciously on the literary nature of the psychoanalytic narrative.

The next block of essays focuses on Fernández Cubas's novels. *El año de Gracia* has been much analyzed. We reprint here Catherine G. Bellver's 1992 essay from *Studies in Twentieth Century Literature*. Linguistic problems and issues of communication, central in Fernández Cubas's first story, "La ventana del jardín," have continued to preoccupy her. Bellver pays special attention to how the 1985 novel undermines both written and oral discourses. The protagonist, Daniel, initially sees himself and the world around him through the lens of the books and stories he has read, notably *Treasure Island, Robinson Crusoe*, and the Bible. His experiences, however, consistently contradict his literary models, which are subverted by inversion and erasure. Similarly, Daniel's knowledge of Greek and Latin is of no help in his attempt to communicate with the island's sole human inhabitant, the shepherd Grock, whose language is a mixture of English and Gaelic, and when Daniel reads the Bible aloud to Grock, it is not the meaning of the words but their sound and rhythm, the semiotic dimension of language, that enthralls the shepherd. Bellver argues in her essay that *El año de Gracia* "reveals a world in which the ability of literature to sustain meaning is problematic and meaning itself becomes irrelevant."

Janet Pérez examines the second novel, *El columpio,* through the lens of Julia Kristeva's concept of the Abject, a concept which illuminates much of the Spanish writer's fiction. According to Kristeva's formulation, everything related to biological reproduction and the physiological (as opposed to the "spiritual" or "clean and proper" side of humanity) becomes unmentionable and therefore marginalized, negated or, in her terminology, "abjected." Abjection defines what may be seen (legitimately observed and acknowledged) and what must remain unseen (silenced and hidden), provoking otherwise inexplicable reversals of behavior, deformations, or metamorphoses of perception, and the denial of events or characters previously "seen." Pérez demonstrates that such instances abound in *El columpio,* where perceptions turn murky, incidents previously discussed are negated or distorted, the faces in portraits cease to be identifiable, and an initially transparent world becomes opaque. The gap between appearance and reality widens as the narrator moves into a realm where nothing is what it first seems to be. In addition, Pérez detects in the novel a subtext of generational differences. The status of the daughter, who is free to mature, contrasts with that of women of her mother's generation, treated as perpetual children by the Franco regime.

Psychoanalytical feminist theory grounds the subsequent essay, in which Silvia Bermúdez studies the ambivalent ways in which *El columpio* addresses the complex mother-daughter bond. She finds useful Marianne Hirsch's assertion that the two figures form a double self, "a continuous multiple being of monstrous proportions stretched across generations, parts of which try desperately to separate and delineate their own boundaries." While *El columpio* establishes, at one level, the daughter's identification with the mother, Bermúdez argues in her essay that a desire for autonomy ultimately sustains the novel. She contends that by foregrounding the unconscious and the uncanny in a hauntingly spectral encounter between the daughter and the dead mother, the novel challenges the oedipal story of cultural development and forces us to recognize the ambivalence of our cultural desires in relation to mothers and motherhood.

John B. Margenot III approaches the 1995 novel from another angle, that of the problematics surrounding authorship and composition in a text that is highly self-conscious and whose narrator must constantly employ strategies to frustrate other characters' efforts to dominate her. Margenot considers a number of narrative strategies that lay bare the fictional artifice, in particular those related to epistolary writing, role-playing, and games. The level of playfulness exhibited by characters who behave like children and inhabit insular spaces highlights the centripetal nature of discourse in *El columpio*. Margenot also discusses the narrator's use of a semantic field related to literature, especially the theatrical presentation of characters on the world stage, as well as their awareness of literary models and novelistic devices.

Although *Hermanas de sangre* has not yet been staged, the play has been transformed into a made-for-television movie filmed in Catalan and then dubbed to Castilian Spanish. Phyllis Zatlin analyzes the original drama and compares it to the film adaptation, which amplifies the story line and expands the role of certain characters. The play's plot centers on the reunion of seven women, now in their forties, who attended Catholic boarding school together as children. Zatlin observes that the basic situation holds out the potential pitfall of having a narrative voice take command as the women remember the past and recount their lives, and the structure runs the risk of being unoriginal: the reunion of old classmates is hardly a new device. Fernández Cubas, however, adroitly avoids these pitfalls and creates a dramatic work that offers a gripping psychological suspense tale.

Our final essay concerns *Cosas que ya no existen*. David K. Herzberger reminds us that contemporary literature often seems to efface history, leaving the reader with nothing but the artifice of text. Herzberger sees Fernández Cubas as both affirming and denying the availability of the past in *Cosas que ya no existen*. The awareness that parts of her own past have disappeared from consciousnesss and comprehension is countered by her desire to make them reappear through narration. Her awareness of an irrecoverable past allows her to exploit uncertainty in her favor. She understands that the past persists as a correlative of both the need and desire of an unformed self in the present, but she also perceives how that past is constructed by memory and narration and thus shaped by contingency, ambiguity, and even deceit. Within her writing she asserts the forceful need to make some sense of the past, in part simply to rescue the facts from oblivion. *Cosas que ya no existen* emerges for her as a very personal book in which the exploration of textual memory as the object and the subject of narration becomes paramount.

The scholars who have contributed to this book engage one another in dialogue as they examine from varying theoretical perspectives the intellectual preoccupations, narrative strategies, and rhetorical devices that distinguish the fiction of Cristina Fernández Cubas. Beyond trying to cover as many aspects of Fernández Cubas's work as possible, the editors have respected the intellectual freedom of the contributors, preferring not to impose or limit topics or approaches. The occasional treatment of a given text by more than one contributor results not so much in overlap as in alternative perspectives on that text, demonstrating the richness of hermeneutics offered by this author's ambiguous and sometimes indecipherable writings. Thus both the critical essays and Fernández Cubas's texts dialogue as well among themselves. We trust that this dialogue will inspire in readers a desire for further elucidation and celebration of the work of this gifted writer.

NOTES

1. Vicente Carmona, Jeffrey Lamb, Sherry Velasco, and Barbara Zecchi, "Conversando con Mercedes Abad, Cristina Fernández Cubas y Soledad Puértolas: 'Feminismo y literatura no tienen nada que ver,'" *Mester* 20:2 (1991): 158.
2. Ibid., 162.
3. See, for example, Geraldine C. Nichols, "Entrevista a Cristina Fernández Cubas," *España Contemporánea* 6 (1993): 59, and María del Mar López-Cabrales, "Cristina Fernández Cubas: Los horrores de la memoria," *Palabras de mujeres: Escritoras españolas contemporáneas* (Madrid: Narcea, 2000), 172.
4. *Cosas que ya no existen* (Barcelona: Lumen, 2001), 125. Subsequent references to this work will be cited parenthetically in the text.
5. Jochen Heymann and Montserrat Mullor-Heymann, "Cristina Fernández Cubas," *Retratos de escritorio: Entrevistas a autores españoles* (Frankfurt: Vervuert, 1991), 127.
6. Ibid., 121.
7. López-Cabrales, "Cristina Fernández Cubas," 175.
8. Kathleen M. Glenn, "Conversación con Cristina Fernández Cubas," *Anales de la Literatura Española Contemporánea* 18 (1993): 360.
9. Heymann and Mullor-Heymann, 120–21.

Effects of the Double in Cristina Fernández Cubas's Short Fiction

Ana Rueda

WE ARE FAMILIAR WITH THE LITERARY MOTIF OF THE DOUBLE OR *DOPPEL-gänger* through such classic examples as *The Strange Case of Dr. Jekyll and Mr. Hyde* by Robert Louis Stevenson, *The Double* by Fyodor Dostoevsky, *The Picture of Dorian Gray* by Oscar Wilde, and *The Woman in White* by Wilkie Collins. In these works, the authors often enlist the double to dramatize how such timeless contraries as the conscious and the unconscious, sanity and madness, good and evil, masculine and feminine, or even life and death, remain joined in oscillating relations of both strife and mutual dependence. What is more, these authors use these oppositions to explore the hidden sources of our sense of mystery, the uncanny, or the fearsome supernatural: that element that is so crucial for the human imagination.

According to Robert Rogers, the double conventionally presents an antithetical "I," configured either as a guardian angel or tempter demon.[1] This view, however canonical it may be, creates an impression that the motif of the double operates according to one rigid pattern. In fact, stories featuring doubles represent a wide range of configurational possibilities: they can be about split personalities inside the same identity (e.g., Dr. Jekyll and Mr. Hyde), about visions in which the "I" is reflected in an exact replica (e.g., Narcissus), about separate entities that physically resemble each other (e.g., the half-sisters in *The Woman in White)*, about multiple and semiautonomous characters that belong to a psychologically unified entity (e.g., the four Karamazov brothers or the three Miau sisters in the work of Galdós). The double, therefore, may refer to half of a duality, to a pair, or even to a group of interdependent characters. At times, the double signifies hostility between two antagonistic parts of the individual, symptomatic of the disintegration of the modern personality (the Freudian field of the rational and the irrational, the ego and

25

the alter ego). At other times, however, the division signifies comple-
mentarity, such as occurs with the primitive forces that represent the
soul (phantoms, voodoo dolls, the Golem, robots, and manne-
quins). But it is important to add that, beyond Rogers's categorical
division of the double as angel or devil, literary doubles may also
assume more complex patterns that combine various degrees of the
helpful, harmful, desirable, or undesirable.

In its pure form, or allied with other approaches, Freudian psychology has influenced the majority of studies on the literary double. With Rogers's short, classically Freudian study are aligned those
of Paul Coates, Carl F. Keppler, and Otto Rank.[2] The approach to
this topic used by Wilhelmine Krauss and Ralph Tymms brings literary and historical issues together.[3] Masao Miyoshi's *The Divided Self*
focuses on the psychology and sociology of nineteenth-century England, while *Fearful Symmetry,* the collection of essays edited by Eugene J. Crook, includes studies that combine psychology with
literary criticism.[4] From the psychological perspective, doubles relate more to the author of the tale than to the characters in it. In
this view, doubles derive from some conflict or repressed hostility
within the tale's creator:

> the figure of the second self is created by its author, either consciously
> or unconsciously, to express in fictional form the division within his own
> psyche, whether caused by purely personal problems or by the wider
> problems of his culture or by both. This figure usually embodies the au-
> thor's own shortcomings, his "darker side," the self which he really is
> . . . as against the self that he would like to be, or at least would like to
> be thought to be: "pure," outgoing, ageless, immortal, infinite, enlight-
> enedly rational, transcendently irrational, wholesome, and whole.[5]

Thus, the double is configured as a mental projection of its creator,
symptomatic of his maladjustment or internal conflicts.[6] The literary
and historical perspective, however, treats the double as a rhetorical
strategy, designed not so much to exorcise internal demons as to
present the darker side—although at times the lighter one as
well—of the poetic imagination. In this essay, I base my analysis of
the figure of the double in the short stories of Cristina Fernández
Cubas on a theoretical approach derived from both disciplines,
avoiding the necessity to limit myself to the classical Freudian idea
that every character in a fictional text is merely a double of the author.

In an interview, Fernández Cubas admitted that her characters tend to form a specular image: "I always had a distorted reflection, a mirror."[7] The projection of the self defined as one belonging to another appears in several of her stories: "Lúnula y Violeta" [Lunula and Violet] and "La ventana del jardín" [The Garden Window], both in *Mi hermana Elba* [My Sister Elba] (1980); in "La noche de Jezabel" [The Night of Jezebel] and "En el hemisferio sur" [In the Southern Hemisphere], both in *Los altillos de Brumal* [The Attics of Brumal] (1983); in "La mujer de verde" [The Woman in Green] and "Con Agatha en Estambul" [With Agatha in Istanbul], both in *Con Agatha en Estambul* (1994); as well as in the short novel *El año de Gracia* [The Year of Grace] (1985). Fernández Cubas creates highly effective games with the image of the double, behind which we can perceive the disintegration of the modern identity. Whether the doubles are simple or compound, complementary or antagonistic, only similar in appearance or exact replicas, their bifurcated consciousnesses set up a battle between the conflicting impulses within the "I" generally hidden behind the mask of friendship or of love for the other. The double operates as a tool through which the characters become aware of the dissolution of their identity, for one's identity is always perceived more accurately as projected onto an "other." In addition, besides exploring the maladjustments of the self, the double also works as a rhetorical strategy that has as its goal the representation of the poetic imagination. Kathleen Glenn has taken a decisive step in this direction in linking the doubles in Fernández Cubas's stories to the conventions of Gothic literature. Besides the coherence that Glenn observes between Anglo-American Gothic fiction and the stories of this writer from Barcelona, the effects of the double articulate complex literary preoccupations around this critical insight.[8] In my view, Fernández Cubas uses the double in her fiction to embody four metafictional concerns: the contradictory origins of writing, the dangerous practices of imitation and of artistic rivalry, the insuperable mismatch between oral and written discourses, and the comic effects of artistic redoubling or what one may call doubling the double. The result is, in each case, a split story: a story that duplicates (doubles) and exemplifies the thematics of doubleness in its very structure. Insofar as they are stories about stories, with positions in favor of and against the act of telling stories, Fernández Cubas's stories adopt a "Siamese discourse," composed of discourses and story lines that split in two. They point, therefore, to the impossibility of their producing Edgar

Allan Poe's famous "single, unifying effect," a formula invoked by authors and critics of the short story to describe that genre's presumptive "essence."[9]

The doubles of Fernández Cubas reveal, in the fractures of the "I," the work of writing, the characters' awareness of discourse. In fact, in these self-conscious works, the antagonism between the doubles is usually related to the desire to appropriate the words of another. As I examined in "Cristina Fernández Cubas: una narrativa de voces extinguidas" [Cristina Fernández Cubas: A Narrative of Suppressed Voices] (1988), the rivalry between the "I" and the other grows out of the fictional writer's desire to appropriate the skill with spoken language that he envies in the other. Each being undergoes transformations that result from having supplanted the other or from having made incursions into the text of the other, in sum, from having wished to become the other. The break between the "I" and the other whom the "I" desires to imitate forms a structure of alienating incompatibility that culminates in the renunciation of writing or in death. As a result, in this contest over possession of the word, the balance between oral speech and written language cannot be restored.

However, in some stories Fernández Cubas further deepens the metaliterary aspects of the motif of the double by folding the figure of the double over on itself; that is, she doubles the double. With this strategy, she complicates the practices of artistic imitation and rivalry, stroking the fatalism inherent in writing and in the creative identity with a touch of humor. The stories braid together two parasitic texts with a mutual need for each other, but crossed by the red thread of hatred. The violent and contradictory origin of writing creates stories that separate themselves narratologically into two. They not only dramatize their own thematics but also produce a reading experience with multiple effects, in which each signifier splits into pairs of values that oscillate between profundity and lightness. To see more precisely how this metaliterary use of the double functions, let us turn to "Lúnula y Violeta" and "Helicón."[10]

"Lúnula y Violeta"

The protagonists who lend their names to the title of this story give rise to complementary but opposing mirror images. Violeta, the narrator, is introverted and modest, like the flower for which she is

named. When the story opens, she lives in a boardinghouse in the
city, but, after shattering the "detested image" (14) that she sees in
her mirror, she moves to the country house that is owned by her new
friend, Lúnula. Eventually, timidly, she shows Lúnula the notebook
of her writings. Lúnula, on the other hand, is described as sure of
herself, uninhibited, and exuberantly obese, like the semitropical
flower associated with her, the jacaranda. Under the evil shade of a
jacaranda tree, Lúnula relentlessly tells stories of selfish and incon-
stant lovers. Lúnula, whose name connotes another "looking glass,"
functions like the reflection of Narcissus, restoring the broken
image in Violeta's mirror.[11] The two women's life together seems to
be ideal. When one of them falls ill, the other, who enjoys full health
and an immeasurable vitality, cares for her. While one allows the
house to become stuffed with objects and covered in dust, the other
carefully tidies up after her. But this apparently reciprocal friendship hinges on Violeta's voluntary and servile submission before Lúnula's overwhelming personality. Little by little, Lúnula dominates
the relationship. She is decisive when it is time to slaughter the rab-
bits, the aspect of farm work that intimidates Violeta. Lúnula takes
over the largest and sunniest room, putting Violeta in a dark and
stuffy corner of the house. Above all, Lúnula "avidly devours" the
manuscript that Violeta, the apprentice in the art of writing, shows
her.

While Violeta is associated with writing, Lúnula's supremacy
jumps into the foreground in her sphere of the spoken word. Violeta, who keeps a diary, is fascinated by Lúnula's verbal skill in telling
stories: "Mi amiga pertenecía a la estirpe casi extinguida de narra-
dores. El arte de la palabra, el dominio del tono, el conocimiento de
la pausa y el silencio, eran terrenos en los que se movía con absoluta
seguridad" [My friend belonged to the nearly extinguished tradition of storytellers: the art of the word, the control over the tone,
the knowledge of the pause and of silence, was a terrain through
which she moved with absolute confidence] (21). Just as Otto Rank
establishes in his theory of the double, Violeta's fascination for the
other turns to disgust when she discovers the corrections that Lúnula has written on her manuscript:

Lo que en algunas hojas no son más que simples indicaciones escritas a
lápiz, . . . en otras se convierten en verdaderos textos superpuestos, con
su propia identidad, sus propias llamadas y subanotaciones. A medida
que avanzo en la lectura veo que el lápiz, tímido y respetuoso, ha sido

sustituido por una agresiva tinta roja. En algunos puntos apenas puedo
reconocer lo que yo había escrito. En otros tal operación es sencilla-
mente imposible: mis párrafos han sido tachados y destruidos.

[What on some pages are no more than simple indications written in
pencil . . . on others become actual superimposed texts, with their own
identity, their own reference marks and subnotations. As I read further,
I see that the timid and respectful pencil has been replaced by an aggressive red ink. At some points I can hardly recognize what I have written.
In others such an operation is simply impossible: my paragraphs have
been crossed out and destroyed.] (20)

Violeta asks: "¿Dónde termino yo y dónde empieza ella? [Where
do I end and where does she begin?] (29), diffusing the limits between the doubles and underscoring the rivalry over the authorial
word. Lúnula, the stronger one, demands the destruction of Violeta,
who huddles near the doorway, waiting like a watchdog for the return of her friend, until she dies of starvation. Lúnula leaves on a
trip, i.e., she "dies" in narratological terms, meaning that there is
no possibility of salvation for the divided "I."

More important still for the metaliterary quality of the story, for
the refinement of the motif of the double in Fernández Cubas's
hands, is the shift in narrator that occurs at this point. The voice of
Violeta gives way to another voice, whose story competes directly
with that of Violeta through the medium of an Editor's Note. By the
act of storytelling this new voice creates in turn another pair of rival
doubles. The Editor's Note claims to be an *objective* retelling of the
subjective experience narrated by Violeta. The reader, used to the
convention that an Editor's Note stands outside of the fiction, ex-
pects that this new voice of logical reality will clarify the imaginative
impressions that Violeta wrote both as diarist and as first-person narrator of the story. But the reader's hopes for clarity evaporate. The
Editor makes no attempt to decipher the state in which her papers
were found on the floor of the farmhouse, "scattered" and "ram-
bling," although placed horizontally suggesting an enigmatic type
of order (31). He establishes precise rules to resolve the identity of
the corpse (depending on locating the documents that certify her
identity), but then he violates his own stated rules: for example, his
dismissing the testimony of the witnesses as a "dead letter" makes a
mockery of his claims to be objective. In fact, he ends up insisting
on the lack of a signature either among her papers or on any docu-
ment that might identify the corpse found near the doorway. More-

over, he states that the forensic report leaves unexplained whether one or two people were living on the farm: the papers mention two names, but it might simply be a case of a single woman with a compound name, thereby reinforcing the paradox of the simultaneous unity and duality of the doubles. Neighbors in the village identify the initials V. L. on the shirt of the corpse as belonging to a certain Miss Victoria, while others attribute them to a certain Mrs. Luz: "Hubo alguien, en fin, para quien el nombre de Victoria Luz no resultó del todo desconocido" [Well, there was even somebody for whom the name Victoria Luz did not turn out to be wholly unknown] (32). The careful construction of the doubles, based largely upon Violeta's diary, disappears like magic in the Editor's Note: "los nombres de Violeta y Lúnula no despertaron en los encuestados ningún tipo de recuerdo" [the names of Violeta and Lúnula did not stir up any type of memory in the people who were asked about them] (32). Thus, the double Violeta–Lúnula is displaced by that of Victoria–Luz. This new single or compound entity echoes, in its lack of specificity, that of the first set of doubles and yet it is empowered with the ability of having invented the former pair. Which set of doubles is the original and which the replica? Which is factual and which chimerical? This ambivalence of the double emerges clearly from the sequential presentation of the two competing texts.

Thus, far from clearing up the mystery, the "facts" that the Editor presents only serve to strengthen the fiction. The Editor not only disappoints the reader's expectation that he will create the ability to make sense of Violeta's story, but his text also imitates hers through a subtle game of narrative duplicity that sets both texts against each other. Isn't the unknown double Victoria–Luz infected with a self-delusion similar to that of Violeta? By assimilating Violeta's internal conflict about imitation and rivalry over the possession of language, the Editor reveals himself as another double. He ends his Note with a reference to the capricious and inexplicable flowering of a jacaranda in an arid land, which is nothing more than an echo of Violeta's last thoughts: "(oh, árbol maravilloso ¿florecerás?, y dime, tú que sabes de la vida y de la muerte, ¿volverá pronto Lúnula?") [(oh, wonderful tree, are you going to bloom? Tell me, you who know life and death, will Lúnula return soon?)]" (30). Thus, both texts "respond" to the demand on Violeta that Lúnula made: to formulate, sitting in the shade of the jacaranda tree with her eyes closed, a "deseo inédito," that is, a desire both original and unpublished. In turn, the obedience of both narrators to Lúnula's dictation underscores the intense rivalry between the two competing pairs of doubles. Far from having supreme authority over his characters, the voice of the Editor reveals a dependency and a desire for independence that parallel those of Violeta. The story produces, through the ambivalent structure of imitation and rejection, a complex mediation that links the psychological and narratological levels, infecting both discursive modalities—the intimate diary and the editorial note—with a disquieting duality.

"HELICÓN"

This story duplicates the paradox of the double by working the theme from two sides, multiplying the doubles into two pairs of twins: a real pair and an imaginary one. Marcos invents his twin brother (Cosme), while Angela really has a twin sister (Eva). In both cases, the twin represents the hidden face of the "I": a being that is slovenly and motivated by elemental passions; in sum, the unpresentable and disreputable sibling that no one would like to have.

Once again, we are faced with an unreliable first-person narrator. Marcos, the narrator-protagonist of "Helicón," scrupulously notes everything that happens to him in his pocket diary, but begins his narration this way: "Si la memoria no me engaña y puedo considerarme un hombre cuerdo . . ." [If memory doesn't deceive me, and I can still consider myself a sane man . . ."] (13). He is a timid person, yet adopts a persona in order to dazzle women.[12] He confesses that he met Angela, his new girlfriend, through his own "error": the invention of his twin, the brother that he doesn't have, is what brought them together. Angela, sipping a milkshake made with a double banana, reveals her obsession with disturbing dualities: double bananas and other twin fruits and vegetables, eggs with double yolks, and other monstrosities of the natural world that make her think with anguish of the fusion of the two halves at the expense of the essential, but disquieting difference between them. The egg with two yolks stirs in her a fearful, yet comical, thought. These embryonic selves

> estaban condenadas a contemplarse la una en la otra. Una, en cierta forma, era parte de la otra. Y su fin, el lógico fin para el que nacieron, para el que estaban destinadas, parecía todavía más angustioso: fundirse fatalmente en una tortilla, abandonar sus rasgos primigenios—iguales,

idénticos, calcados—entregarse a un abrazo mortal y reparador, y volver a lo que nunca fueron pero tenían que haber sido. Un Algo Único, Indivisible.

[were doomed to contemplate each other. One, in a certain way, was part of the other. And its end, the logical end for which they were born, for which they were destined, seemed still more anguishing: melting fatally in an omelet, abandoning their original features—equal, identical carbon copies—surrendering to a fatal and restorative embrace, and returning to what they never were but were destined to be. A Single Thing, Indivisible.] (17–18)

Her deep-seated fear of the "fatal embrace" of the two halves, her unwillingness to be confused with her own twin sister, explains her excessive pleasure in words like "*binomio, dicotomía, dualidad, reflejo, bisección... e incluso fotocopia*" [*binomial, dichotomy, duality, reflection, bisection . . . and even photocopy*] (36). Angela's obsession mirrors or duplicates that of Marcos, who had already invented his double before he met her: "Cosme es mi hermano—dije sonriendo—mi hermano gemelo" [Cosme is my brother—I said, smiling—my twin brother] (22). Marcos will project his mania and madness on this undesirable brother, while he devotes himself to alcohol in order to forget who he is and to flee from the monothematic Angela, who makes him nervous.

Marcos's uneasiness about Angela's "Siamese" discourse increases when she takes out of her handbag a newspaper clipping reporting the suicides of a pair of twins:

Los cadáveres de María Asunción y María de las Mercedes Puig Llofriu presentaban el aspecto de dos momias cuando, en la mañana de ayer, fueron descubiertas por la policía tras forzar las puertas del piso. Hacía siete meses que no se sabía nada de ellas. Impresos y facturas se amontonaban en el buzón y las ventanas exteriores de la vivienda aparecían cerradas desde entonces. Esos extremos, sin embargo, no habían puesto en guardia a los vecinos. Las gemelas, solteras y de unos cincuenta años de edad, no solían relacionarse con nadie, apenas ventilaban la casa, y, en los últimos años, les había sido cortado el suministro de luz y de agua. Todo parece indicar que incapaces de solventar su penosa situación económica, optaron, a mediados de agosto, por poner fin a sus vidas.

[*The bodies of María Asunción and María de las Mercedes Puig Llofriu looked like those of two mummies when they were discovered yesterday morning by the police who forced open the doors of their apartment. No one had seen the women for the past seven months. Since then, printed matter and bills had piled up in*

the mailbox, and the outside windows of the dwelling had appeared closed. These
extreme circumstances, however, had not alerted the neighbors. The twin sisters,
spinsters around fifty years old, did not socialize with anyone, hardly ever aired
out the house, and, in their last years, their electricity and water had been cut off.
Everything seems to indicate that, sometime in the middle of August, unable to
find a solution for their difficult economic situation, they decided to end their
lives.] (20–21)

As occurred with the Editor's Note in "Lúnula y Violeta," the language of this clipping is informative—its headline reports TWO TWIN
SISTERS FOUND DEAD IN THE BEDROOM OF THEIR HOUSE—and purports to challenge the mad discourse of the protagonist. But it is also
infected with the same madness. Permeated by the motif of the double, the news story rehearses the suicide of the sisters without even
providing facts about the means employed: "¿Veneno? ¿Corte de
venas? ¿Inanición?" [Poison? Opening a vein? Starvation?] (21), Angela wonders. Through its two pairs of inseparable siblings, "Helicón" symmetrically dramatizes the idiosyncrasies of the "I"
reflected in the other, real or invented. Eventually, as "Lúnula y Violeta" does, "Helicón" aims at rehabilitating the storytelling capacity
of mankind. The "unexpressed desire," the source of the ability to
create stories, does not give rise to a jacaranda flower this time, but
to a helicon, a figure with a double meaning: "Helicon" designates
not only a musical instrument but also the seat of the Muses or the
place in which one seeks and finds artistic inspiration.[13] When he
plays the helicon, Marcos descends to layers of existence which do
not conform to the normal and arbitrary limits of reality. The helicon draws out "las tonalidades más burdas, más tétricas, más im-
pensables" [the coarsest, gloomiest, most unthinkable tonalities],
perfectly tuned to the foul filth of his naked skin and the stench to
which he prefers to abandon himself in loneliness: "era muy semejante a descender a los infiernos" [it was very similar to going down
into Hell] (30). Both the grunting of the helicon and the filth in
which Marcos takes such delight have something of the abyss about
them. They are "invocaciones a elementales, a íncubos de la más
baja estofa, a poderes de la peor categoría" [invocations to the most
primitive elements, to the incubus of the lowest sort, to the powers
of the worst category] (30), which, notwithstanding, allow him to be
reborn from his miasmas like a new man. The abject twin being that
he creates for himself perfectly fits those feelings that grow out of
his sessions with the helicon. Accidentally discovered in one of those

sessions by his former girlfriend, Violeta, to whom he had given his house keys in order to seduce her with his best poem and other qualities of his soul, he offers his particular interpretation of Jekyll-Hyde: "Marcos no está en casa. . . . Soy su hermano" [Marcos is not at home. . . . I am his brother] (31). From this point on, doubling follows an inexorable movement, like that suggested by the spiral movement that the image of the helicon imposes on the action of the story.[14]

Marcos nourishes his madness by dressing up as Cosme and by allowing himself to be seen in front of his usual bar with the outlandish and dangerously disturbed appearance of his "twin" brother. His brilliant interpretation of Cosme is spurred on by his attraction to Violeta, a woman who is prone to retell life as fiction. Violeta, in turn, responds to the challenge posed by Marcos's theatrics with changes in her physique that he attributes to the nonexisting brother, the replica: "un amago de estrangulamiento, desgarrones brutales en su delicado traje de seda, y una pasión y un deseo capaces de aterrorizar a la mujer más bregada componían ahora el cuadro de sufrimientos y penalidades por los que había pasado la dulce heroína" [a feigned attempt at strangulation, brutal tears in her delicate silk suit, and a passion and a desire capable of terrorizing the toughest woman formed part of the new picture of suffering and hardships that the gentle heroine had endured] (35). In other words, Violeta inscribes her body with physical markings which could never be traced to Marcos, the "normal" brother, but which are presumptive attributes of Cosme, "aquella copia ruin y abyecta, aquel animal desbocado" [that ruined and abject copy, that unrestrained animal] (35). In order to teach Violeta a lesson and put an end to her fictions, Marcos commits his imaginary twin to a sanatorium. Clearly, Cosme is born out of Marcos's desire to imitate and compete with Violeta's stories. Marcos then uses his creation—Cosme—as a tool of seduction aimed at Angela. He intends to convince Angela, who projects the need to assert the difference inherent in repetition, of his genius and self-sufficiency over Cosme (and over her as well). However, in the end, his struggle for power over both women sinks him deeper into dependence.

A lucky accident that Marcos suffers precipitates the solution to this contagious spiral of inventions. Just when he is sure that he has secured Angela's admiration for his invention of a twin brother, a pot of nauseating vegetable soup is emptied on his head while he is walking in the street. Angela bumps into him and, naturally, thinks that he is Cosme. She embraces him and kisses him so hard that his lips begin to bleed. Marcos wonders: Is Angela crazy, or is she an outstanding psychologist collecting sample data for her dissertation on identical twins? Ready to unmask her, he arranges to meet her in a bar and, sure of his triumph, he purposely arrives late in order to ensure Angela's defeat. Standing outside the bar, Marcos observes that

> su desaforada pasión por la simetría la había conducido a sentarse frente al espejo, junto a dos sillas vacías. ¿Qué podía hacer yo? ¿Ocupar la de la derecha, probablemente reservada a Marcos? ¿O acomodarme en la de la izquierda, con una media sonrisa entre inquietante y compasiva?

> [her boundless passion for symmetry had led her to sit down in front of the mirror, near two empty chairs. What could I do? Occupy the one on the right, probably reserved for Marcos? Or make myself comfortable on the left one, with a hint of a smile of mixed disquiet and compassion?] (46).

But Angela has a surprise for Marcos, as well as for the reader:

> de pronto el rostro en el que me recreaba había adquirido un aspecto demasiado alterado. . . . Y enseguida, mientras un sudor frío empezaba a deslizarse por mi frente, comprendí consternado que en aquella mesa del rincón, frente a Angela y a las dos sillas que me aguardaban, no había existido jamás un espejo.

> [suddenly the face in which I had taken such pleasure acquired an extremely altered appearance. . . . And immediately, while a cold sweat slid down my forehead, looking at Angela and at the two chairs that awaited me, I realized with consternation that there had never been a mirror near that corner table.] (46–47).

Angela has kept the twin sister, who is now discovered sitting facing her, a secret. If Angela has hidden her, it is because of the shame that she feels in possibly being compared to her, since her double, as in *The Picture of Dorian Gray,* allows others to detect what passes unperceived in herself. For example, the twin—Eva—picks her nose in public and lets her bra straps droop. The reader deduces that the brutal kiss that has bloodied Marcos was given to him by Eva, not Angela. Eva now becomes her sister's sexual rival, duplicating the rivalry between Cosme and Marcos. In the violent and unsymmetrical kiss that seals the destiny of the two couples, neither party correctly identifies the other (Marcos is "dressed" as Cosme, thanks to the disgusting soup, and Eva is confounded with Angela) and the hidden faces of the two protagonists, that is, the denied beings incarnated by Cosme and Eva, join each other. However, this union destabilizes the symmetry of the identities, since Cosme, unlike Eva, remains fictional, and the reality of a whole, superior "I" is revealed as an illusion.

Deciding to end the masquerade that has caused him so much anxiety, Marcos determines that "me aceptaría tal como soy" [I will accept myself just as I am] (51). He opens the closet to which he has banished the helicon, the cause of his evil fate, and dials a telephone number. "—¿Marcos?," asks Angela hopefully, from the other side of the telephone connection, "Porque eres Marcos ¿verdad?" [Because you are Marcos, aren't you?]. "—No—dije con voz firme. Y pregunté por Eva" ["No," I said with a firm voice. And I asked for Eva] (52). Marcos's accepting the hidden face of his being, which corresponds to Eva, is a jump into abjection that symbolically kills Marcos and destroys the symmetry of the "two" pairs of siblings.[15] The copy (Cosme) triumphs over the original (Marcos), although he must bear the weight of the betrayal involved in assimilating his being to that of the other. In effect, Marcos finally becomes indistinguishable from Cosme. Thus, the story problematizes this thorny question about the ambivalence of the double: Which is the original and which is the replica? Choosing to name the secret twin Eva—the "first" woman—suggests in effect that the *other* is the first-born and that the invention precedes the reality.

On the textual level, is there an objective and logical framework in "Helicón" that refutes the disturbed illusions of the characters? Let us recall the first words of the story: "If memory doesn't deceive me, and I can still consider myself a sane man." Are these cautious words spoken by a sane man who recognizes the dark side of his being, or do they belong to a narrator who, hidden behind the personality of an other, is making fun of the reader? The hesitancy of the narrator infects the reader, who is left deeply troubled, split by the ambivalence of dual, dissociated meanings. The text in turn breaks in two. The newspaper clipping of the suicide of the twin sisters is not part of Marcos's story, but it inserts itself into "Helicón" as a notice of the theme of the death of the double. It reproduces, with apparent rationality, the madness of the "Siamese" discourse to which it attaches itself. Such juxtaposition can be viewed as a parasitic act that ratifies the congenital and disturbing duality of both types of discourses, the objective and the subjective, the rational and the irrational, the reliable and the schizoid. "Helicón" is, therefore, a text that "echoes," like a zygote that will give rise to identical twins, the egg with a double yolk.

Conclusions

With this strategy of doubling the double, Fernández Cubas connects her stories to valid psychological theories, but without accepting the limits prescribed by any particular one. She organizes the narratological level of her stories according to the same ambivalent structure of imitation and rejection that characterizes not only her characters' problems of identity but also their need to create fiction. Her stories look for a balanced anchorage with respect to the authorial word, threading together "objective" and rational texts that attempt to clarify the "Siamese" discourse obsessed with doubling. Notwithstanding their split situation, her stories cannot resist the implications of the double. Far from providing a framework for reflection, the rational justification sets up a *tour de force* with the marvelous that reveals their mutual dependence. Rationality challenges the zygotic discourse, but ends up swept away by it. At the very end, the imbalance of zygotic discourse is apparently restored to vindicate a fiction of the marvelous, of life and death, fabricated under the protection of the inexplicable jacaranda or of the enormous helicon. Given these narratological and thematic similarities, the reader might think of "Helicón" and "Lúnula y Violeta" as twin narratives. Such reading is plausible and finds further support in the small mirrors that Cristina Fernández Cubas places between both stories, reflecting and refracting common motifs. For instance, the settings for the death of the double reveal a marked preference for isolated, stuffy dwellings. And Violeta is a recurring name to designate females who go to extremes to tell their stories.

The fractures in the integrity of the personality represented by the double allow us to see in the stories of Cristina Fernández Cubas the violent and contradictory origin of writing. They threaten the principle of unity of the genre, ruining the "single, unifying effect" that Poe found so persuasive. Far from submitting themselves to a compact and unifying effect of a preestablished design, her stories adopt a "Siamese discourse," with structural components and story lines that split in two. This double bifurcation suggests that the fantastic stories of today do not necessarily have to be governed by romantic laws. Even so, they show the breach, always open, between literature and its double: life. They put to the test our notions of "reality" and replace them with a *double* reality, a fantastic one less susceptible of being regulated. Fernández Cubas seems to be leading us, through the helicon and the jacaranda, to the source of fiction. Why not suspend the rationality of the everyday world (of editors and journalists) and make a space for the irrational, as Marcos does in twisting the helicon around his body, or as Lúnula does, closing her eyes under the jacaranda? In Cristina Fernández Cubas's stories, the double is a box of surprises, of multiple effects, which reveal the maladjustments of the modern mind, but that, above all, lead us also to the everlasting sources of fantasy.

NOTES

Preliminary versions of this essay, originally written in Spanish, were read at the conference on *Narradoras españolas actuales*, Saint Louis University, Madrid, April 10, 2002; and at the *Second International Conference on Literature Written by Women in the Fields of Spanish and Portuguese*, Stockholm, Sweden, April 11–13, 2002. This version of the essay, including all selections from the work of Cristina Fernández Cubas, was translated with the help of Sandy Camargo of the Department of English at the University of Illinois, Urbana-Champaign.

1. Robert Rogers, *A Psychoanalytic Study of the Double in Literature* (Detroit, Mich.: Wayne State University Press, 1970).

2. Paul Coates, *The Double and the Other: Identity as Ideology in Post-Romantic Fiction* (New York: St. Martin's Press, 1988); Carl F. Keppler, *The Literature of the Second Self* (Tucson: University of Arizona Press, 1972); Otto Rank, *The Double: A Psychoanalytic Study* (Chapel Hill: University of North Carolina Press, 1971); *Don Juan: Une étude sur le double* (Paris: Denöel et Steele, 1932); and "The Double as Immortal Self," chap. 2 in *Beyond Psychology* (New York: Dover Publications, 1958).

3. Wilhelmine Krauss, *Das Doppelgängermotiv in der Romantik: Studien zum romantischen Idealismus* (Berlin: E. Ebering, 1930); Ralph Tymms, *Doubles in Literary Psychology* (Cambridge: Bowes & Bowes, 1949).

4. Masao Miyoshi, *The Divided Self: A Perspective on the Literature of the Victorians* (New York: New York University Press, 1969); Eugene J. Crook, ed., *Fearful Symmetry: Doubles and Doubling in Literature and Film. Papers from the Fifth Annual Florida State University Conference on Literature and Film* (Tallahassee: University Presses of Florida, 1982). Among the studies of clinical psychology that Miyoshi discusses are *The Dissociation of a Personality: A Biographical Study in Abnormal Psychology* by Morton Prince (New York: Longmans, Green, 1908) and *The Three Faces of Eve* by Corbett H. Thigpen and Hervey M. Cleckley (New York: McGraw-Hill, 1957).

5. Keppler, *The Literature of the Second Self*, 189.

6. Freud, in "The Relation of the Poet to Day-Dreaming" (1908), underlined "the tendency of modern writers to split up their ego by self-observation into many component-egos, and in this way to personify the conflicting trends in their own mental life in many heroes" (*Collected Papers*, 5 vols., trans. under the supervision of Joan Riviere, ed. Ernest Jones [London: Hogarth Press and the Institute of Psychoanalysis, 1953, 180]), cited in Rogers, 11.

7. Interview with Kathleen M. Glenn, Barcelona, April 26, 1991, cited in "Gothic Indecipherability and Doubling in the Fiction of Cristina Fernández Cubas," *Monographic Review/Revista Monográfica* 8 (1992): 125–41.

8. See Ana Rueda, "Cristina Fernández Cubas: una narrativa de voces extinguidas," *Monographic Review/Revista Monográfica* 4 (1988): 257–67. Jessica Folkart has examined, in turn, the link between psychological fissures and identity: "Desire, Doubling, and Difference in Cristina Fernández Cubas's *El ángulo del horror*," *Revista Canadiense de Estudios Hispánicos* 24:2 (Winter 2000): 343–62.

9. Going obsessively into the causes of an incident that are not revealed until the end—the "single, unifying effect" of Poe—constituted, in spite of its vagueness, the primary and canonical defining characteristic of the genre. Brander Matthews bases his influential theory on the "single effect" (*The Philosophy of the Short Story* [New York: Longmans, Green, 1901]), while Charles May (*Short Story Theories* [Athens: Ohio University Press, 1976]) and Frank O'Connor (*The Lonely Voice. A Study of the Short Story* [Cleveland, Ohio: World Publishing Co., 1963]) expand their respective theories to include other romantic principles. Cited in Ana Rueda, *Relatos desde el vacío: Un nuevo espacio crítico para el cuento actual* (Madrid: Orígenes, 1992), 98.

10. For "Lúnula y Violeta," published originally in 1980, I used *Mi hermana Elba y Los altillos de Brumal* (Barcelona: Tusquets, 1988), 13–32. The references to "Helicón" come from *El ángulo del horror* (Barcelona: Tusquets, 1990), 13–52. All references to these works will be cited parenthetically in the text.

11. The name "Lúnula" is associated with "luna," which in Spanish means "looking glass" and "mirror" as well as "moon."

12. What is certain is that the invention of Cosme dazzles the women that Marcos wants to seduce. They quickly feel that they are in a "triangular desire" in which, in René Girard's terms, they do not want the other, Marcos, nor the object of his desire, but his desire itself. See René Girard, *Deceit, Desire, and the Novel: Self and Other in Literary Structure*, trans. Yvonne Freccero (Baltimore: Johns Hopkins University Press, 1965).

13. According to H. G. Liddell and R. Scott, *Greek-English Lexicon with a Revised Supplement* (Oxford: Clarendon Press, 1996), these meanings correspond to two different words: Ελ κων, "Helicon, a hill in Boeotia, the seat of the Muses"; and ελίκων 1. "thread spun from the distaff to the spindle"; 2. "a nine-stringed instrument."

14. The figure of the spiral is common in Cristina Fernández Cubas's short stories in order to mark the entry into the layers of existence. Besides "Helicón," whose plot implies the enormous spiral of the instrument in the title and the drain of the sink that swallows Angela's two zygotic yolks, the figure of the spiral is observed in "En el hemisferio sur" (as a tornado), in "Los altillos de Brumal" (in the playful reversal of the names Adriana-Anairda), in "El ángulo del horror" (in the angle of vision), and in other stories.

15. Janet Pérez's article "Fernández Cubas, Abjection and the 'retórica del horror,'" *Explicación de Textos Literarios* 24 (1995–96): 159–71, analyzes stories from *El ángulo del horror*, including "Helicón," as examples of abjection in Kristeva's sense.

Reading the Sign of Spain: Negotiating Nationality, Language, and Gender

Maryellen Bieder

National identity is a recurrent preoccupation in Spanish fiction in the last decades of the twentieth century. One critic points to "the interplay of geographic representation, of nation formation, and of postmodern identity politics" that characterizes contemporary narrative and film in Spain.[1] Cristina Fernández Cubas interrogates this postmodern interplay of geography, nationality, and identity in two extraordinary stories, "La Flor de España" [The Flower of Spain], from the collection *El ángulo del horror* [The Angle of Horror] (1990) and "Con Agatha en Estambul" [With Agatha in Istanbul], from the volume of the same title (1994).[2] Both stories have a first-person narrator, a Spanish woman who communicates her struggle to constitute herself as subject from outside Spain and, as one narrator specifies, from within "una ciudad de idioma incomprensible" [a city with an unintelligible language] ("La Flor" 119). The narrator of "La Flor" is in her first winter of teaching in a Scandinavian country, while the narrator of "Con Agatha" makes an impromptu visit to Istanbul with her husband. Isolation from a familiar culture and a common language in these two stories shapes the narrators' construction of identity, destabilizes their reading of cultural signs, and calls into question the portability of national identity. In her fine study of Fernández Cubas's fiction, Jessica Folkart speaks of the significance of "cultural adaptations to space and time." In Folkart's reading of "La Flor," the story dramatizes "the effect that repositioning the subject in 'another time, another place' has on the subject's visual construction of itself and its others."[3]

My discussion of national cultures in these two stories borrows Helen Graham and Jo Labanyi's definition of "culture" as "both lived practices and artifacts or performances, understood as symbolic systems."[4] In these works, as in others, Fernández Cubas builds

41

on the postmodern awareness that representations, including artifacts and performances, are politically and culturally constructed, although the narrators of her fictions are frequently oblivious to this
constructedness. Robert C. Spires has remarked perceptively on the
postmodern nature of Fernández Cubas's narratives and her laying
bare of "the absurdity underlying class consciousness, national identity, linguistic communities, and gender attitudes."[5] In the two stories treated in this essay, nationality, language, and gender are
performances—sustained at times, at others transitory—that produce a possible if constantly shifting construction of Spanishness as
an other of the foreign culture in which each story takes place. In
Stuart Hall's pithy statement, identification is "a construction, a
process never completed—always 'in process.'"[6] Nevertheless,
within this ongoing project of identity formation, Fernández Cubas's narrators are subjects always in search of a center in order to
be able to act at all.

In analyzing "the *postmodern* problem of identity" Zygmunt Bauman asserts that the "hub of postmodern life strategy is not identity
building" but an avoidance of fixedness.[7] He names the postmodern
types that jointly comprise "the metaphor for the postmodern strategy moved by the horror of being bound and fixed": the stroller,
the vagabond, the tourist, and the player.[8] The narrators of "La
Flor" and "Con Agatha" may be seen as embodying two of Bauman's types, the "vagabond" and the "tourist," respectively. As Bauman observes, "[o]ne thinks of identity whenever one is not sure of
where one belongs, that is, one is not sure how to place oneself
among the evident variety of behavioural styles and patterns, and
how to make sure that people around would accept this placement
as right and proper, so that both sides would know how to go on in
each other's presence."[9] The vagabond is always the stranger, never
integrated into new communities. As a variation on Bauman's vagabond, the narrator of "La Flor" tests integration into different facets
of Scandinavian culture while nevertheless toying with a return to
Spain, never feeling herself at home in one place or the other. The
tourist, like the vagabond, is "nowhere *of* the place he is in," but
unlike the vagabond he is "a conscious and systematic seeker of experience, of a new and different experience."[10] Tourists, Bauman
adds, "want to immerse themselves in a strange and bizarre element
. . .—on condition, though, that it will not stick to the skin and thus
can be shaken off whenever they wish." A tourist, the narrator of
"Con Agatha" immerses herself in the language and customs of Is-

tanbul and shakes off her bonds to other Spaniards. Although Bauman posits that "[e]ntertaining a dream of going native can only end in mutual recrimination and bitterness,"[11] each of Fernández Cubas's narrators resolves "going native" very differently. Vagabond and tourist, Fernández Cubas's two narrators inhabit transitory communities into which they project their identities in flux as an escape from one nexus of nationality, culture, and language and an excursion into another.

In writing about Spanish women authors at the beginning of the twentieth century, Mary Lee Bretz makes the interesting observation that women took advantage of their increased freedom of movement to travel and cultivate travel writing. The spread of hotels for the new middle-class tourist created "new spaces for the production of community across national and linguistic barriers."[12] Fernández Cubas, in stories from the end of the same century, continues to exploit the intersection of travel writing with women, travel, and the production of community outside national borders and national languages. Travel to unfamiliar places is a frequent motif in her fiction, as critics have noted. Kay Pritchett, for example, recognizes that in Fernández Cubas's stories "travel becomes an exploration of external and internal spaces."[13] In a broader context, Kathleen Glenn discerningly remarks that the "exploration of boundaries and the testing of limits" are constants in Fernández Cubas's plotting, as is "an interest in problems of communication."[14]

Critics have repeatedly affirmed the indeterminacy of Fernández Cubas's fictional worlds, drawing attention to "indecipherability" in her fiction and more specifically to "the (in)decipherability of a variety of signs" in "La Flor."[15] This "indecipherability" functions not only in the protagonist's inability to read cultural and linguistic signs but also in the indeterminacy of the author's postmodern texts that resist stable, univocal signification. Critics have similarly emphasized the role that doubling plays in her narrative. Jo Labanyi labels her early fiction "horror stories" and concludes that they dramatize a "fear of invasion by the other."[16] The author, she asserts, "uses the horror story to undermine the opposition between self and feared/desired Other."[17] She includes Fernández Cubas among those Spanish women writers "interested in the falsity or instability of identity" and posits that these authors "do not seem much interested in relating the postmodernist deconstruction of identity to gender issues." She credits gay writers and filmmakers with having "embraced postmodernism as a release from fixed identities" and denounces feminist writers and filmmakers for seeming "more concerned with uncovering some kind of authentic female self."[18] Nevertheless, Fernández Cubas's stories go well beyond the recovery of an "authentic female self" cited by Labanyi. They set gender instability into play alongside unstable national and linguistic identity, even as the author deploys the cultural signifiers of fixed gender and national identity. It could even be argued that in "La Flor" and "Con Agatha" Fernández Cubas appropriates "postmodernist pastiche," a form that Labanyi does not detect in the work of other Spanish women authors.

Subjects constituted, in Lacanian terms, in and through language, the first-person narrators of "La Flor" and "Con Agatha" are inherently fluid subjects. Each produces the spoken and unspoken language that expresses her perception of herself and her experience in a foreign land, but even this language, and especially the interpretative strategies it records, is unstable. Each narrator also fluctuates between using the native Spanish integral to her identity and the foreign language that speaks her alien status. Both women are decentered subjects, to employ Derrida's formulation, and thus not organized around a fixed identity or consciousness. Each narrator's dependence on the Spanish language maps her geographical displacement and her response to national, linguistic, and gender difference as well as impelling her search for an interlocutor in a foreign culture and across the barrier of language. Each seeks herself in a double, a complementary self who mirrors both her sameness and her difference. This specularity of self and other articulates the construction of national identity in both stories. Jo Labanyi has formulated succinctly the problem of Spanish national identity in postmodern texts: "Postmodernist theory deconstructs the concept of unity—and by extension that of identity, in its sense of 'sameness'—exposing it as a political manoeuvre designed to suppress recognition of difference within. . . . 'Spanishness' is a shifting concept, encompassing plurality and contradiction."[19]

The geographical and linguistic marginality of Fernández Cubas's narrators in these two stories—strangers in a strange land—complicates the postmodern play of nationality in an exploration of what it means to be Spanish at the end of the twentieth century. The two narratives destabilize identity markers—the concept of a fixed center—and articulate the constructedness of their subjects-information through their ceaseless mutability across time and space. Fernández Cubas's characters perceive nation and nationality in privileged moments of seeing themselves in, and against, others. Both narratives coincide with Baudrillard's perception that everything in a text is image, a surface without depth. For her part, Labanyi reminds us that "identities are strategic constructions: neither inherent nor imposed, but negotiated."[20] This continuous negotiation of identity, including national identity, suggests that, within the dissonance between one's native culture and a foreign culture, nationality, like gender as defined by Judith Butler, is "a constituted social temporality."[21] Articulating the relationship of gender to urban space, David Lynch contends that "city space is mapped by its inhabitants," so that "contradictory urban spaces provide the conditions for what Butler calls a 'proliferative catachresis,' permitting the production of new gendered identities."[22] Both "La Flor" and "Con Agatha," I will argue, explore the process of negotiation of national and gender identity by a postmodern, decentered subject situated outside Spain. In both stories the play of nationality, identity, urban space, and national language produces new arenas for the "politics of location" and for the "postmodern identity politics" of vagabond and tourist.

The women who narrate these two stories—both women's nationality and native language are Spanish—lack the linguistic competence to negotiate their subjectivity in a foreign culture, but each woman confronts the problem in a different way. Here playing off of Benedict Anderson's concept of nationality as an "imagined community" may be productive. Defining nationality as "a socio-cultural concept," Anderson opines that "in the modern world everyone can, should, will 'have' a nationality."[23] Thus, as critics have commented, Anderson views nationality as "a relationship term" based on "a system of differences."[24] Although for him nationality is a stable, fixed identity marker, he also argues that as a cultural artifact it is "'modular,' capable of being transplanted, with varying degrees of self-consciousness, to a great variety of social terrains."[25] Anderson's concepts of transplantation and identification with an extended, unseen, and unknowable community will help elucidate Fernández Cubas's stories. In "La Flor" the narrator rejects participation in the community of expatriate Spaniards and "imagines" herself an integral part of a community of Scandinavian women married to Spanish men, temporarily suspending her Spanish identity to share a common gender, language, and nationality. Although the community of women is finite in the story, the narrator's immersion in it implies her identification with the larger, invisible community of Scandinavian women. In "Con Agatha" the narrator, believing herself competent in the Turkish language, "imagines" herself part of the Turkish-speaking "community" represented by her Istanbul taxi driver. Since in neither story does the local community of Spanish speakers reflect back to the narrator a satisfying subject position for her to occupy, each narrator seeks to merge in her own way with a gendered, linguistic community alien to her Spanish nationality and language.

While language mediates the process of self-construction, in these stories as in life, it does not resolve its inherent instability. Peter Brooker's remark that "difference, and therefore meaning, are in a constant process of being constructed" is instructive here.[26] I have suggested that nationality, like gender, is performative: "an identity tenuously constituted in time, instituted in an exterior space through a *stylized repetition of acts*," as Butler stipulates with regard to gender.[27] In Fernández Cubas's narratives nationality is negotiated both through language and in the absence of a mediating language, both through and in the absence of an interlocutor. Language, as Butler reiterates in *Gender Trouble*, "is not an *exterior medium or instrument* into which I pour a self and from which I glean a reflection of that self." It is not a question of agency, since, as in the process Fernández Cubas's narrators enact in these stories, "the 'doer' is variably constructed in and through the deed."[28]

If reliability is problematic in all first-person narratives, the indeterminacy and contradictions of postmodern texts only render it more so. As readers, we have only the narrator's words, only her understanding of herself, her decoding of her circumstances and the foreign world around her, to guide our reading. In both "La Flor" and "Con Agatha" Fernández Cubas immerses us in the flow of her narrators' thoughts as they traverse, read, and try to make sense of their experiences, negotiating their way through the snow and fog of unfamiliar lands.[29] She signals the unreliability of both narrators as they struggle to locate their subjectivity in the otherness of the world around them. Their constant vision and re-vision communicates to readers, if not to the narrators themselves, the misunderstandings and flawed comprehension that engulf them. In the absence of the cultural markers of Spain, each narrator attempts to define for herself her Spanishness, both in relation to other Spaniards and to the foreign women and men with whom she comes into contact.[30] Each navigates the unknown waters in an unceasing flow of interpretation and reinterpretation, as she deciphers glances, cultural artifacts and practices, and written words.

Each of the narrators grasps a reflection of herself in a mirroring surface in an effort to fix her identity in that moment and capture the way others perceive her. In "La Flor" the narrator sees her reflection in a shop window: "El cristal de una de las vitrinas me devolvió la imagen de una mujer desaseada y deprimida" [The glass of one of the shopwindows reflected back to me the image of an unkempt and depressed woman] (145). She also uses the window glass to read others in the act of reading her:

> El cristal me devolvió un reflejo, un gesto apenas perceptible, el mentón de la visitante proyectado súbitamente hacia delante—hacia mí, hacia mi espalda encorvada sobre la vitrina—en una interrogación exagerada que sólo podía interpretarse como un "¿Quién es ésa?" "¿Qué quiere?"
>
> [The glass showed me a reflection, a scarcely perceptible gesture, the chin of the woman visitor suddenly jutting forward—towards me, towards my back bent toward the window—in an exaggerated question that could only be interpreted as "Who is that woman?" "What does she want?"] (139)

The desire for a stable identity and a fixed relationship to the world around her leads the narrator of "La Flor" to impose inalterable readings on the body language her gaze intercepts; a gesture "sólo podía interpretarse como" [could only be interpreted as] (139), she concludes more than once. She firmly attaches meaning to each gesture until another equally fleeting motion—"gesto apenas perceptible" [a scarcely perceptible gesture] (130)—catches her eye and challenges the fixedness of her initial reading.[31] Among the mirrors in which each narrator attempts to read her reflection is another Spanish woman, a woman who is both like and unlike her and who becomes both her alter ego and her nemesis. For the narrator of "Con Agatha" the glass of the hotel aquarium in Istanbul serves as the reflecting surface on which she spies a surprising view of her Spanish other, Flora: "un reflejo que me devolvió el cristal, unos labios fruncidos, una expresión desmadejada, insulsa" [a reflection that the glass showed me, a pair of pursed lips, a lifeless, insipid expression] (210). Then face to face with Flora she projects onto her the reflected image that, to the narrator's mind, reveals the hidden truth that gives the lie to Flora's superficial beauty. The narrator circles the fish tank, trying to reconcile the two faces of her foe, to catch the moment in which the two coexist: "un momento, un instante acaso, en que se vislumbra un león-tigre. Y ése era el punto. Preciso, indefinible. La fracción de segundos, total, reveladora . . ." [one moment, perhaps an instant, in which one can glimpse a lion-tiger. And that was the point. Precise, indefinable. The fraction of a second, total, revealing . . .] (214). In both stories, each subsequent experience undermines the narrator's brief moment of confident insight and calls for reevaluation.

The names of the women whom the narrators identify as mirrors of themselves signal another level of doubling that connects the two stories: one is Flora, a tourist in Istanbul, and the other, Rosita, the owner of "La Flor de España," a store selling Spanish products. Fernández Cubas doubles both the name—Flor/Flora—and the floral signifiers—Flora/Rosita. While flowers are traditional emblems of femininity, the two female narrators are nontraditional women outside the space of nation and domesticity—one an expatriate vagabond and the other a tourist—who undercut the conventional association of women with the short-lived, fragile beauty of flowers. As postmodern texts, these stories contest such essentialist construction of women and femininity. Even the scent the narrator purchases in Istanbul—the appropriately named Egoïste, supposedly a Chanel product—realigns perfume's traditional enhancement of feminine qualities and allure. According to her husband, it stinks, and deployed with premeditation it clears the area around the narrator on the airplane. Language is slippery in all its manifestations in Fernández Cubas's narratives.

"LA FLOR DE ESPAÑA"

In "La Flor de España" the narrator's identity oscillates as she moves between teaching Spanish in Scandinavia and living immersed in a new language, between the "imagined community" of Spanish expatriates and the "imagined community" of Scandinavian women, between her Scandinavian women friends and her Scandinavian male lovers, between her former lovers and the same two men as *novios*, between the foreign city and Rosita's Spanish store, between the cultural icons of Scandinavia and the shop with its surfeit of cultural markers of Spanish "difference." Wandering the streets of a Scandinavian city, the narrator suddenly and unexpectedly finds herself face to face with "Spain." The store that gives

title to the story offers its customers the best of Spain—*la flor de España*—in the form of imported food products that are cultural signifiers of Spain's difference. Before her breath fogs up the window
and "Spain" disappears from sight, the narrator enumerates the cultural artifacts in the shop window: "tres cabezas de toro, dos trajes
de faralaes, innumerables peinetas, algunas barretinas, un montón
de chapelas, panderetas, castañuelas, abanicos, vírgenes del Pilar de
todos los tamaños, una virgen de Covadonga empecinada en mostrarse siempre en el mismo tamaño" [three bulls' heads, two Fla-
menco dresses, innumerable large combs, some Catalan caps, a lot
of Basque berets, tambourines, castanets, fans, statues of the Virgin
of Pilar of every size, a Virgin of Covadonga stubbornly remaining
always the same size] (121–22). We might view the contents of the
shop's display window as a still life, rendered in the story as a verbal
painting. Rosemary Lloyd's penetrating recognition that "the still
life, in art and literature, becomes a means for transferring the anxiety aroused by the contingency of a society in flux onto objects
whose stubborn thereness is at once a reality and an illusion"[32] cap-
tures the narrator's visual response to artifacts whose "thereness"
seems to arrest the aimless fluidity of her life. The subject matter of
still life, Lloyd contends, invites "contemplation of other and
broader cultural domains, questions of class, of race, or of gender,"[33] as do the cultural signifiers in Fernández Cubas's story. The
cultural artifacts in Rosita's store—a pastiche of Spain's unique national identity on sale in the shop—stand in counterpoint to the
high culture embodied in the academic and professional circle of
Spanish expatriates.[34] Nevertheless, the country these artifacts con-
note is the postmodern, fragmented Spain comprised of autonomous regions; juxtaposed in the window the cultural markers coexist
without coalescing into a seamless whole. This is not a Spain constructed from the center, from the bureaucratic model of integration, but from the plural markers of identity of its peripheral
regions. Even the expatriate Spaniards at the dinner party name
themselves by naming their "lugar de origen" [place of origin],
rather like specifying the provenance of a bottle of wine: stating
one's "lugar de origen, parecía un requisito ineludible" [place of
origin seemed to be an unavoidable requirement] (130). Their
"Spain" is an empty signifier of a mythic national culture belied by
the proliferation of sites of origin.

The store's owner, Rosita, occupies a mediating position between
the circle of Spanish professionals with their Scandinavian wives and

the products she purveys. While to the narrator Rosita's shop iconically embodies traditional Spain, outside time and history, the blond Spaniard Rosita seems stranded midway between Spain and Scandinavia, between integration into Scandinavian culture and cultural isolation, as does her shop with its location on an unprepossessing street between two broad avenues. Although the narrator recognizes herself in the products that, like her, signify Spain, she does not initially identify the owner as a Spanish speaker. Rosita's Scandinavian blondness belies the stereotypical construction of Spanishness to which the narrator falls prey. Challenging Rosita's control of cultural signs and her power to select the components of cultural difference, the narrator vies with her to identify those signs—*botellas de Rioja* [bottles of Rioja wine] (126), *turrón de coco* [coconut nougat] (141), *pimientos del pico* [pico peppers] (157), and the missing *pimientos del piquillo* [piquillo peppers] (157)—that comprise an inclusive, unmutilated Spain. Culture, as Graham and Labanyi remind us, is "a site of power that is always negotiated and contested."[35] Rosita's power derives from the products that surround her and remind the narrator of what she has lost both in her geographical displacement and in her changing self-definitions: Spain, a dispersed but still recognizable Spain. It is Rosita, "una buena chica" [a nice girl] (134) in the eyes of the expatriates, who enjoys the acceptance of the Spanish community in Scandinavia that the narrator scorns.

Rosita and her shop reconnect the narrator with "Spain" in a foreign land, but the owner's refusal to acknowledge the narrator's Spanishness denies her identity by denying their sameness. The narrator's musings to herself about the possible "distinción inexistente" (nonexistent distinction) between *pimientos del pico* and *pimientos del piquillo* reiterates her questioning of sameness and difference, of herself and Rosita: "¿Había en realidad alguna diferencia entre los unos y los otros?" [Was there really any difference between the two?] (157) Does she, like the various producers of canned peppers who replicate "el error, la distinción inexistente en agresivas letras de molde y etiquetas" [the error, the nonexistent distinction in aggressive print and on labels] (157), err when she persists in drawing distinctions between Rosita and herself? Similarly, in both stories grape and grain—Rioja en "La Flor" and raki in "Con Agatha"—function not only as cultural markers but as markers of difference and, at the same time, repetition. Spain's rich heritage of wine production, perhaps the defining artifact of Spanish culture, is reduced in "La Flor" to a single Rioja that the narrator, and other

Spanish expatriates, purchase from Rosita's shop. Like *pimientos del pico* and *pimientos del piquillo* difference may be a question of sameness, in this case, a similar nostalgia for iconic Spain and a resistance to Scandinavian patterns of consumption. In "Con Agatha" both the narrator's husband and Flora simulate an immersion into the local culture by drinking raki, while the narrator resists this tourist ploy by sticking to wine and whiskey. The bond of raki creates a sense of community between Julio and Flora that leaves the narrator feeling isolated, a nontouristy tourist in Istanbul: "Se estableció una comunicación de la que yo, sola ante mi whisky tibio, quedaba automáticamente excluida" [A connection was established from which I, alone with my warm whisky, was automatically excluded] (188).

When the narrator of "La Flor" first spies the neon sign in front of Rosita's shop, its defective *ñ* flickers between "España" and "Espana" while the sign itself sputters between its approximation of "Spain" and undifferentiated darkness. With its grotesque *ñ* and "curiosos guiños" [curious winks] (120)—now a simulacrum of "España," now a mutilated "Espana"—the sign is an unstable signifier of negotiation, of a subject always in process. "Espana" is the trace of "España" in the polysemic sign, as the shop itself is a trace of Spain in a Scandinavian city. The tilde figures this instability of representation and the possibility of plurisignification. The neon sign's ill-formed and mutable letters visually and literally communicate the constructedness of "Spain" and correspondingly the store's inevitable condition as, in Spires's words, "a defective imitation of the real thing."[36] The name "Spain" itself disappears and reappears, like facets of the narrator's shifting identity. The bizarre, disproportionate tilde suggests not only the uneven relationship between Spain's component regions but the narrator's unease, her feeling of not belonging, of being and not being a part of the local culture:

Aquélla no era una tilde normal y corriente. Una onda apenas esbozada, un signo ligero, sugerente, sino un auténtico disparate, un trazo desmesurado, toscamente añadido a una inocente e indefensa ene.

[That was not a normal, run-of-the-mill tilde. A barely sketched wave, a slight, suggestive sign, but something truly ridiculous, a disproportionate line, crudely added to an innocent and defenseless *n*.] (120–21)

Peter Brooks reminds us in *Body Work* that "the use of the linguistic sign implies the absence of the thing for which it stands."[37] The shop "La Flor de España" makes a simulacrum of Spain present in its accumulation of cultural icons, "but always within the context of its absence." If nationality as cultural artifact is, as Anderson states, "'modular,' capable of being transplanted," then Fernández Cubas's scenarios interrogate the ways in which this occurs.

In a postmodern world, "La Flor de España" is the space of Spanish difference always on the verge of becoming other, "Espana," or disappearing altogether. Like Flor and Flora in the two stories, "Españ/na" signals both difference and sameness. The duality of "España"/"Espana" literalizes Derrida's concept of "under erasure," a marking that calls attention to the absence of univocal meaning, truth, or origin. The word is both there and not there, "operating 'under erasure' in the interval between reversal and emergence; an idea which cannot be thought in the old way, but without which certain key questions cannot be thought at all."[38] The shop sign also mirrors the impossibility of the narrator's quest for coherence as a subject; she both does and does not see herself reflected in it, does and does not recognize herself in Rosita. The shop symbolically encodes "Spain" and "Spanishness" but Rosita does not; she fails to respond to the narrator's need for a reflected image of herself. The distinction between the self as observer (a subject in process) and the self as reflected back by others (object) does not collapse into unity.

From the unfamiliar space of the city made more vast and less hospitable by the snow, the narrator moves into the cozy interior of Rosita's store with its nostalgic recreation of a Spain outside history. Rosita is a counterpoint to the female community of Scandinavian women: her shop simulates Spain, whereas the women construct the narrator as a simulacrum of themselves. The narrator first perceives her bond with the wives when she intuits in their silence a communal confession of opposition to Rosita that gestures toward embracing her: "'A nosotras *tampoco* nos gusta Rosa de España'" [We don't like Rosa from Spain *either*] (138). It is the wives who invite the narrator to join them and whose gift of an embroidered collar, the icon of their national costume, is a way of saying: "'Ahora empiezas a ser un poco de las nuestras'" [Now you are beginning to be just a little like us] (155). The gift signals the narrator's boundary crossing: "Una frontera o aduana entre las aborígenes y las extranjeras, las integradas y las turistas, las mujeres de bien, en definitiva... y las otras" [A frontier or customs post between aboriginal women and foreign women, integrated women and women tourists, in short, proper women . . . and the others] (155).

In contrast, the narrator takes the initiative in identifying Rosita as her imagined community of *nosotras* [we women]. Reduced to speaking "mitad con gestos, mitad con palabras" [half in gestures, half in words] (123) and to "ridículos balbuceos" [ridiculous babblings] (125) when she first tries to converse with Rosita in the local language, on her subsequent visit the narrator feels overwhelmed by a desire to speak, to regain her own language and the control it gives her: "De repente sentía unas ganas tremendas de hablar" [Suddenly I felt a tremendous desire to speak] (126). In Rosita's laconic responses, the story's unreliable narrator initially reads a ploy by Rosita to interpellate her and make her reveal her identity: "Aquellas palabras no eran más que un lazo, una trampa ingeniosa para hacerme intervenir; para estrechar un círculo; para arrancarme de una vez por todas mi tarjeta de visita" [Those words were only a snare, an ingenious trap to make me participate [in the conversation]; to tighten a circle; to wrest my visiting card from me once and for all] (140). Hall emphasizes that identities arise partly in the field of fantasy: "the belongingness, the 'suturing into the story' through which identities arise is, partly, in the imaginary (as well as the symbolic) and therefore, always, partly constructed in fantasy, or at least within a fantasmatic field."[39] The narrator's truncated, one-sided dialogues with Rosita operate to a large degree "within a fantasmatic field." Language itself fascinates the narrator as her overdetermined readings of Rosita's scant utterances demonstrate. She toys with its surface by repeating words like *pimientos de piquillo* and *contratiempo* [contretemps] (142) until, the arbitrary nexus between signifier and signified dissolved, the sounds cease to convey anything other than themselves.

The narrator's obsessive stalking of Rosita is another kind of mirroring, her attempt to recover her Spanishness by provoking Rosita into a recognition of their sameness. Rosita's impassivity arouses in the narrator the need for an interlocutor, a perverse desire to engage the silent woman in conversation with her. Attempting to make Rosita return her gaze, she ponders strategies that underscore her similarity to the sputtering *ñ*: "¿Por qué no pensar en un mensaje, un guiño, un reto, un 'aquí estoy,' encantador y desafiante?" [Why not think of a message, a wink, a challenge, a charming and defiant "here I am"?] (159). The protagonist, like the store's neon sign with its winks and fluctuating messages, is, in Spires's phrasing, "a carica-

ture of her transported Spanish self."[40] Rosita's resistance gives the
narrator a space for the exploration of identity, for winnowing self
from other within the parameters of sameness. The narrator's insis-
tent response to the challenge posed by Rosita confirms Ernesto
Laclau's dictum that "the constitution of a social identity is an act of
power."[41] The narrator's power play opens a space within which she
can negotiate her identity against a resistant other, against Rosita's
marking of difference within their sameness of geography, language, gender, and nationality.

Gender identity as well as national identity is unstable and open
to misreading in these stories. The narrator's initial path toward
integration into the world of the other comes in her affairs with
Scandinavian men: first with Olav, whose incomprehensible abandonment of her—"me preguntaba . . . *por qué* Olav me había abandonado" [I asked myself . . . *why* Olav had abandoned me]
(119)—sets in motion her disoriented quest for a centered identity,
and then with Gert, whom she dramatically abandons—"Lo hice de
un soberbio portazo, recordando . . . que mi relación con Gert había
tenido mucho de teatro" [I did it with a magnificent slamming of
the door, remembering . . . that my relationship with Gert had been
very theatrical] (144). The isolation of the solitary individual in a
foreign community remains: "Olav y Gert, ¿existía en el fondo alguna diferencia entre abandonar o ser abandonado?" [Olav and
Gert, was there deep down any difference between abandoning and
being abandoned?] (144). From being her lovers, the two men move
into an exclusive relationship with each other which she first reads
as "amigos inseparables" [inseparable friends] (152) and then as
novios [lovers] (159). The sexual bonding of two Scandinavian men
seemingly closes the ranks of nationality and gender against her and
calls her own gender identity into question. As Hall observes, identities are "never singular but multiply constructed across different,
often intersecting and antagonistic, discourses, practices and positions."[42]

At the end of the story gender and sexuality resurface in the narrator's curiously mocking query to Rosita about the possibility that
"nuestra querida tilde, tan islámica, tan cumplidora y equitativa en
sus deberes conyugales, se haya decantado por una de sus esposas
con el consabido perjuicio para la otra?" [our dear tilde, so Islamic,
so reliable and equitable in its conjugal duties, has decanted itself
toward one of its wives to the obvious detriment of the other?]
(159). Here her fixation with the tilde overlaps with her obsession

with Rosita as she inscribes both in sexual language. Her question associates her attraction to her blond double with sexual fascination and pairs the two women in a conjugal bond with the polygamous tilde that brought them together and ties them to each other. By fixating on the shopkeeper, the narrator duplicates the Olav/Gert quest for sameness as she searches for her reflection in the mirror of another Spanish woman, a woman seemingly at home in both the autochthonous community and its Spanish-speaking community, while retaining and purveying the signs of Spanishness. Indeed, the narrator's encounters with Rosita occur in the intervals between her relationships with Olav and Gert and trigger a desire for release from a foreign tongue and a return to Spanish. In the light of Olav and Gert's pairing, do we read the narrator's obsessive dependence on Rosita—and on Rosita's recalcitrance—as "a stylized repetition of acts" that performs gender even as it performs nationality? The narrator's probing of difference within sameness, marking the boundaries between self and other, suggests the destabilization of gender as well as language and nationality. She is experiencing "category crisis," as Marjorie Garber terms the "failure of definitional distinction . . . that permits border crossings from one (apparently distinct) category to another."[43]

In the end the challenge posed by the desire to read the signs of Spanishness and otherness that are Rosita allows the narrator finally to see herself as process and to project interlocution as the space for the construction of her future: "me sentía bien en mi piel y ante nosotras, sobre todo, se abría un largo, frío, imprevisible invierno" [I felt good in my skin and ahead of us women stretched, above all, a long, cold, unpredictable winter] (160). The undifferentiated, isolating sameness of winter, once viewed as so unwelcoming, has become the opportunity for the narrator to probe the sameness and difference of gender, language, and nationality and her dependence on and desired control of a disinterested Rosita. She imagines a nuclear community of herself and Rosita that is, as Anderson envisioned, a "deep, horizontal comradeship" with "cultural roots," "regardless of the actual inequality and exploitation that may prevail."[44] This distillation of a common nationality does not produce reciprocity or communication in either story. The border crossings—both literal and figurative—in both stories produce subjects that embody and at the same time contest Jo Labanyi's observation that in the new, postmodern Spain, "to be Spanish is to be Spanish and international at the same time."[45]

"Con Agatha en Estambul"

In both of Fernández Cubas's stories, the narrators stare through
glass at a world outside their grasp, either from the street looking in
at "Spain" in "La Flor de España" or from the hotel looking out at
"Istanbul." If in "La Flor" the shop window frames "Spain," in
"Con Agatha en Estambul" the window of the hotel bar tantalizes
the immobilized narrator with the possibility of visual access to an
"Istanbul" obliterated by mist. Unable to confirm the existence of
Istanbul by looking outward, she looks into the aquarium in the hotel's bar. A simulacrum of the Golden Horn that gives Istanbul its
unique identity, as the store in "La Flor" is a simulacrum of Spain,
the aquarium is both reflecting surface and the space of discovery
that prompts her meditations on the instability of identity. While
Rosita's shop reduces Spain to its distinctive artifacts, the aquarium
with its single fish is a *reductio ad absurdum* of the Bosporus. But
whereas in "La Flor" the narrator comes face to face with the signs
of Spain, the cultural signifiers of Istanbul are invisible to the narrator of "Con Agatha" in the fog that shrouds the city. Rather than
affirming the identity of the city, their absence mocks the tourist's
quest to see firsthand what is already familiar from representations.
Instead of viewing "the real thing," the narrator eyes the city in the
paintings of its most famous cultural artifacts that hang on the hotel
walls: "A mi espalda unos cuantos grabados reproducían retazos de
aquella ciudad que se negaba a mostrarse en conjunto. El Gran
Bazar, el Harem de Topkapi, Santa Sofía" [At my back some pictures
reproduced fragments of that city which refused to show its whole
self. The Grand Bazaar, the Topkapi Harem, Saint Sophia] (176).
Like the paintings, the names of famous visitors to the city, its cultural icons—Agatha Christie, Sarah Bernhardt, Mata Hari, Ata-
turk—exist only as textual memories (176). These representations
of cultural absence throw into sharper focus the process of identity
construction and raise the question of whether something exists if
the narrator cannot see it or whether nothing exists beyond language: "¿Existía Estambul? . . . ¿estaba yo realmente allí? O mejor:
¿qué era *allí?*" [Did Istanbul exist? . . . was I really there? Or better
yet: what did *there* mean?] (176). They also figure the layering of
time and cultures in an Istanbul whose Pera Palas Hotel effaces its
historic 1941 bomb damage. This interplay of physical reality, memory, representation, and the power of imagination underlies Fernán-

dez Cubas's story. The narrator's decision to accept the identity of
the invisible city—"El decidir que aquello era Estambul como podía
ser cualquier otra ciudad del mundo" [Deciding that that was Istanbul just as it could be any other city in the world] (180)—sets in
motion the chain of interpretation and reinterpretation that constitutes the story of a tourist continually (re)inventing the city as Istanbul and not Istanbul and herself as Spanish and not Spanish. The
end of the story makes explicit the link between memory and verbal
invention, between past, present, and future, in the narrator's "recordando, fabulando" [remembering, telling] (233). Language
gives form to memory, and memory and storytelling—linguistic invention—shape the construction of subjectivity.

Searching for the "real" Istanbul in the enveloping fog, the narrator discovers the duplicity of surface appearances from the chimerical fish in the fish tank/sea. As the narrator stares dumbly, the fish
metamorphoses from a strange, ugly creature into a youthful, ap-
pealing *Campanilla* [Tinkerbell], exercising the same fascination for
her as Rosita does for the narrator in the earlier story. Its transformations convey the possibility of decoding what lies hidden beneath
visible surfaces. Identity is mutable and reveals its multiple facets
only in privileged moments. Her gaze deflected through the glass of
the aquarium, the narrator experiences the optical illusion of seeing
both her nemesis, Flora, and Flora's double, a duality that in turn
duplicates her doubled view of the aquarium's fish and *Campanilla.*
Flora is both doubled and, as a Spanish woman tourist in Istanbul,
the narrator's double, reproducing the split the narrator does not
detect in herself, a split similar to the one that propels the narrator
of "La Flor" in her pursuit of Rosita. In "Con Agatha" the narrator's fixation on Flora replicates her perception of Flora's vamping
of her husband. "[U]na mujer pendiente de las reacciones de un
pez" [A woman waiting for the reactions of a fish] (210), the narrator believes she is learning to read the mutability of the people and
objects around her by watching the fish change form. On one level
Flora is the perfect tourist, evincing "la amable disponibilidad de los
viajeros en un país extraño" [the amiable flexibility of travelers in a
foreign country] (181) that the narrator cannot muster. On another
level, in unguarded moments Flora's face displays what the narrator
deciphers as her hidden agenda. Flora's name and the Spanish she
speaks offer the only markers of her nationality. The requisite
"lugar de origen" [place of origin] that situates the members of the
Spanish-speaking community in "La Flor" plays no role in "Con

Agatha." Here language, the Spanish language, is identity, and as
the narrator slips from Spanish into Turkish she loosens her ties to
her husband, to Flora, and to Spain.

Both the display window and the aquarium are reflecting surfaces
that give access to a magical space in which multiple others—
multiple enactments of Spain—shape the way each narrator sees
herself. As mirrors they reflect back the narrators' constructions of
self and other and within their depths they hold the space that
allows each narrator to conceive alternate subject positions. In both
stories a bell [*campanilla*] breaks the narrator's reverie: the bell on
the shop door in "La Flor," and the bellboy's signature bell in "Con
Agatha." Both bells interrupt the narrator's mental fabrications, the
chain of linguistic signifiers that is the narrator's processing of herself. In "Con Agatha" there is both the sound of a real bell and the
glimpse of its complement, Tinkerbell. With the fog, the narrator of
"Con Agatha" cannot confirm the identity of Istanbul or the
Golden Horn, but within the miniature "sea" of the aquarium she
perceives a duality beneath the surface of the visible. From this
awareness she spins her web of language. Her identity formation
centers on a series of cultural icons: "Agatha Christie," the Spanish
tourist, Flora, and the taxi driver, Faruk. "Agatha Christie" is the
visible space—the narrator literally peers through the keyhole into
an empty hotel room—onto which the narrator projects an alter
ego, another self, imagined as similar in experience to her, yet different. The narrator bonds with this codified memory of Agatha
Christie, whose visit to the Pera Palas Hotel is improbably memorialized on the door of one of the small rooms on an upper floor. From
this locked space and remembered scenes from the film *Agatha*, the
narrator invents an "Agatha" with whom she shares identity mark-
ᴇrs—a woman in her late thirties (the narrator is forty), in an unfamiliar country, without her husband, uncertain of her future—in
much the same way that the narrator of "La Flor" adopts Rosita as
the site of her identity-in-construction. Through the closed door of
the room, the narrator perceives "Agatha" smiling back at her,
much as the fish seems to return her gaze, whereas in "La Flor" the
flesh-and-blood Rosita steadfastly resists the narrator's attempts to
impose a story on her. In her mental fabrications the narrator plots
Flora as she imagines Agatha Christie plotting the characters in her
fiction. Her eyes riveted on the aquarium, the narrator seeks the
privileged moment in which the two, incompatible identities of the
fish/*Campanilla* coexist, the moment in which she can hold simulta-

neously both Floras or both the fish and Tinkerbell in her field of vision. It is the impossibility of capturing in a single moment in time all manifestations of identity that Fernández Cubas's story dramatizes.

Instead of the conventional story of a tourist visually consuming an unknown—but nevertheless familiar—city, "Con Agatha" explores interior spaces: hotel rooms, bars and restaurants, the back seat of a taxi, Faruk's house, and finally the plane en route to Barcelona. The narrator's claustrophobic sojourn and evident paranoia contrast with her freedom of movement and initiative in Barcelona as the story opens. She imagines language as another interior space awaiting exploration: "el turco, como todas las lenguas, era un castillo del que no se conocen los planos" [Turkish, like all languages, was a castle for which no one has the plans] (206). With the prevailing mist and her swollen ankle, the narrator misses the opportunity to "go native" and map the city space for herself. Instead it is language that challenges her to map its unknown dimensions: "Tenía que hacerme con el manojo de llaves y desvelar los secretos de todas las cerraduras" [I had to get hold of the bunch of keys and unveil the secrets of all the locks] (206). Language tempts her to penetrate its inner recesses just as the narrator of "La Flor" rises to the challenge of penetrating Rosita's silences. Like the Turkish language, the geographical space of Istanbul holds the illusion that it can be apprehended:

¿Existía Estambul? ¿O no era nada más ni menos que un espacio sin límites que todos, en algún momento, llevábamos en la espalda, pegado como una mochila? . . . ¿O se trataba únicamente de un eco? Un eco distinto para cada uno de nosotros que no hacía más que enfrentarnos a nuestras vidas.

[Did Istanbul exist? Or was it no more and no less than a limitless space that we all, at some moment, carry on our backs, adhering to us like a backpack? . . . Or was it only an echo? A different echo for each one of us that only brought us face to face with our own lives.] (222–23)

Istanbul becomes the space of self-discovery, an echo of the narrator's desires. Like Flora, Agatha, and Faruk, the city is the other of the Spanish narrator, an unknown and unknowable space, tantalizingly close but unbridgeable by language, memory, or representation.

While the narrator of "La Flor" fixates on another woman, in an obsession that mirrors the same-sex coupling of Olav and Gert, in "Con Agatha" the narrator convinces herself that she is conversing in Turkish with Faruk. She invents a subject position that cuts across nationality, language, gender, and most particularly class. It is the lack of reciprocity in the passenger-driver relationship that eludes the narrator as she imagines herself entering a language community of Turkish speakers. The physical presence of Faruk is always displaced, first by the taxi's rearview mirror, then by her failure to decipher his words, by the old photograph he shows her, and finally by her distant musing on "la posibilidad de una aventura con Faruk" [the possibility of an adventure with Faruk] (231). Like Istanbul, Flora, and Julio, Faruk is a mystery, an unknown space obscured by fog which she mythifies through successive interpretations of his only vaguely understood conversation. In the game the narrator plays—the game in which she speaks and comprehends Turkish— Faruk is displaced by the "Faruk" that filters through her limited language skills. He is as unknowable to her as she is to him. As Bauman specifies with regard to "players" in the postmodern world: "Each game is made of conventions of its own; each is a separate 'province of meaning'—a little universe of its own, self-enclosed and self-contained."[46] In the narrator's game that she forms part of a Turkish-speaking community, she perceived her moves, in Bauman's terminology, as "clever" and "shrewd," rather than "misguided" and in error. Only from the airplane on her flight back to Barcelona—quite literally a "flight" that leaves her husband behind—does the narrator appreciate the extent of her miscommunication and her failure to create a community between Faruk and herself. Contradicting her confident view of herself is Julio's portrayal: a woman drugged by pain pills, "empeñada en chapurrear un idioma que desconoces, en usar un perfume pestilente" [determined to babble away in a language you don't know, to use a foul-smelling perfume], and suffering from "un ataque de celos" [an attack of jealousy] (221). What Julio reads as jealousy of Flora can be understood as a complex mix of attraction and rejection grounded in a common national identity that, as in "La Flor," masks a desire at once to dominate the other and to occupy her place.

   In the story's circular structure which takes the narrator from her impulsive purchase of a ticket to Istanbul to her return to Barcelona alone, her personal circumstances alter but her capacity for language and invention remains undiminished. Having failed at "going native" in Istanbul and having broken her bonds to her Spanish compatriots, Julio and Flora, she resists conforming to the dictates of courtesy and douses herself in the Egoïste perfume that is as unconvincing as her performance in Istanbul and equally alien to Spanish middle-class cultural norms. In the airspace that is neither Spain nor Turkey, she continues to negotiate her identity, projecting future variations on her relationship to Faruk and pondering ways to regain control of a story that, unexpectedly for her, he turns out to have written. One alternative is to relocate the story to Barcelona and recast it as a sexual adventure. When linguistic compatibility proves illusory, sexual difference offers a more conventional plot line. As a story about identity formation, "Con Agatha" interrogates the construction of cities—Barcelona and Istanbul, not countries as "La Flor" does, but nevertheless an absent Spain links the narrator and Flora. The tension between the two women and the narrator's sense that Flora is making a play for Julio—is he literally the conquering Caesar or ironically Flora's conquest?—cloak another identity conflict, one that characterizes the historical and cultural ties binding and dividing Barcelona and Spain.

Conclusion

In "La Flor de España" the narrator's conflicted response to her displaced Spanishness, her attempts to center her identity and occupy a stable subject position, do not resolve gender, linguistic, and national differences and come to rest on the specularity of another woman. In "Con Agatha en Estambul" the narrator's attempted integration into a community of Turkish speakers, initially interpreted by her as entirely successful, subsequently unravels into a recognition of self-deception. Both narrators are subjects perpetually in pursuit of the illusions of both selfhood and community, constantly negotiating between languages and nationalities. Like the ever-flickering ñ of "España" and the fish that is both fish and Tinkerbell, both women by turns are—and are not—Spanish, are—and are not—other, as they enact Garber's "category crisis" in their continuously shifting relationships to language, gender, and nation. Fernández Cubas's postmodern world dramatizes Spanishness as an unending process of identity (re)construction through differentiation and doubling. Language marks the boundaries of nationality and otherness and holds the promise of a "shared community." The fact that the author, a Spanish-language writer, lives and publishes in the capital city of the autonomous region of Catalonia adds a further layer of doubling and differentiation to my reading of her stories. The two great port cities in "Con Agatha," Barcelona and Istanbul, once capitals of their respective empires and now positioned at the margins of late twentieth-century geopolitics, mirror each other in terms of their geographical, historical, and linguistic displacement on the global stage. Their empires remain alive only in the national imaginary and, especially in the case of Istanbul, in the monuments that constitute cultural capital in the tourist economy. In some sense, Fernández Cubas, by writing of Istanbul, displaces onto foreign terrain the fraught relationship between Spanish and Catalan in her native Barcelona. In both stories the unstable positions of linguistic dominance and subordination can be read as reflecting the uncertainties facing a native Spanish speaker navigating the unsettled waters of language politics in post-Franco Barcelona.

In this essay I have treated Spain as the nation of origin of both narrators, but in fact each story constructs Spain from its periphery. The cultural artifacts and practices that identify "Spain" originate at the margins of its geographical space. The absence of a unifying center, like the physical absence of Spain in the stories (except in the opening paragraph of "Con Agatha"), figures a plural, decentered Spain that is both geographically distant and always other. Fernández Cubas's recognition in these two stories that identity, as Graham and Labanyi define it, is "difference within" and her postmodern construction of "Spanishness" as the negotiation of "plurality and contradiction" suggest the possibility of reading both stories as allegories of the national, linguistic, and gender politics not only of Spain but also of her native city, Barcelona, where Spanish and Catalan coexist in an uneasy and unresolved tension.

NOTES

1. Nathan E. Richardson, *Postmodern "Paletos": Immigration, Democracy, and Globalization in Spanish Narrative and Film, 1950–2000* (Lewisburg, Pa.: Bucknell University Press, 2002), 23.

2. Cristina Fernández Cubas, "La Flor de España," *El ángulo del horror* (Barcelona: Tusquets, 1990), 118–60, and "Con Agatha en Estambul," *Con Agatha en Estambul* (Barcelona: Tusquets, 1994), 171–233. As I will discuss later, no single translation of the title of "La Flor de España" reflects its polysemy. Hereafter whenever clarity permits I will shorten the titles of the stories to "La Flor" and "Con

Agatha." In her study of *El ángulo del horror*, Jessica A. Folkart comments that the author "playfully problematizes the connection between language, national identity, and world view" ("Desire, Doubling, and Difference in Cristina Fernández Cubas's *El ángulo del horror*," *Revista Canadiense de Estudios Hispánicos* 24:2 [Winter 2000]: 356).

3. Folkart, "Desire, Doubling, and Difference," 354.

4. Helen Graham and Jo Labanyi, eds., *Spanish Cultural Studies: An Introduction. The Struggle for Modernity* (Oxford: Oxford University Press, 1995), 5.

5. Robert C. Spires, "Postmodernism/Paralogism: *El ángulo del horror* by Cristina Fernández Cubas," *Journal of Interdisciplinary Literary Studies* 7 (1995): 234.

6. Stuart Hall, "Who Needs 'Identity'?" *Questions of Cultural Identity*, ed. Stuart Hall and Paul Du Gay (London: Sage, 1996), 2.

7. Zygmunt Bauman, "From Pilgrim to Tourist—or a Short History of Identity," *Questions of Cultural Identity*, ed. Stuart Hall and Paul Du Gay (London: Sage, 1996), 24.

8. Ibid., 26.

9. Ibid., 19.

10. Ibid., 28–29. For Bauman "the catchword of postmodernity is recycling" (18). Hence in his view the postmodern individual seeks to keep identity in flux: "the *postmodern* 'problem of identity' is primarily how to avoid fixation and keep the options open" (18).

11. Ibid., 28.

12. Mary Lee Bretz, *Encounters Across Borders: The Changing Visions of Spanish Modernism, 1890–1930* (Lewisburg, Pa.: Bucknell University Press, 2001), 326.

13. Kay Pritchett, "Cristina Fernández Cubas's 'Con Agatha en Estambul': Traveling into Mist and Mystery," *Monographic Review/Revista Monográfica* 12 (1996): 247.

14. Kathleen M. Glenn, "Gothic Indecipherability and Doubling in the Fiction of Cristina Fernández Cubas," *Monographic Review/Revista Monográfica* 8 (1992): 139; "Narrative Designs in Cristina Fernández Cubas's 'Mundo,'" *Romance Languages Annual* 9 (1997): 504.

15. Pritchett, "Cristina Fernández Cubas," 247; Glenn, "Gothic Indecipherability and Doubling," 131. Folkart identifies Fernández Cubas as "one of the key writers who express the exploration of identity in post-totalitarian Spain" and affirms that "[i]n all her fiction, Fernández Cubas investigates how society influences the formation of identity" (343).

16. Jo Labanyi, "Narrative in Culture: 1975–1996," *The Cambridge Companion to Modern Spanish Culture*, ed. David T. Gies (Cambridge: Cambridge University Press, 1999), 156. Labanyi adds that Fernández Cubas's first two books "remain her best." I consider the two stories treated in this essay to be among her finest work to date.

17. Labanyi, "Postmodernism and the Problem of Cultural Identity," *Spanish Cultural Studies: An Introduction*, ed. Helen Graham and Jo Labanyi (Oxford: Oxford University Press, 1995), 403–5.

18. Ibid., 404. Labanyi opines that "the only successful feminist appropriation of postmodernist pastiche is the performance art of the singer Martirio" (405).

19. Ibid., 397.

20. Ibid.

21. Judith Butler, *Bodies That Matter: On the Discursive Limits of "Sex"* (New York: Routledge, 1993), 3.

22. David Lynch, *The Image of the City* (Cambridge: MIT Press, 1960), 65.

23. Benedict Anderson, *Imagined Communities: Reflections on the Origin and Spread of Nationalism*, 2nd ed. (London: Verso, 1991), 5. In Anderson's widely cited definition, the nation is "an imagined political community": "It is *imagined* because the members of even the smallest nation will never know most of their fellow-members, meet them, or even hear of them, yet in the minds of each lives the image of their communion" (6). Anderson equates national identity with what to him is the fixed, stable nature of gender identity. I reject this aspect of his definition.

24. Andrew Parker, Mary Russo, Doris Sommer, and Patricia Yaeger, eds. *Nationalisms and Sexualities* (New York: Routledge, 1992), 5.

25. Anderson, *Imagined Communities*, 4.

26. Peter Brooker, *A Concise Glossary of Cultural Theory* (London: Arnold, 1999), 64.

27. Butler, *Gender Trouble: Feminism and the Subversion of Identity* (New York: Routledge, 1990), 140; emphasis in the original.

28. Ibid., 143 and 142.

29. Janet Pérez has studied narrative unreliability and the "dense atmospheres of ambiguity" in Fernández Cubas's fiction, including *Con Agatha en Estambul* ("Cristina Fernández Cubas: Narrative Unreliability and the Flight from Clarity, or, the Quest for Knowledge in the Fog," *Hispanófila* 122 [1998]: 30). Pérez concludes that as Fernández Cubas moves away from the Fantastic and the Gothic "towards seemingly more mundane, quotidian 'realities,' her fictional world moves paradoxically further from the reader's grasp, slipping from the unknown into the unknowable" (37).

30. For the narrator of "La Flor" the reduction of Spanish identity to "nombre, apellidos, profesión, años de residencia y lugar de origen" [name, last names, profession, length of residence and place of origin] (130) is unsatisfactory.

31. Glenn recognizes the instability of the interpretative act in this story when she questions "how much faith we should place in the narrator's reading of other people and her decoding of the verbal or non-verbal messages they transmit." She concludes that the text "remains unstable" ("Gothic Indecipherability and Doubling," 132).

32. See Rosemary Lloyd, "Objects in the Mirror: Gendering the Still Life," *Yearbook of Comparative and General Literature* 49 (2001): 39–55.

33. Lloyd, "Objects," 41.

34. As Labanyi observes, "'low culture' is that which is enjoyed for its functional qualities" (*Constructing Identity in Contemporary Spain: Theoretical Debates and Cultural Practice* [Oxford: Oxford University Press, 2002], 2).

35. Graham and Labanyi, *Spanish Cultural Studies*, 5.

36. Spires, "Postmodernism/Paralogism," 238.

37. Peter Brooks, *Body Work: Objects of Desire in Modern Narrative* (Cambridge: Harvard University Press, 1993), 8.

38. Hall, "Who Needs 'Identity'?," 2.

39. Ibid., 4.

40. Spires, "Postmodernism/Paralogism," 236.

41. Quoted in Hall, "Who Needs 'Identity'?," 5.

42. Hall, "Who Needs 'Identity'?," 4.

43. Marjorie Garber, "The Occidental Tourist: *M. Butterfly* and the Scandal of

Transvestism," *Nationalisms and Sexualities,* ed. Andrew Parker, Mary Russo, Doris Sommer, and Patricia Yaeger (New York: Routledge, 1992), 125.

44. Anderson, *Imagined Communities,* 7.

45. Labanyi, "Postmodernism," 397. Discussing border crossing, Spires concludes that in "La Flor de España" it conveys "the illogic of language and national identity" ("Postmodernism/Paralogism," 236) and reveals "the absurd inconsistencies in language, communication, national identity, and deductive reasoning" (238).

46. Bauman, "From Pilgrim to Tourist," 31.

Being Other in Another/'s Place:
Uncanny Adventures in *Con Agatha en Estambul*

Nancy Vosburg

CON AGATHA EN ESTAMBUL [WITH AGATHA IN ISTANBUL], CRISTINA FERNÁN-
dez Cubas's 1994 collection of five short stories, presents the reader
with a rhetoric of ambiguity and uncertainty and an absence of
closed, stable meaning that we have come to expect from this writer
of what some have identified as "fantastic" short fiction.[1] Yet, particularly in this collection, the stories seem to be adventures in the uncanny rather than the fantastic. Most of the extant criticism on
Fernández Cubas's stories notes the recurrent theme of the double
or the repressed self, often configured as the abject, that inhabits
many of her tales.[2] While this theme is explored again in the 1994
collection, what seems to link these five tales is the creation of uncanny effects that are centered on the desire to "be other in another
place." While this notion is explicitly stated in the fourth story of
the collection, "Ausencia" [Absence], the other four stories explore
as well the desire to appropriate another place, another life, one
that each protagonist feels rightly belongs to her or to him. As the
characters cross boundaries, concrete or abstract, they enter uncanny worlds that eventually lead to "home," configured literally or
metaphorically.

Fernández Cubas's stories have fascinated and/or unsettled readers since the publication of her first collection, *Mi hermana Elba* [My
Sister Elba], in 1980. This was followed by the short stories of *Los
altillos de Brumal* [The Attics of Brumal] in 1983, the novel *El año de
Gracia* [The Year of Grace] in 1985, and a subsequent collection of
short stories, *El ángulo del horror* [The Angle of Horror], in 1990.
Early criticism of the initial short story collections attempted to situate them within the realm of the Fantastic, even while acknowledg-
ing the difficulties of defining the genre.[3] But, as Janet Pérez has
affirmed in relation to Fernández Cubas's subsequent writings, the

author "progresses away from or beyond the fantastic terrain and sometimes Gothic ambients glimpsed in her initial collections toward seemingly more mundane, quotidian 'realities'" in her later writings. Paradoxically, Pérez notes, this shift does not result in greater epistemological clarity, but rather creates an even greater "shifting ontological ground" than that encountered in earlier writings.[4]

In many of Fernández Cubas's tales, particularly those of the 1990 *El ángulo del horror,* the sense of horror arises from the increasing dominance of those elements that tend toward "the dark side or repressed aspects of personality."[5] A certain malevolence haunts these stories, creating an ominous mood that contributes to the vague Gothic atmosphere of the stories. This, however, is not the predominant mood four years later in the *Agatha* collection, with perhaps the exception of the second story, "La mujer de verde" [The Woman in Green]. In fact, in all the stories, we are reminded of Freud's 1919 essay in which he explored the nature of *unheimlich,* or the "uncanny."[6] In one of his numerous forays into aesthetics, Freud began by affirming that the uncanny is "undoubtedly related to what is frightening—to what arouses dread and horror."[7] Yet he goes on to describe the uncanny as "that class of the frightening which leads back to what is known of old and long familiar." Freud discovered that the root of the uncanny is more inextricably linked to its apparent opposite, *heimlich,* or "'familiar,' 'native,' 'belonging to the home,'" than the simple negating prefix of the German word implies. The prefix tempts us "to conclude that what is 'uncanny' is frightening precisely because it is *not* known and familiar."[8] *Heimlich,* which designates a quality found within the bounds of a specific place that is at once familiar and intimate, is, as Freud noted, "a word the meaning of which develops in the direction of ambivalence, until it finally coincides with its opposite, *unheimlich.*" For Freud, the *unheimlich,* or uncanny, is "in some way or other a subspecies of *heimlich.*"[9] Freud's exploration of the uncanny is a useful tool for delving into this phenomenon in Fernández Cubas's *Agatha* collection. For we find in these stories that the desire to be other in another place, or in another's place, propels the fictional characters toward "home," toward that which they have "long known" to be familiar.

While "Ausencia" is the fourth story of the *Agatha* collection, it seems pertinent to begin here since the desire to be other in another place is explicitly stated. The story is narrated in the second-person singular, a technique that recalls for any Hispanist Carlos Fuentes's moribund Artemio Cruz, and his exploration of his subconscious desires. In Fernández Cubas's story, an apparently amnesia-stricken female addresses an "other" that she knows to be herself yet is incapable of identifying by the usual markers (name, nationality, age, address, profession, etc.). Her confusion is accompanied by a creeping dread that is introduced in the first paragraph:

> "¿Qué hago yo aquí?", te sorprendes pensando. Pero un sudor frío te hace notar que la pregunta es absurda, encubridora, falsa. Porque lo que menos importa en este momento es recorder lo que estás haciendo allí, sino algo mucho más sencillo. Saber *quién* eres tú.

> ["What am I doing here?," you surprise yourself thinking. But a cold sweat makes you aware that the question is absurd, concealing, false. Because what matters at this moment is not remembering what you are doing there, but rather something much more simple. Knowing *who* you are.] [10]

As the narrator slowly unravels her own identity, in both space and time, through the objects with her and around her (mirrors, credit cards, her identity card, a club membership card with her address and phone number, newspapers, clocks), she continues to experience dread as the essential question changes from that of her own identity to the motive of her apparent amnesia. Arriving at the front door of her *home,* she hesitates: "¿No será precisamente *lo que hay aquí* la causa de tu huida, lo que no deseas recordar por nada del mundo?" [Couldn't it be that it is precisely *what is here* that is the cause of your flight, what you do not want to remember for anything in the world?] (163–64).

The narrator's search for her own identity eventually reveals to her some sort of truth about her own existence: "Constantemente disgustada. Deseando ser otra en otro lugar. Sin apreciar lo que tienes por lo que ensueñas. Ausente, una eterna e irremediable ausente" [Constantly displeased. Desiring to be another in another place. Without appreciating what you have because of what you long for. Absent, eternally and irremediably absent] (170). In this tale of a fragmented identity, absence and presence are revealed to be two sides of the same coin. Indeed, absence defines the narrator's presence in the world. Her flight from reality/identity can be read as a compensation for a life she deems "gris, marrón, violácea" [gray, brown, violet] (170) in its routine and banality. The tone of apprehension and the emphasis on the "unfamiliar" situates it firmly within the realm of the uncanny. But her temporary absence, with its attendant "unfamiliarity," becomes "home-like" and familiar when she recalls the number of times she has invoked this state of absence throughout her life. The *unheimlich* develops toward and eventually coincides with the *heimlich.* Embracing her desire to be other, she does become temporarily an "other" that is paradoxically more definitive of the self.

Preceding and following "Ausencia" are two stories ("El lugar" [The Place] and the title story "Con Agatha en Estambul" [With Agatha in Istanbul], respectively) in which the characters share a preoccupation with "place," and with making "home-like" a reality configured as "unreal." Their quests will take them into "foreign" terrains, yet it is what they carry with them that transforms the *unheimlich* into something already known and familiar that has merely been waiting to reveal itself. In both stories, boundaries are crossed, yet this is accompanied by a paradoxical erasure of boundaries which leaves the reader with unsettled questions about the nature of the world, or worlds, presented.

In "El lugar," we encounter deceased characters speaking from beyond the grave (or in this case, a family mausoleum). The title of the story is closely associated with the idea of the *heimlich,* as the narrator's new wife, Clarisa, surprisingly abandons her professional life to install herself as a happy housewife:

El *lugar,* para Clarisa, era algo semejante a un talismán, un amuleto; la palabra mágica en la que se concretaba el secreto de la felicidad en el mundo. A veces era sinónimo de "sitio"; otras no. Acudía con frecuencia a una retahíla de frases hechas que, en su boca, parecían de pronto cargadas de significado, contundentes, definitivas. Encontrar el lugar, estar en su lugar, poner en su lugar, hallarse fuera de lugar. . . No había inocencia en su voz. Lejos del lugar—en sentido espacial o en cualquier otro sentido—se hallaba el abismo, las arenas movedizas, la inconcreción, el desasosiego. . . . Su lugar éramos la casa y yo, su marido.

[*Place,* for Clarisa, was something similar to a talisman, an amulet; the magic word in which the secret of happiness in the world was defined. At times it was synonymous with *sitio* (location, situation); at other times not. She turned frequently to a series of stock phrases that, in her mouth, seemed suddenly loaded with meaning, forceful, definitive. To find one's place, to be in one's place, to put in one's place, to find oneself out of place . . . There was no innocence in her voice. Beyond place—in the spatial sense or any other—was the abyss, the quicksand, the unsolidified, uneasiness. . . . The house and I, her husband, were her place.] (105–6)

Clarisa even appears to meld into a living room chair, erasing the boundaries between self and environment as she appropriates her new *lugar.* "No se sabía dónde acababa su vestido y empezaba el si-llón, pero lo mismo se podía afirmar de sus cabellos, de su piel, de los pies descalzos" [It was hard to tell where her dress ended and the chair began, but the same thing could be said about her hair, her skin, her bare feet] (102).[11]

After introducing Clarisa to his family pantheon, the narrator becomes disturbed when he notices an abrupt change in both her character and her health. Clarisa begins to dwell on the idea of her own death, and seems preoccupied with the fact that, upon dying, she will be placed in her husband's family pantheon, surrounded by unfamiliar souls. Within days she does die, and the narrator, characterizing his actions as the "tonterías" [foolishness] typical of the bereaved, slips into her coffin articles which belonged to his ancestors, hoping in this way to prepare a warm welcome for her.

It is at this point that the story takes on a supernatural quality, as the narrator begins to "converse" with his deceased wife in dreams. Initially disoriented, Clarisa slowly begins to discern the contours and characters of her new *lugar.* "*la casa,* decía ella" [*the house,* she called it] (138). Clarisa gradually begins to seize control of her new environment, to the point where she even contradicts the narrator's images and memories of his own family. While for Clarisa the mausoleum becomes more "home-like," the narrator begins to have his own uncanny sensation of displacement. What was once familiar, particularly the story of the mausoleum's tyrannical matriarch, Aunt Ricarda, becomes suddenly unfamiliar when Clarisa reports that Ricarda is nothing more than a servant. Gathering the items that he hopes will ensure his welcome reception in the pantheon, the narrator muses: "Clarisa había encontrado *su* lugar. Bien. Pero yo, desde ahora, estaba haciendo lo posible por asegurar el mío" [Clarisa had found *her* place. Fine. But I, from this moment on, would do everything possible to assure my own] (149).

While this story welcomes a psychological reading (the emotional stress suffered by a bereaved husband), as many of the author's stories do, it is also linked to the other tales in the collection by the desire, both Clarisa's and the narrator's, to be other in another/'s place. Clarisa, an orphan, not only appropriates the narrator's family pantheon, she appropriates "another/'s" place there (for the narrator, his own; for Clarisa, perhaps that of the matriarch Aunt Ricarda). The narrator must now find a way to assure his spot in that "other" place.

If Clarisa has an obsession with *el lugar* [place], an obsession that the narrator appropriates as his own, the narrator of the title story, "Con Agatha en Estambul," has a similar obsession with *el sitio* [location]. The narrator and her husband of fifteen years, Julio, cross a geographical frontier on a vacation trip from Barcelona to Istanbul. They also seem to pass into another "reality" due to the dense fog that envelops the city upon their arrival:

> ¿Existía Estambul? La sensación de irrealidad que me había embargado en el aeropuerto, nada más bajar del avión, no había hecho en aquellos días sino acrecentarse. Pero ahora ¿estaba yo realmente allí? O mejor: ¿qué era *allí?*

> [Did Istanbul exist? The sensation of unreality that had overpowered me in the airport, as soon as I got off the plane, had only increased in the following days. But now, was I really there? Or more accurately: what was *there?*] (176)

Strangeness is accentuated through the accumulation of additional uncanny effects that make the narrator feel "other" in this alien world she has entered. Most uncanny is her sudden discovery that she speaks fluent Turkish (or so she thinks); she also believes she has acquired "una extraña sabiduría" [a strange wisdom] (183) that converses with her, making her question what she observes; time seems to slow down; an accident leaves her with a sprained ankle, impeding her from moving freely around Istanbul with her husband; and objects, such as the fish in the hotel's lobby aquarium, gradually metamorphose into something else. All of these events seem to be provoked by the appearance of another woman, Flora, with whom the narrator gradually becomes obsessed, convinced that she is trying to seduce Julio. In addition, all the events are marked by a sense of disproportion—a disproportionate swelling of her ankle, a disproportionate change in the size and shape of the fish, disproportionate jealous imaginings when the narrator is forced to stay in the hotel while Julio and Flora explore the city.

The narrator is equally obsessed with an episode from the life of

Agatha Christie, who frequently stayed in the same hotel where the narrator and her husband have found *sitio*—the Pera Palas. The narrative of Agatha's ten-day "disappearance" in 1926 becomes an important subtext in the story:

> Diez días en los que el mundo la dio por muerta y en los que posiblemente la autora perdiera la razón o sufriera—y esto parece lo más probable—un agudo ataque de amnesia. Aunque, según algunas versiones, todo se redujo a una astuta estratagema para llamar la atención—de su marido fundamentalmente—y evitar lo que en aquellos momentos se le presentaba como una catástrofe. La separación. El abandono. Pero si eso fue realmente así, de nada le sirvió (al poco tiempo el marido conseguía el divorcio y se casaba con una amiga común).

> [Ten days in which the world thought her dead and in which the author possibly went insane or suffered—and this seems the most probable—a sudden attack of amnesia. Although, according to some versions, it all came down to an astute strategy to get the attention—of her husband fundamentally—and avoid what at that moment seemed like a catastrophe. Separation. Abandonment. But if that were really true, it didn't work (shortly afterward her husband obtained a divorce and married one of their mutual friends).] (185)

The episode acquires additional impact as the narrator begins to feel increasingly "other" as she is left behind by Julio and Flora.

As the story reaches the climactic moment of the confrontation between wife and husband, Istanbul itself becomes "other," its ontological status in the world questioned once again:

> ¿Existía Estambul? ¿O no era nada más ni nada menos que un espacio sin límites que todos, en algún momento, llevábamos en la espalda, pegado como una mochila? ¿Era Estambul un castigo o un premio? ¿O se trataba únicamente de un eco? Un eco distinto para cada uno de nosotros que no hacía más que enfrentarnos a nuestras vidas. No llegué a ninguna conclusión. En aquel espacio impreciso desfilaron antiguas historias, viejas reyertas, episodios olvidados. Julio me insultó, yo provoqué que me insultara.

> [Did Istanbul exist? Or was it neither more nor less than a space without limits that all of us, at some moment, carried on our back, stuck to us like a backpack? Was Istanbul a punishment or a reward? Or was it only an echo? A different echo for each of us whose purpose was to make us confront our lives. I didn't reach any conclusion. In that imprecise

space, ancient histories, old quarrels, forgotten episodes paraded by.
Julio insulted me, I provoked him to insult me.] (222–23)

The once-unfamiliar city is now recognized as a site long known and
familiar, an echo of "the truth" of the narrator's own character, her
desires, and her marital relationship.

Returning alone to Barcelona, the narrator muses that she has
somehow responded to some sinister desire to make Agatha's anguish her own: "¿Por qué hice mías sus angustias, el momento en
que el mundo se le vino abajo?" [Why did I make Agatha's anguish,
the moment in which the world collapsed on her, my own?] (228).
But Agatha's own happy ending, her second marriage, seems to animate and give hope to the narrator, who now feels that she can get
on with the adventure of life: "Decidiendo, en fin, que aquellos
pocos días, en Estambul, yo me lo había pasado en grande" [Decid-
ing, finally, that in those few days, in Istanbul, I had had a fabulous
time] (233). More importantly, she acknowledges and assumes that
other voice, the voice of "mature wisdom," as her own, embracing
her new-found insight into her own desires.

As we've seen in the previous stories, crossing boundaries,
whether physical or metaphysical, seems to signal a fragmentation
or doubling of the self. As Kathleen Glenn has noted in other writings by Fernández Cubas, the "idea that the self is a coherent, stable,
and unified whole is subverted, and the boundary between self and
other is blurred."[12] It is this crossing into the "unfamiliar," or the
unheimlich, which produces an ominous dread, yet the characters'
initial horror is dispelled as they come to recognize the space as another reality that is simply the other side of a familiar coin. It is here
that the characters confront repressed or subconscious desires and
find their "place," for better or worse.

Returning to the first narrative, "Mundo" [World], we find a narrator who becomes "other" not only in another place, but perhaps
in "another/'s" place, or even "others'" places. Narrated by Carolina, "Mundo" tells the story of her life from the moment she enters
a convent at the age of fifteen. This tale contains many of the elements Eve Sedgwick has identified as pertaining to the Gothic, such
as the priesthood and monastic institutions, sleeplike and deathlike
states, doubles, affinities between narrative and pictorial art, and unintelligible writings.[13] We also find in this story many of the inter-
twining themes that recur throughout the *Con Agatha* collection: the
crossing of boundaries into another "world" which is initially full
of dread; the erasure of boundaries between art/life, truth/fiction,

presence/absence, and Self/Other; the desire to appropriate another's place; and the vying for authorial control. Meaning in this narrative, as in many of Fernández Cubas's tales, is unstable. We quickly discover, for example, that "mundo" is not just "world," but refers as well to *baúl*, or the trunk that Carolina takes with her. The constant and intentional slippage between the two meanings, one familiar, one not, destabilizes the possibility of ascertaining the meaning of the entire narrative, just as it suggests a fusion of incompatible or opposite ideas. For if, as Carolina states on entering the convent, she has left behind "el mundo" [the world], she takes with her her own particular "mundo," with its secret drawers and enigmatic imagery. The predominant image on the trunk is that of a sailor holding a painting of himself holding a painting of himself in an infinitely diminishing spiral, a splendid sun on his left, a sinister storm to his right. The painting, with its *ad infinitum* regression, suggests the doubling and redoubling of the central character that occurs in the story. Throughout the tale, we are never quite sure *who* Carolina is, as she seems to usurp surrounding identities. Additionally, the infinite regression may represent the peeling away of the layers of the unconscious, suggesting a movement toward greater self-knowledge. But the question of interpreting the movement remains: is it progress toward a positive outcome (the sun) or a negative one (the storm) for the individual situated at this important crossroad?

The story begins with the narrator crossing the boundary between the familiar, her childhood home, also significantly called La Carolina, and the unfamiliar world of the convent, a world of "sombras" [shadows], of "seres invisibles" [invisible beings] (27). Crossing the garden of La Carolina, she steps through the creaking gate, then endures a hot and dusty journey through the countryside in a hired car before arriving at the heavy convent doorway. It is a movement away from what was initially *heimlich*, or familiar. The name identification of the protagonist with her childhood home suggests that her journey is one not only away from home and that which is *heimlich* but also away from self. The family housekeeper's lament to Carolina—"a ti también te han engañado" [they have deceived you as well] (20)—as she departs suggests that the narrative will unfold as a redemptive quest for the Truth, despite the "death-in-life" dread that initially accompanies her. In this sense, the narrative structure coincides with the imagery of "el mundo," as the layers of "deceptions" are exposed and the truth of her apparent expulsion from patriarchal culture is slowly revealed.

Operating from the "shadows," Carolina gradually acquires the power and authority over Self and others that she lacked when living with her avaricious father. Her appropriation of the convent as her own space is a process that depends on the appropriation of the Other, those who inhabit and control the convent. Carolina first usurps the status of Mother Pequeña as the youngest one in the convent, then takes control of the Mother Superior's keys to knowledge (the books, maps, and encyclopedias she keeps locked away) as the nuns await the arrival of a new member, Mother Perú. Carolina eventually gains authorial control over Mother Perú's "text" [her life narrative etched on a gourd], and finally assumes Mother Angélica's powers as the Mother Superior. Throughout the years, Carolina stows away her rage and impotence at the paternal, authoritarian figures of her past (her father and the priest) and the cruel Mother Pequeña in the secret drawers of "el mundo," until finally, her control complete, she empties out and disinfects them. The cleansing of "el mundo" coincides with the cleansing of the convent and its cruel and/or criminal elements.

The mirror plays an important role in the narrative, suggesting the separation and subsequent fusion of Self/Other. Before entering the convent, Carolina repeatedly glimpses her fifteen-year-old image in the mirror, first on the wall in her bedroom and then in the rearview mirror as she crosses into her new world. The mirror suggests not only the dual nature of the narrator, as "engañada/engañadora" [deceived/deceiver], but also the fusion of Self and Other. Upon entering the convent, she is given one last opportunity to gaze at her image, the image she will carry with her throughout her remaining years. Seated in the convent garden, Carolina is contemplating her reflection when another image unexpectedly appears:

Entonces la vi. El revuelo de un hábito negro, un mandil a mis espaldas, una mano enguantada que se posó en mi hombro, y la evidencia de que frente a mí, allí, en el huerto, ya no faenaba nadie. Era madre Pequeña. Quise volverme y saludar, pero el espejo se me adelantó y por unos momentos la luna se llenó de un rostro viejo, el rostro más viejo y arrugado que había visto en mi vida, unos ojos sin luz, una sonrisa desdentada, inmensa. Y enseguida, con un movimiento casi imperceptible, volví a ser yo.

[Then I saw her. The fluttering of a black habit, a leather apron behind me, a gloved hand that rested on my shoulder, and the evidence that

before me, there, in the orchard, no one was working any longer. It was
Mother Pequeña. I tried to turn around and greet her, but the mirror
got ahead of me and for a few moments it was filled by an old face, the
oldest and most wrinkled face I had ever seen, eyes without light, an immense, toothless smile. And then, quickly, with an almost imperceptible
movement, I became myself again.] (26–27)

The uncanny melding of the images of Self and Other, the familiar
and the unfamiliar, of Carolina and Mother Pequeña, the youngest
one (until Carolina's arrival) and nefarious killer of stray cats, fills
the young Carolina with horror as it portends her own future image.
It is a prophecy fulfilled when, years later, Mother Perú thrusts a mirror into Carolina's face and she sees

> un rostro arrugado, sorprendido, aterrado. Y aunque todavía no puedo
> explicarme cómo ocurrió, sí sé que de inmediato lo reconocí. Allí estaba
> ella. Su rostro olvidado. Allí estaba—¡otra vez!—madre Pequeña.

> [a wrinkled, surprised, terrified face. And even though I still can't ex-
> plain to myself how it happened, I do know that I recognized the face
> immediately. There she was. Her forgotten face. There she was—
> again!—Mother Pequeña.] (64)

But Carolina, freed by this time by the knowledge of the past, and
the knowledge of Mother Perú's true identity, chooses to "rewrite"
the history of the Self/Other, by welcoming into the convent once
more the stray and abandoned cats.[14]

Likewise, Carolina, originally the most adept "reader" of Mother
Perú's "text" (as well as of Mother Angélica's texts) takes authorial
control over the gourd etchings, fashioning a new legend for the
convent. In essence, she usurps the "life text," the life and text, of
the Other, seizing her "arte" and her "prestigio" [art and prestige]
and making them her own. Carolina's authorial control of the legend (a fictional world) seems to give her the ultimate power over
the material realm of the convent. In addition, the author seems to
suggest that a "written" history, which makes visible the existence of
the convent and its inhabitants, will ensure their escape from the
shadows of oblivion.[15]

Ensconced in the all-female world of the convent, empowered by
textual knowledge, Carolina has become "another" in another/'s
place. Initially the impotent victim of patriarchal culture, then an
invisible being in a world condemned to oblivion, she seizes

"author-ity" of a world that will live on, that will exist, through its legends. The taunting words of Mother Perú that still ring in the narrator's ears—"meticona, vieja, revieja" [meddler, old woman, old hag] (72)—serve to remind us of Carolina's dual nature. For just as time periods become confused in the convent, so do identities. If she has "abjected" the cruel side of Mother Pequeña (the Other glimpsed in the mirror) by welcoming in the abandoned cats, she has also participated in the removal of another "stray," Mother Perú, by changing the final imagery of her life narrative. Her ascension to power over the material realm of the convent, through her access to and control over the "texts" of others (Mothers Angélica and Perú), is not completely innocent: the narrator hints at her own capacity to "deceive" at two moments in the story.[16] These admissions, in fact, serve to cast doubt on the narrator's reliability, and thus on the reader's ability to decode the ambiguity of "Mundo." But one thing is clear: "el mundo," with its secret drawers likened to the cells of the convent, belongs to Carolina. It is her "home." Again, the *unheimlich* develops toward the *heimlich* until it coincides with it.

While the four stories I've discussed share a seemingly felicitous outcome for the characters, the second story in the collection, "La mujer de verde," seems more similar in mood and shares a common theme of obsession with the stories in Fernández Cubas's 1990 *El ángulo del horror*.[17] The first line in the story ("Lo siento—dice la chica—. Se ha confundido usted" [I'm sorry—the girl says. You're mistaken]) (75) plunges the reader immediately into the confusion, uncertainty, and apprehension that we've come to expect from this author's narratives. Of all the stories in the *Agatha* collection, "La mujer de verde" is the one that initially appears to come closest to fulfilling Todorov's definition of the Fantastic. The reliability of the first-person narrator, who tells us she is "una ejecutiva respetada" [a respected executive] (78), is undermined by her confusion, insomnia, incomprehension, and frayed nerves.[18]

The action of the story centers on the narrator's repeated sightings of a woman dressed in green, whom she mistakes for Dina Dachs, a new secretary in her office. With each sighting, the woman seems to be visibly degenerating, her appearance becoming gradually more grotesque. The fact that one of these "sightings" is in a bathroom mirror suggests the possibility that the narrator is, in fact, the woman in green, perhaps even Dina Dachs. The fusion of Self/Other is suggested at various points in the story, particularly when the narrator reaches into Dina's purse and finds letters that she herself has supposedly written to her boss (and married lover) Eduardo. Is she Dina Dachs, who yearns for the status and love the narrator proclaims, or does she simply *want to be* Dina, the efficient, polished secretary who in reality is Eduardo's lover?

Despite the fantastic framework of "La mujer de verde," a telling phrase in the *denouement* brings the reader back to an uncanny explanation:

> Recuerdos que no recuerdo. *Nunca olvidaré la primera noche, en el hotel frente al mar.* . . Frases absurdas, ridículas, obscenas. Promesas de amor entremezcladas con ruidos de pasos, llaves, puertas que se abren, que se cierran, los vecinos del piso de arriba arrastrando muebles, un hombre con bata blanca diciéndome: "Está usted agotada. Serénese."

> [Memories that I don't remember. *I'll never forget the first night, in the hotel facing the sea.* . . . Absurd, ridiculous, obscene phrases. Promises of love mixed in with the sounds of steps, keys, doors opening and closing, the upstairs neighbors dragging furniture about, a man with a white smock telling me: "You're exhausted. Calm down."] (97)

While the reference to the upstairs neighbors suggests that the narrator is back "home," the presence of the man "con bata blanca" points instead to a hospital or mental institution. *Heimlich* and *unheimlich* converge at this and the other moments described above. As in some of her earlier tales, such as "Lúnula y Violeta" in Fernández Cubas's first book (*Mi hermana Elba*), the explanatory ending shifts the tale away from the fantastic, providing instead an interpretation which rests on the narrator's apparent insanity.[19] While the ending leaves the reader still in doubt about the narrator's final action toward "Dina" (attempted homicide or attempted suicide?), the lingering impression is that of a tragic character with a desperate desire to be "other" than what she is. So despite its different mood, "La mujer de verde" does find a "home" in *Con Agatha en Estambul.*

Throughout the stories brought together in *Con Agatha en Estambul,* the desire to be "other" and/or the desire to be in "another/'s" place result in situations that initially produce dread yet eventually are recognized as familiar. Carolina plays out her desire to control self and others in "Mundo"; the narrators of "Ausencia" and "La mujer de verde" are propelled toward amnesia and insanity, respectively, in their desire to be "other"; Clarisa appropriates "another/'s" place in "El lugar"; and the narrator of "Con Agatha" performs an emotional reenactment of Agatha Christie's marital "catastrophe." Indeed, in retrospect, the theme of the desire to be "other" can be found in many of Fernández Cubas's writings, including such stories as "Lúnula y Violeta," "En el hemisferio sur," "Los altillos de Brumal," and "Helicón." Fernández Cubas's tales of the uncanny propel the reader toward complex psychological realms, where the nature of human desire and its relationship to "identity" is explored. As each of the characters stumbles into a reality initially sensed as "other," each moves toward an appropriation of the "Other" as Self. Fernández Cubas's writings remind us that reality, and our "place" and identity within it, is fluid, unstable, and often deceptive.

NOTES

1. See, for example, the following articles: Phyllis Zatlin, "Tales from Fernández Cubas: Adventure in the Fantastic," *Monographic Review/Revista Monográfica* 3:1–2 (1987): 107–18; Mary Lee Bretz, "Cristina Fernández Cubas and the Recuperation of the Semiotic in *Los altillos de Brumal,*" *Anales de la Literatura Española Contemporánea* 13 (1988): 177–88; and José Ortega, "La dimensión fantástica en los cuentos de Fernández Cubas," *Monographic Review/Revista Monográfica* 8 (1992): 157–63.

2. The theme of the double is explored in the following articles: Kathleen M. Glenn, "Fantastic Doubles in Cristina Fernández Cubas's Tales for Children," in *Visions of the Fantastic,* ed. Allienne R. Becker (Westport, Conn.: Greenwood Press, 1996), 57–62, and "Gothic Indecipherability and Doubling in the Fiction of Cristina Fernández Cubas," *Monographic Review/Revista Monográfica* 8 (1992): 125–41; Janet Pérez, "Cristina Fernández Cubas: Narrative Unreliability and the Flight from Clarity, or, the Quest for Knowledge in the Fog," *Hispanófila* 122 (January 1998): 29–39, and "Fernández Cubas, Abjection, and the 'retórica del horror,'" *Explicación de Textos Literarios* 24 (1995–96): 159–71; José Ortega (see note 1); Ana Rueda, "Cristina Fernández Cubas: Una narrativa de voces extinguidas," *Monographic Review/Revista Monográfica* 4 (1988): 257–67; Julie Gleue, "The Epistemological and Ontological Implications in Cristina Fernández Cubas's *El año de Gracia,*" *Monographic Review/Revista Monográfica* 8 (1992): 142–56; and Mary Lee Bretz (see note 1).

3. For an exhaustive summary of the competing theories of the Fantastic, I recommend Allienne Becker's introduction to *Visions of the Fantastic,* ed. Allienne R. Becker (Westport, Conn.: Greenwood Press, 1996), xi–xxi.

4. Pérez, "Narrative Unreliability," 37.

5. Pérez, "Fernández Cubas, Abjection," 160.

6. *Unheimlich* translates literally to English as "unhomely." Alix Strachey, the translator of Freud's article, chose instead the English "uncanny." Freud's article centers on the use of this psychological device by E.T.A. Hoffmann, whom he declares "the unrivalled master of the uncanny in literature" (233). See Sigmund

Freud, "The 'Uncanny,'" in vol. 17, *The Standard Edition of the Complete Psychological Works of Sigmund Freud*, ed. James Strachey (London: Hogarth Press, 1955), 217–56.

7. Freud, "The 'Uncanny,'" 219.

8. Ibid., 220.

9. Ibid., 226.

10. Cristina Fernández Cubas, *Con Agatha en Estambul* (Barcelona: Tusquets, 1994), 153. Subsequent references to this work will be cited parenthetically in the text. All translations are mine unless otherwise noted. Words in italics are italicized in the original unless otherwise noted.

11. This image recalls many of Remedios Varo's paintings, particularly the 1960 *Mimesis*, in which a Varo character undergoes a metamorphosis into the fleur-de-lis pattern of her chair. As in numerous Varo paintings, the most mundane objects and environments become the locus for transcendent moments and profound psychological insights. See Janet A. Kaplan, *Unexpected Journeys: The Art and Life of Remedios Varo* (New York: Abbeville Press, 1988) for an introduction to this prolific Spanish painter, who spent most of her adult life in Mexico.

12. Glenn, "Gothic Indecipherability," 132. Both of Glenn's articles included in note 2 explore in depth the theme of the double in Fernández Cubas's fiction, relating it primarily to the Gothic tradition, even though the author herself rejects this categorization of her work.

13. Eve Kosofsky Sedgwick, *The Coherence of Gothic Conventions* (New York: Methuen, 1986), 9–10.

14. Fernández Cubas's writings are rich in intertextuality, and the interweaving of the abandoned cat story here may be a wink at Esther Tusquets's children's story, *La reina de los gatos* (Barcelona: Lumen, 1993). In Tusquets's story, the "reina" represents the loving maternal figure that is lacking (as is also the case with Carolina, whose mother died in childbirth) and a return to the preoedipal. She is configured as a powerful female voice and positive female role model. The "reina de los gatos" motif also appears in Tusquets's novels *El amor es un juego solitario* (Barcelona: Lumen, 1979) and *Varada tras el último naufragio* (Barcelona: Lumen, 1980).

15. In Catherine G. Bellver's analysis of *El año de Gracia*, she recalls Todorov's affirmation that "Narrative equals life, absence of narrative, death" when addressing the apparent function of Daniel's storytelling. There seems to be a similar supposition in "El mundo." See Bellver, "*El año de Gracia* and the Displacement of the Word," *Studies in Twentieth Century Literature* 16:2 (1992): 221–32.

16. Upon remembering the housekeeper's words as she left home, Carolina reflects: "Pero qué podía saber doña Eulalia de quién engañaba a quién, de cómo era yo, de lo que era capaz de imaginar aunque fuera en sueños" [But what could Doña Eulalia know about who was deceiving whom, about me, about what I was capable of imagining even if it were only in dreams?] (20). Carolina makes a similar comment about the lawyer ("¿qué podía saber él de engaños?" [what could he know about deceptions?] [52]), when told of her deceased father's financial dishonesty.

17. There is no explanation in the collection about the arrangement of the stories for publication; one can only speculate about the chronological sequence.

18. Janet Pérez's article on narrative unreliability in Fernández Cubas's later fiction (see note 2) highlights the narrator's expressions of doubt and confusion in this particular story, one of several devices employed by the author to undermine traditional epistemological premises (33).

19. In an early article (1987) on the author's first book (see note 1), Phyllis Zatlin suggests that Fernández Cubas's insertion of an explanatory epilogue to "Lúnula y Violeta" could be attributed to a lack of confidence in her ability to handle the Fantastic mode (118). As Fernández Cubas's writings have progressed, however, fewer critics are attempting to situate them in the category of the Fantastic.

The Arab/Islamic Other in the Fiction of Cristina Fernández Cubas

Elizabeth Scarlett

CROSS-CULTURAL EXPERIENCE AND INTERNATIONAL TRAVEL HAVE EN-
abled many prominent women writers of modern Spain to move beyond the paradigms of gender roles that were limiting to them in
the pursuit of goals outside of private family life. Rosa Chacel wrote
her first novel while living in Italy with her husband, who was there
on an art scholarship. Mercè Rodoreda's life was shattered by the
Civil War and exile necessitated by her political affiliations, yet writing from outside of her country and region appears to have transformed her writing and given it the elegiac quality for which it is
noted. Poet María Victoria Atencia was fortunate to have a pilot's
license that allowed her to crisscross national borders for a swift
change of perspective. Carmen Martín Gaite lived as an exchange
student in both Portugal and France.

If one examines the formative years of women writers born during
the Civil War and in the first decade of the Francoist dictatorship,
one continues to find extended stays in foreign countries that have
had a strong impact on their subsequent writing. Soledad Puértolas
studied in California for three years; Carme Riera taught classes in
France; Ana Diosdado spent her childhood in the Río de la Plata
region and returned to Spain at the age of twelve; Adelaida García
Morales worked as a translator in Algiers; Clara Janés took classes in
Italy, England, and France.[1]

The majority of these examples involve contact with another Western culture that was thought to be more progressive in its norms for
female behavior at the time, and might be assumed to have had a
liberating or empowering effect on the young writer. It is striking in
the case of Cristina Fernández Cubas, however, that the foreign culture that most clearly manifests itself is one associated with male
privilege (including polygamy), cloistering and overprotection of

women (to the extreme of female genital mutilation in some areas), and a generally more circumscribed domain of female activity. While Fernández Cubas also spent time in Latin America, it is her stay of nine months in Cairo that left the more explicit thematic mark on her fiction (one could argue that her exposure to Latin American magical realism could compete in esthetic importance with her Egyptian sojourn). From the astonishing story "Omar, amor," which heads the now-historic *Doce relatos de mujeres* anthology edited by Ymelda Navajo, through the title story in *Con Agatha en Estambul,* the present essay seeks an understanding of the meaning of Islam and of Arabic and Near Eastern cultures in her work by returning to each of her texts in which Near Eastern or Islamic settings or characters play an important role.

For a writer who has worked mainly in the short story genre, the Middle East must be seen in connection with Scheherazade and the *Thousand and One Nights.* As one of the central origins of the supernatural tale, Arabic culture often appears textually for Fernández Cubas, as it did for Borges, in tandem with the prevalence of mystery, magic, and horror. Studies by Kathleen Glenn, Phyllis Zatlin, Janet Pérez, and others establish the Fantastic and the Gothic as uniting threads among Fernández Cubas's stories and novels.[2] It is not surprising that in the four stories and one novel in which the Arab/Islamic Other figures prominently, it is closely entwined with the Fantastic. To associate magic and horror with the Middle East calls forth the critique of Orientalism in Western culture as elaborated by Edward Said and others, but in Fernández Cubas's work there is usually a twist that shows awareness of Western cultural hegemony in representations of the Orient from a European perspective. Thus, one reads the Islamic Other from without and from within, destabilizing the point of view in a way that contributes to the fluctuating effect of the Fantastic as it was defined by Todorov.

The author writes of her stay in Cairo that while she had initially intended to produce a series of foreign-correspondent pieces on well-defined topics that would be of interest to periodicals back home, she found herself mesmerized instead by the small details of life, and sought deeper meanings in the tiniest sounds and symbols of her surroundings. The encouragement for the Fantastic direction her writing would soon take is clear:

En el mundo en el que vivía, en la superposición de decorados faraónicos, coptos e islámicos, existía entre cajas un código desconocido que

vislumbraba sin entender y que, de momento, me intrigaba y me con-
fundía.

[In the world in which I lived, in the layering of Dynastic, Coptic, and
Islamic backdrops, there existed between the sets an unknown code that
I glimpsed without understanding and that, for the moment, intrigued
and confused me.][3]

"Omar, amor" [Omar, My Love] (1982) portrays a male/female
couple in a life-or-death struggle that ranges in time from Egypt's
ancient Dynastic Age through early Christianity to modern times,
and in space from the pyramids along the Nile at Luxor and Giza
to a monastic community in the desert of Scete to urban Cairo. Its
discursive fields are similarly eclectic, assimilating Arabic words and
Muslim, Hindu, Jewish, and Christian elements. It portrays Egypt as
a site of syncretism so absolute that temporal and spatial boundaries
are blurred in the best Fantastic tradition, accompanied by a blending of the erotic and the maternal, of love/creation and hatred/de-
struction, of the Symbolic and the Real, of male and female, and of
Self and Other.

The blending of time frames that is related in the Fantastic mode
in this story can be observed as part of the holiday bustle in the author's description of Cairo in 1978, when she lived there. Writing
some twenty years later, she recalls the combination of automobiles,
lambs, bicycles, and camel caravans clogging the streets, all seeming
to get nowhere ("Días de jamasín," 149). The jarring juxtaposition
of the ancient and the modern makes a similar impression on the
author as she crosses the desert and approaches the monastery-city
of Wadi Natrún, the model for San Macarios in "Omar, amor." She
sees a novice friar running alongside the road toward the lone city,
carrying an old telephone, and she wonders where in the desert he
could have begun this strange errand. Above all she remembers his
expression: "Me pareció la viva imagen de una felicidad que tenía
mucho de ultraterrena" [It looked to me like the living image of a
largely otherworldly happiness] ("Días de jamasín," 153). In addition to the scrambling of discursive fields, the Egyptian collision of
time frames is another key that unlocks the Fantastic for the author.

The opening of "Omar, amor" has the lovers frolicking inside the
pyramid at Keops. The opulence of the contents of the chambers
and the lovers' freedom of movement after bribing a guard place
this episode in the Dynastic Age, before these monuments were

sealed and soon afterward, spoiled. The lovers are able to defile the sacred purpose of the pyramid by making love for three nights in its gallery and offering their rapture up as a sacrifice. Omar has sprung directly from the narrator's imagination (though one later learns that he was born in Cairo), giving her a godlike control over him: "Yo lo había planeado todo, Omar. El color de tu galabía, tu sonrisa, el corte de tus cabellos" [I had planned everything, Omar. The color of your jhellaba, your smile, your haircut].[4] Their supernatural intersubjectivity seems nearly complete, and she can anticipate his every move as in a dream. He speaks perfect Arabic and she addresses him as "Hub" [Love] and "Habibi" [Darling]. But while she declares him totally hers, he soon begins to display signs of a growing independence that troubles the narrator: "Jadeabas, *ya* Omar, en unas contracciones que a ratos se me antojaron extrañas e irreales" [You were panting, oh Omar, in contractions that struck me at times as strange and unreal] (17). Their enjoyment at this stage is still boundless, however, and they can even slide down the eye of the Sphinx, introducing a female monster who is notorious for devouring men who fail to pass her test.

In preparation for a change in setting, the lovers change into Bedouin garb, and the narrator masks her femininity by hiding her hair under a turban: "Yo cubrí mis cabellos con un turbante y fingí ser hombre ante las dunas" [I covered my hair with a turban and pretended to be a man before the dunes] (18). The gender-crossing disguise is reminiscent of Isabelle Eberhardt's exploits in North Africa. Disguised as a man and often going by the name Mahmoud Saadi, the Swiss writer (1877–1904) learned Arabic, crossed the deserts of Magreb on horseback with Bedouins, converted to Islam, and even accompanied her male companions to bordellos, where she watched them indulge themselves.[5] The second section of "Omar, amor" imaginatively parallels the transformation Eberhardt underwent in changing from European to Arab and from woman to man. Although the narrator permits herself greater freedom by donning the disguise, it introduces a gender-based inequality within the couple, since Omar does not need to change identity to make himself acceptable in the next social context.

When the two awaken after sleeping for several days, they have traveled far in time and space. The desert monastic community where they find themselves is one dedicated to St. Macarius the Great of Egypt, a fourth-century anchorite who opposed the heresy of Arianism (as Islam would later contend, Arianism held that God could not be born as a mortal), ate once a week, and left behind several thousand followers in the monastery he founded.[6] Present-day monasteries devoted to Macarius are located in the desert between Cairo and Alexandria (such as Wadi Natrún, visited by the author when the remains of St. John the Baptist were reportedly unearthed there ["Días de jamasín," 152]), and in Libya. The site as described in the story suggests a medieval Christian ascetic context as the setting for the lovers' second romp. Here they commit transgressions against the chastity of the religious order for whom they are pilgrim guests by visiting each other's cell and kissing secretly in the hallways. Despite their deceit, the narrator is increasingly restricted in her activities as the young men begin to sense her difference from them. Her interactions with Omar take on a maternal tone: "Y seguiste riendo, con esa sonrisa que yo deseaba, . . . bebiendo de mí, siempre, cada noche, minutos antes de que yo vendase mis pechos con un lienzo y tú regresases silencioso a la soledad de tu celda" [And you kept on smiling that smile I desired, . . . drinking from me, always, each night, minutes before I bound my breasts with a cloth and you returned quietly to the solitude of your cell] (18).

Finally, the monastic life proves intolerable, and the lovers reassume their Bedouin apparel and flee on horseback to the banks of the Nile. Here the narrator adopts a double identity. By day she is Ibrahim, a name that echoes as the patriarch of two major world religions: the Judaic (through Isaac) and the Islamic (through Ishmael). By night she is Kalíma again, explaining that, "Te gustaba llamarme así y tenías razón. Porque yo, Kalíma, te había dado la palabra" [You liked calling me that and you were right. Because I, Kalíma, had given you the Word] (19). Once again Omar remains unchanged. His liking for the name Kalíma, meaning "word" in Arabic, and her linking it to "the Word," connects the choice to the series of Arabic prayers called Kalima(h), meaning "the (Divine) Word." They express the most fundamental articles of faith for Muslims; the principal one, Kalima(h) Shaharadat, states, "There is no god but God, and Muhammad is God's apostle."[7] The narrator thus claims the role of initiator into the Symbolic order for Omar in addition to her role as a divinity, since she is his creator and her name echoes his most sacred prayer. Furthermore, in their relationship she harbors overtones of both the paternal role (as Ibrahim), and of the maternal (when he drinks from her breasts), and of course the role of his lover. But from this point onward her position of absolute power and control over Omar quickly disintegrates as the story unravels.

In a contemporary context, the name Kalima is a favorite of psychics, tarot readers, tattoo parlors, and the Western occult and Gothic countercultures in general. Its popularity in this regard springs from its connection to Kali, Hindu goddess of transformations and particularly of the cycle of birth and death. Known as both the Dark Mother and the Warrior or Blood-Drinking Goddess, Kali is often depicted with three eyes (one each for the past, the present, and the future), stepping on her husband Shiva's body and sticking out her tongue. Shiva, god of destruction, must work in conjunction with Kali, whose name derives from the Sanskrit "Kala," meaning time. Gavin Flood terms her "the light of pure consciousness from which the universe manifests and to which it returns."[8] The narrator as Kalíma combines the Word of Islam with the Dark Mother of Hinduism, a discursive field that is not out-of-place here since Indian culture is one of the main sources for Scheherazade's tales. The destructiveness of the Dark Mother comes to the fore after Kalíma finds herself slighted by her love, forsaken and imprisoned in the pyramid of Amenophis III, then left to await her love in a boat beside a perilous waterfall.

Plotting revenge against her privileged male lover, she invites him back to his birthplace in modern Cairo. Once there, he is too caught up in the narcissism of Westernized urban life (watching his reflection in passing mirrors and flirting with boys and women) to notice the trap she is setting. Like the Hindu goddess Kali, she will not be content until she stands over her lover's inert body, and to accomplish this she resorts to the magically performative dimension of the Word that emanates from Islamic culture, which equates the uttering of the Kalima Shaharadat with Muslim identity and belief. Once she hurls Omar to the pavement and pronounces, within earshot of passersby, that his name was/used to be Omar ("Se llamaba Omar" [20]), he must obediently cease to exist. Her words, particularly the past imperfect tense of "to be," have the power of life and death over him, despite the male privilege he has increasingly lorded over her in the social contexts of the second half of the story.

The chilling and fablelike ending carries a strong metafictive connotation (any author, like this narrator, causes characters to exist or cease to exist with words). It also works as a gender-based inversion of several Arabic paradigms. This could be Scheherazade taking the upper hand with her husband Shahryar, whose habit of executing his wives after the wedding night keeps her weaving stories that she leaves unfinished at the dawn of each day. Here the female story-teller seals her partner's fate with words. It is also possible to see a reversal of the well-known "repudiation" of marriage vows that can be enacted in Arab society by the husband. By merely saying so, with or without cause and with no recourse for the wife, the husband may pronounce their union dissolved, keeping the children and all property except for her bride-price and often sending the wife back into dependence upon her parents.[9]

After murdering her companion with the magical power of the Word, the narrator returns to the sacred Christian site of St. Macarius to offer alms in Omar's memory. Her betrayal of the Islamic Other is thus linked to the Christian facet of her shifting identity. This link seems to acknowledge the Orientalizing, colonialist view that the West has taken of Egypt. After exploiting the Islamic Other in a series of exotic adventures, she disposes of him just as he begins to declare his autonomy: "¡Ya no te pertenezco!" [I no longer belong to you!] (19). Ironically, the narrator has taken advantage of the information supplied by her Arab lover about his culture (the horror of decomposition that will ensure a quick burial with few questions asked) to betray him. The betrayal is not only one of female against male, but of West against East. In obliterating Omar, her companion through the ages, Kalíma fulfills a role similar in some ways to that of the modernization process brought to Islamic countries by the West to transform cities and towns beyond recognition, often causing people to feel lost in their own land.[10]

The twisted love of "Omar, amor" is visible in transposing the letters of *amor* into *Omar*. In terms of subject/object relations this love shifts through a sequence of paradigms, facilitated by converging discursive fields. The narrator may be seen as the mother who refuses autonomy to her offspring, the woman in Arab society who exacts retribution for her disenfranchisement, the Symbolic that obliterates the Real, the feminine force of destruction within Nature as envisioned by Hinduism, or the Western position that marginalizes the Arab/Islamic Other as Oriental, to exist only as a function of the need for the exotic or the despotic against which Western culture may define itself.

Published shortly after the author's stay in Cairo, the title story of *Mi hermana Elba* [My Sister Elba] (1980) relates magical powers in children to a religious eclecticism that also resonates with the layering of polytheistic, Christian, and Islamic discourses that had captured Fernández Cubas's attention in the Egyptian capital. The narrator looks back on herself as an eleven-year-old with the help of a diary from that time, and on her relationship with her younger sister Elba, who was developmentally challenged and subsequently died in a fall. The girls find themselves at a lonely crossroads, with their parents working out a divorce while they are left to fend for themselves at a convent boarding school. The narrator befriends Fátima (a name that is thoroughly ancient, Christian, and Arabic at once), a somewhat older girl who has been held back in school, but who sometimes speaks from a wide-ranging perspective far beyond her years. In catechism class she feigns ignorance, but when the pupils discuss points of contention among themselves, Fátima surprises them with an erudition that broadens their knowledge of non-Christian belief systems. She is able to compare the idol worship condemned by Moses with Muhammad's destruction of the idols at Mecca, and provides her companions with a brief history of comparative religion by tracing the Egyptian ox-god Apis on the ground, proceeding through key myths of Babylonia, Classical Greece, and Arabia. The nuns have apparently been giving her failing marks for her heterodoxy in order to preserve the univocal discourse of the convent. Unlike the arch-conservative Marcelino Menéndez Pelayo, who explored beliefs that differed from Roman Catholicism in *Historia de los heterodoxos españoles* [History of Spanish Heterodoxy] and dutifully censured each alternative viewpoint, the more tolerant Fátima fails to privilege the dominant discourse of her social context.

Naturally it is Fátima who introduces the Fantastic into the text, by teaching the sisters about secret passageways and magical hiding places that make them invisible. Though scholastically backward, Elba excels at these games. This points to a distinction between the intellect and the ability to defy the laws of physics in the logic of the story. Childhood is presented as an oasis, for when Fátima returns the next school year she has entered adolescence and has become more interested in appearing grown up than she is in religious diversity or the magical powers associated with it. Entering the heterosexual exchange economy, which will eventually give her access to the power of the phallus, also supplants the importance of the Fantastic in the narrator's youthful mind. The kiss she receives from a boy on the day of her sister's funeral makes her record this as the happiest day of her life.

"El reloj de Bagdad," from the author's following collection, *Los altillos de Brumal* [The Clock from Baghdad, in The Attics of Brumal]

(1983), presents the Fantastic as emanating from contact between Christianity and Islam. The two discursive fields, along with the substratum of ancient animism, collide, and the narrator is caught in the crossfire. Throughout the story it remains unclear whether the calamities that plague her family, their servants, and their home after the introduction of the stately grandfather clock (completed in 1700 by Iraqi craftsmen for a European patron) are the result of powers residing within the uncanny object, manipulations by the two servants who reject the clock as the work of heathen souls, or the outcome of simple misfortune. Viewed from either of the latter two perspectives, the Arab artifact is a scapegoat or "cabeza de turco" (literally, turbaned head formerly used for target practice), and it is offered up as a sacrifice at the end.

Much as preadolescent childhood emerges as the domain for games involving the Fantastic in "Elba," in "Bagdad" it is advanced age that renders the family servants Matilde and Olvido sensitive to the presence of spirits of the dead ("ánimas"). The youthfulness of the narrator makes her receptive to their miraculous beliefs and tales. Whether they decant age-old wisdom or ancient superstition is left undecided, along with the debatable guilt of the clock itself. The antique clock seems pathetic at first: "un gigante humillado" [a humiliated giant] or "un descomunal juguete" [an enormous toy], a piece of Islamic culture held captive within the straight-laced bourgeois Spanish home.[11] This Arab/Islamic Other, when set on a stairway landing that is tellingly between the floors of the house (holding sway over both levels but belonging to neither one), seems to exert a destabilizing influence. On the one hand, the clock constitutes a commanding sight to behold; timeless, harmonious, and complete unto itself:

> Parecía como si se hallara en el mismo lugar desde tiempos inmemoriales, como si sólo él estuviera en su puesto, tal era el altivez de su porte, su seguridad, el respeto que nos infundía cuando, al caer la noche, abandonábamos la plácida cocina para alcanzar los dormitorios del último piso.

> [It seemed as though it had been in the same place since time immemorial, as though only it was in the right place, such was the nobility of its stance, its security, the respect it instilled in us when, at nightfall, we left the peaceful kitchen to reach the bedrooms on the top floor.] (120)

On the other hand, the established order of the household is soon disturbed and changed forever when Olvido refuses to clean the clock and withdraws into silence and fear. Matilde falls while polishing the clock's celestial designs, retreating into paranoia as well. Matilde soon leaves her position, giving an improbable excuse, and Olvido weakens and presumably dies during one of the narrator's absences. The children now live in terror of the clock, and they dream at night of "el Señor Innombrado, el Amo y Propietario de nuestras viejas e infantiles vidas" [the Unnamed Lord, the Master and Owner of our old yet infantile lives] (124–25). Fittingly, the presence of the clock, and/or the maids' fanatical rejection of it, have so decentered their religious discourse that it no longer sounds either Christian or Islamic.

Absolute chaos ensues, with objects falling and breaking, food rotting ahead of time, and the house finally going up in flames, perhaps from the carelessness of its distressed residents. The assessment of the clock's role in all of this remains subject to change and questioning. To the narrator's ears, its chiming after the fire sounds like perverse laughter. The antique dealer from whom it was purchased refuses to buy it back and denies ever having possessed it. It becomes taboo to speak of the clock at home and, as the family moves out of the town for good, the narrator sees it in the middle of a bonfire on St. John's Night, a time when flames purge evil and make way for the new. The spectral figure of Olvido is also seen dancing and flying about it. The clock is again pathetic; with its pendulum missing it looks like a beheaded giant (129). The narrator's father adds fuel to the fire and cheerfully turns her head forward so that she cannot see the fire, the clock, or her beloved Olvido. She would never see spirits again: "Aquélla fue la última vez que, entornando los ojos, supe verlas" [That was the last time when, half-closing my eyes, I was able to see them] (130).

The Iraqi clock is an object distressingly secure and complete to modern eyes because of its antiquity; it is free from contingency and other forms of connection and must be interpreted on its own terms. An interesting reverse figure is found in the author's memoir of her life in Cairo. There, the modern refrigerator was a focal point for Egyptian households privileged enough to possess one. The refrigerator bestowed social status and was festooned, pampered, and awarded a position of honor, such as placement in the living room or dining room ("Días de jamasín," 144). However, though it brought convenience and comfort, it also contributed to the breakdown of traditional social ties in Arab society, separating those who could afford refrigerators from those who could not. Both the grandfather clock—originating in Baghdad, the setting for many stories in the *Thousand and One Nights*—and the modern appliance associated with Westernization are foreign objects that dominate their new surroundings for different reasons and subsequently intro-duce change and destruction of old ways.

The clock is consumed in a strange auto-da-fé that harks back to Inquisitorial purging of heresy and heterodoxy. For the maids, who believe in the presence and power of spirits of the dead (from the ancient, pre-Christian belief system of animism), the clock's origin in a Muslim land brings heathen souls into the home, although they never identify the foreign religion with which the clock is associated. Hence, the interaction among Christian, Muslim, and ancient poly-theistic discursive fields is ultimately what produces the Fantastic ef-fect of "El reloj de Bagdad." The irrational or uncanny dimension of each one unleashes a similar reaction in the others. As is the case in the other stories treated here, the Arab/Islamic Other winds up a victim of the Orientalizing gaze of the Western subject, even as Islam forms a necessary piece in the puzzle of the Fantastic.

Of the two novels the author has published to date, *El año de Gracia* [The Year of Grace] (1985) includes an Arab character of some importance in the context of a partly science fiction travel nar-rative. In the novel's problematization of an islandwide biological warfare experiment with anthrax that has gone dreadfully wrong, Robert Spires has found a challenge to "our Western heritage of privileging logic, science, and technology, all of which have played key roles in sustaining a patriarchal legacy."[12] Naguib, the silent and hostile assistant to the captain aboard the *Providence*, the ill-fated craft that the narrator, Daniel, joins as a crew member, is in the main a taciturn balance to the gregarious and avuncular captain, Tío Jean (a possible reference to pirate Jean Lafitte). Daniel soon proves to be in over his head on the vessel; both the unpleasant Egyptian and the friendly European are in cahoots to dispose of the narrator, and only a shipwreck that leaves Daniel stranded on an island for several months appears to prevent them from carrying out their conspiracy.

Naguib's presence aboard the *Providence* harks back to the Eastern resonances of several main characters on the *Pequod* in *Moby Dick*, especially Captain Ahab and the narrator, Ishmael.[13] Melville's char-acter names are chosen not on account of their ethnic origin, but for the Biblical contexts of each. Ishmael was the eventual patriarch of Arabs and Islam. Ahab was a king of Israel who allowed for a de-gree of religious syncretism and freedom that included polytheism,

forged controversial alliances with Damascus, and met with an igno-
minious end.[14] Both are forsaken figures from the narrative perspective of the Old Testament, yet their achievements beyond the
boundaries of Judeo-Christian discourse are considerable. Melville's
Ahab, like the Jewish king, is similarly lured outside of the narrow
limits of his established role, as Nathalia Wright notes: "His voyage is
disastrous when, in the midst of a profitable whale hunt, he becomes
involved in the unequivocal pursuit of supernatural truth."[15] Both
Ahabs attempt to transcend the codes by which they live and thereby
suffer destruction.

Although Fernández Cubas's Naguib has an intertextual tie to
Melville's seafaring heroes with Near Eastern names, his role is that
of a crafty survivor who does not waste words by engaging in
thoughtful conversation. Daniel's attempts to practice his school-
book Arabic with him are met with disdain. Daniel (another name
of Middle Eastern, Biblical resonance) thus cannot begin to share
his soul-searching with his fellow sailor. Naguib probably cannot
read or write, but he is a consummate seaman who makes Daniel
feel quite unnecessary. After the shipwreck, Daniel is able to survive
at first by using the Egyptian's possessions and supplies. Later it is
learned that Naguib has also managed to survive the shipwreck. He
emerges as an authentic, nonliterary Eastern sailor (unlike Melville's
Western seafarers with Biblical shadows) who reinforces the novel's
questioning of erudition and textual authority from the outsider's
standpoint of a non-Westerner who is secure in an independent tradition.

Returning to the Islamic/Eastern Other in the title story of her
most recent collection to date, *Con Agatha en Estambul* [With Agatha
in Istanbul] (1994), the city where East meets West in the universal
discourse of tourism provides the setting for a series of provocative
encounters. Zatlin detects a higher reality content in this group of
five stories than in the author's more fantastical work from the
1980s, as well as a recurring theme of dissatisfaction with set patterns
in life typical of the mid-life crisis.[16] Accordingly, "Con Agatha en
Estambul" begins with the narrator's quest for escape and adventure; she is especially attracted to the Turkish city to spend the holi-
days because she knows that she will not have to deal with the
Christmas rituals in her native Barcelona.

The initial quality of the destination for this travel narrative is thus
one of absence and escape: a place where one can avoid the routines
and rituals associated with one's own culture. Although she is able

to call up mental postcards of Istanbul's monuments while she packs, on her arrival the negative presence of fog and silence surprises her. Concerned at the possible remoteness of her unknown lodgings and the possible lack of heat, she is comforted to find that she and her husband can stay at the Hotel Pera Palas, an establishment with modern conveniences originally built for travelers on the Orient Express. It has an impressive list of former residents that includes Sarah Bernhardt and Agatha Christie, which impresses the narrator.

The most marvelous element of the story is the narrator's perceived sudden ability to say things in Turkish, a language she has never studied. Later she explains this as the result of having leafed through a phrase book during her flight, though she continues to wonder at her gift of instant assimilation of the Turkish language. As fog continues to enshroud the city, she begins to doubt the very existence of Istanbul: "¿Estaba yo realmente allí? O mejor: ¿qué era allí?" [Was I really there? Or better yet: what was there?].[17] The bombing of 1941 gives her a historical basis for believing that the city no longer belongs to reality; this would make ghosts of the hotel employees with whom she has been interacting (178). Her musings recede to the background as her stay progresses and a threat to her already sour marriage enters the scene: Flora, another Spanish tourist, befriends her husband. Flora is very attractive and well acquainted with the sights and places frequented by tourists. She scans a room from right to left, the way one reads in Eastern languages. Julio is annoyed by what he considers to be his wife's clumsy attempts at speaking the local language, but responds positively to Flora's knowledge of the urban landscape and culture of Istanbul (she drinks the local *raki*, while the narrator sticks to Western beverages and gets drunk). A rift widens in the marriage, to which the narrator, intentionally or not, contributes. Immobilized by a sprained ankle she suffered while walking home intoxicated, she gazes at an aquarium in the hotel bar while Julio and Flora explore underground wells and teach each other Turkish.

The references to Agatha Christie (1890–1976) as a former resident of the hotel whose erstwhile room (411) has been consecrated to her like a shrine could easily be misread as an indication that it was there that Christie suffered her famous case of amnesia or mental "fugue." However, evidence points to her having remained in England during the whole episode: after disappearing from her car near her home in 1926, she was discovered eleven days later at the

Hydropathic Hotel in Harrogate, with scarcely a clue to her identity.[18] She did, however, stay at the Pera Palas several times between 1926 and 1932, when she was writing *Murder on the Orient Express.* And she left a statement saying that the answer to the mystery of what happened during her disappearance—never fully explained in her lifetime—was to be found in an unpublished portion of her diary held in a safe place. An old skeleton key was indeed found in her room at the Pera Palas as the result of a 1979 séance, but a corresponding safe box or diary has never been located.[19] Whether the reader connects the fugue state itself or the later séance and key discovery to the Hotel Pera Palas, the story incorporates these remarkable elements from Agatha Christie's colorful biography and assimilates them into the unreal dimension of Istanbul.

For the narrator, the disappearance itself is not the important thing, but the direction Christie's life would take afterwards.[20] Around the time of the episode, the latter's husband was preparing to leave her for another woman; many, including the narrator, have interpreted the amnesia as a reaction to this crisis and/or as Christie's desperate bid for her husband's attention. Yet after this pathetic incident and the inevitable divorce, she wrote a string of her most acclaimed works and met her second husband, Max Mallowan, with whom she would enjoy a fine relationship until the end of her life. The narrator, at the age of forty and in a rapidly deteriorating marriage, begins to look to Christie for guidance. After spending time outside of Christie's old room, she finds that a mysterious voice has metonymically entered her conscience, telling her she must take action (200).

Parallel to Christie's function as inspiration for the narrator's actions in terms of her relationship and her survival of its collapse, one also assumes a relationship between Christie as pioneering woman writer of mysteries, many with Eastern settings she had researched firsthand (*Murder on the Orient Express, Death on the Nile, They Came to Baghdad*), and Fernández Cubas as implied author. The latter takes mystery writing to the realm of the Fantastic, where reality and the marvelous are more permeable than they are in the traditional detective story, of which Christie is an undisputed master. This permeability extends to the treatment of the Eastern/Islamic Other in Fernández Cubas's work; more than just characters and settings that give exotic flavor, they are part of a discursive field that destabilizes basic assumptions. Thus, the underlying metafictive pairing of Christie and the implied author is balanced by the narrator's contact with

Christie's spirit in the hotel. The spirit enters the narrator's mind, urging her repeatedly toward taking direct action—in this case, to escape from her getaway vacation and unloving partner. Could it be that the implied author admits that her plots could benefit from more twists and turns à la Christie? Does the implied author feel the increased pressure of the Spanish 1990s literary market and does she look to the commercially successful Christie as a possible mentor? Certainly the greater dominion of the Real at the expense of the Fantastic in this collection can be seen as a move toward the familiarity and order of Christie's fictional worlds before and after the disruption of murder introduces the need to find out "whodunit." Unlike the other works examined here, the most significant Eastern Other encountered in this story is another Western European woman writer, a precursor with great stamina and longevity who perhaps still has much to teach the contemporary author as she matures.

At the end of "Con Agatha en Estambul," the narrator has refused to stand by and witness the collapse of her marriage, choosing to execute an escape of her own. Through Turkish friends she has gotten to know in the course of the stay, she manages to move up the date of her return flight to Barcelona. With the help of an overpowering local knock-off of the perfume Egoïste (daring to be selfish) bought at a street bazaar, she also secures an entire row of seats on the plane, the better to sleep through the flight. Once back in Barcelona, she can look forward to a visit from Faruk, a suitor who tried to impress her with his muscles and weightlifting trophies. What really impressed her was his offering her the best of himself (230). In contrast to the neat and tidy wrap-ups of a Christie novel, there is no telling what awaits the protagonist as the ultimate outcome of her trip. The only certainties are positive ones: Agatha's voice is now a part of her and she can listen to it or disregard it at will, she has the friendship of a Turkish man and his family, and she has had a great time.

The Eastern/Islamic connection present in all of these texts activates possibilities by offering an alternative code to juxtapose with the Western discursive fields that would otherwise be assumed. In addition, specific beliefs and practices of Islamic and Arabic cultures, such as the performative dimension of language, male privilege and gender segregation, and the origin of the supernatural tale, are worked into Fernández Cubas's texts in a way that facilitates the Fantastic, which often awaits at the juncture between Islam and

Christianity, Islam and Hinduism, or Islam and animism/polytheism. The author's approach to Islamic and Arabic cultures provokes encounters with past women writers who have traveled through similar territory: Agatha Christie, Isabelle Eberhardt, the figure of Scheherazade. Whether the Eastern Other is a lover, a grandfather clock, a sailor, or the spirit of a British writer frequenting a hotel room, there is a persistent awareness of the Western subject's construction of the East as an active process with an impact on East-West relations. Much as Ramón Menéndez Pidal found Spain to be situated between Christianity and Islam, Fernández Cubas situates her texts between these and other belief systems and discursive fields to maximize their potential for eliciting wonder. It is these interstices and areas of cultural contact, rather than any orientalized conception of Islam or Arabic culture itself, that allow the ambiguities, subversions, and mysteries of the Fantastic to develop in her fiction.

NOTES

1. For further biographical information on women writers who were already widely studied and discussed by the late 1980s, see Linda Gould Levine, et al., eds. *Spanish Women Writers: A Bio-Bibliographical Source Book* (Westport, Conn.: Greenwood Press, 1993).

2. For Fantastic and Gothic motifs and related narrative techniques see: Kathleen M. Glenn, "Gothic Indecipherability and Doubling in the Fiction of Cristina Fernández Cubas," *Monographic Review/Revista Monográfica* 8 (1992): 125–41; Janet Pérez, "Cristina Fernández Cubas: Narrative Unreliability and the Flight from Clarity, or, the Quest for Knowledge in the Fog," *Hispanófila* 122 (January 1998): 29–39; Phyllis Zatlin, "Amnesia, Strangulation, Hallucination and Other Mishaps: The Perils of Being Female in Tales of Cristina Fernández Cubas," *Hispania* 79:1 (March 1996): 36–44.

3. "Días de jamasín," *Cosas que ya no existen* (Barcelona: Lumen, 2001), 157. Subsequent references will be made in parentheses in the text of the essay. All translations are mine except where otherwise noted.

4. "Omar, amor," *Doce relatos de mujeres*, ed. Ymelda Navajo (Madrid: Alianza, 1982), 17. Subsequent page references will be made in parentheses in the text of the essay. The analysis of this story comes first because of the specificity of its relation to the present topic, despite the date of its publication following that of the next story to be discussed, "Mi hermana Elba," by two years.

5. For a profile and further references, see Rosa Montero, *Historias de mujeres* (Madrid: Alfaguara, 1995), 159.

6. One of several web pages devoted to the saint is "Saint Macarius the Great of Egypt," *www.roca.org.*

7. For an overview of basic Muslim tenets, see Wilfred Cantwell Smith, *On Understanding Islam* (The Hague, Netherlands: Mouton Publishers, 1981), 28. Prayer

books contain variations of this translation, such as "There is no deity other than Allah, and Muhammad is his servant and his Messenger."

8. *An Introduction to Hinduism* (Cambridge: Cambridge University Press, 1996), 185–86.

9. For Arab customs as they related to women's lives around the time the story was written, see Juliette Minces, *The House of Obedience: Women in Arab Society* (1980), trans. Michael Pallis (London: Zed Press, 1982).

10. Karen Armstrong, *Islam: A Short History* (New York: Modern Library, 2000), 144.

11. *Mi hermana Elba y Los altillos de Brumal* (1980, 1983. Barcelona: Tusquets, 1988), 118. References to "Mi hermana Elba" and to "El reloj de Bagdad" are from this edition. Subsequent references will be made in parentheses in the text of the essay.

12. Robert C. Spires, *Post-Totalitarian Spanish Fiction* (Columbia: University of Missouri Press, 1996), 172.

13. As Nathalia Wright notes (310), an entire group of characters in *Moby Dick* have names that spring from the King Ahab and King Jereboam stories in the Old Testament (Starbuck, Fedallah, etc.). See her chapter "Characters and Types" (1949), *Critical Essays on Herman Melville's Moby Dick*, ed. Brian Higgins and Hershel Parker (New York: G. K. Hall, 1992), 310–15.

14. Ibid., 310.

15. Ibid., 311.

16. Zatlin, "Amnesia, Strangulation, Hallucination and Other Mishaps," 36–37.

17. *Con Agatha en Estambul* (Barcelona: Tusquets, 1994), 176.

18. For a brief account and further sources, see Montero, *Historias de mujeres*, 39.

19. For a commercial rundown of past guests and glories, see "Hotel Pera Palas," www.perapalas.com/English.

20. The fugue state itself, without explicit reference to Christie, takes center stage in another story in the collection, "Ausencia."

Repetition, Remembrance, and the Construction of Subjectivity in the Works of Cristina Fernández Cubas

Akiko Tsuchiya

SINCE CRISTINA FERNÁNDEZ CUBAS MADE HER LITERARY DEBUT IN 1980 with the publication of her short story collection *Mi hermana Elba* [My Sister Elba], she has established herself as one of the most prominent female narrators of the post-Franco era. This and her subsequent books of short stories *Los altillos de Brumal* [The Attics of Brumal] (1983), *El ángulo del horror* [The Angle of Horror] (1990), and *Con Agatha en Estambul* [With Agatha in Istanbul] (1994), as well as her two novels to date, *El año de Gracia* [The Year of Grace] (1985) and *El columpio* [The Swing] (1995), share a preoccupation with the mysterious and disquieting aspects of reality. Often making use of the Fantastic or Gothic paradigms, Fernández Cubas's works set out to test the limits of fiction and subjectivity. Her characters typically find themselves living "on the boundary," struggling with psychic issues of self and otherness, unconscious fears and desires, repressed memories, and uncanny events that defy rational explanation. Her most recent literary endeavors include a dramatic work, *Hermanas de sangre* [Blood Sisters] (1998), a psychological drama set in an atmosphere laden with mystery and perversity; and *Cosas que ya no existen* [Things That No Longer Exist] (2001), a book of memoirs that interweaves personal recollections, oral anecdotes, and travel accounts.

Not surprisingly, many critics have approached Fernández Cubas's fiction from feminist and (Lacanian-influenced) psychoanalytic perspectives, applying concepts such as Kristeva's "semiotic" and "symbolic," abjection, and the Gothic to illuminate the relationship between gender, language, and subjectivity in her works.[1] Likewise, her interviewers have called attention to her recurrent literary preoccupations: doubles and doubling, Gothic spaces (towers, attics, and the like), the uncanny, the Fantastic, the unnamable, and the ex-centric.[2] The relationship between literary representation and the psychoanalytic narrative is key to the understanding of Fernández Cubas's work, given her obsession with the problem of subjectivity and its representation in/through language. In many of her tales, a female protagonist (most frequently, the first-person narrator herself) embarks on a symbolic journey into the past in search of her origin and identity, only to confront a crisis of subjectivity that takes the form of madness, disintegration, or even death. The desire to recover a lost or forgotten past always comes at a price, as the "return of the repressed" poses a threat to one's subjectivity.

Why, then, this obsession with the theme of constant return, dramatized through the construction and deconstruction of subjectivities? It is not only Fernández Cubas's fictional characters who are driven by a compulsion to return to their past in a circular fashion; their journeys also reflect an impulse in the author's own narrative trajectory continually to revisit similar situations and episodes that leave us with an uncanny sense of *déjà vu*. As Freud would remind us, uncanniness is produced by "an unintended recurrence of the same situation," a return to "something which is familiar and old-established in the mind and which has become alienated from it only through the process of repression."[3] The "uncanny" in Fernández Cubas is not limited to a disquieting sensation evoked within a single narrative context, but is, rather, a cumulative effect of the obsessive reenactment of the same scenarios from one work to the next. Narrative, then, becomes a form of repetition-compulsion through which the narrating subject seeks to fill the gaps and absences in memory, in an attempt to recapture an imaginary ideal that has been lost forever: innocence, integrity, and the satisfaction of desire. That is, narration represents an acting out, rather than a "working-through" of the pain of loss, since the repetitive gestures of language are the medium through which the subject elaborates her or his loss.[4]

By drawing on psychoanalytic paradigms to approach Fernández Cubas's texts, my purpose is to explore the function of psychoanalysis *as narrative* within the conventions of the genres that she cultivates. It is not my intention to suggest a direct influence of psychoanalytic theories on Fernández Cubas's own fiction, although in her recent book of memoirs, she confesses her enthusiasm for Freud's work, having lived in Buenos Aires in the 1970s, "en pleno auge del psicoanálisis" [at the high point of psychoanalysis].[5] Nor do I wish to confuse the author's psyche with those of her fictional characters, by suggesting in a simplistic fashion that the latter are projections of the former. What interests me is the way in which Fernández Cubas appropriates the psychoanalytic paradigm to comment on the nature of representation itself, particularly in relation to the formation of subjectivities. Recalling Shoshana Felman's words, uttered in the heyday of psychoanalytic criticism: "in the same way that psychoanalysis points to the unconscious of literature, *literature, in its turn, is the unconscious of psychoanaly*sis."[6] In Fernández Cubas's works, the construction of subjectivities is inseparable from the literary process itself: fiction brings to light what is inherently literary in the narrative of subject-formation, through a recognition of the literary nature of the psychoanalytic master narrative.

I will begin by turning to one of Fernández Cubas's early short stories, "En el hemisferio sur" [In the Southern Hemisphere] (published in *Los altillos de Brumal*), as it is paradigmatic of the "psychoanalytic narrative" in its exploration of the relationship between literature and the (de)construction of subjectivity. The story, told from the perspective of an unnamed male narrator, is about a female writer, Clara, who one day finds herself pursued by a mysterious Voice with a foreign accent. Although the Voice, at first, spurs on Clara's creative activity, it eventually unleashes a crisis of subjectivity, which makes her unable to distinguish her identity from that of Sonia Kraskowa, a novelist who appears already to have written everything that Clara wants to write. In the end, Clara and Sonia become one, and the protagonist, reduced to a state of madness, destroys herself through suicide. This tale, as are many others of Fernández Cubas's creation, is set in a world that tests the limits of established literary, social, and cultural conventions: the boundaries between the real and unreal, subject and object, the self and other, remain completely blurred. Phyllis Zatlin, who considers the "Fantastic" to be the salient characteristic of Fernández Cubas's works, draws on psychoanalytic concepts to elaborate on the relationship between fantasy and the process of ego formation in her early fiction.[7] If fantasy creates a space for the expression of repressed desire, as psychoanalytic critics have claimed, it represents an (impossible) attempt to recapture the ideal state of undifferentiation (Lacan's Imaginary) between self and other, subject and object, before the moment of loss and separation in the process of subject formation.[8] According to Rosemary Jackson, fantasy seeks to reverse the process of the subject's formation by recuperating the realm of the Imaginary.[9] From a Lacanian perspective, Clara's crisis of subjectivity is suggestive of just such a desire for the Imaginary.

The story opens as the male narrator listens to Clara's account of a mysterious female voice that haunts her every time she begins to write. This Voice is relentless in urging on her writing and leads her into a state of "trance, sugestión, arrebato, éxtasis" [trance, suggestion, rapture, ecstasy].[10] In Derridian terms, the voice (as a manifestation of speech) connotes the ideals of "meaning, truth [and] presence."[11] For Hélène Cixous, who (drawing on Derrida) reformulates Lacan's model of sexual identity formation in gendered terms, "woman," or the "mother," has a privileged relationship to the voice; that is, she discerns an essential link between *écriture féminine* and the maternal voice.[12] In Fernández Cubas's tale, the female protagonist's discovery of the Voice—written with a capital "V" and personified through the gendered "Ella"—suggests just such an identification between woman's writing and the maternal presence in the Imaginary. Yet, the same voice that spurs on her creative activity also instills a disquieting fear in her, and she soon feels a need to escape from its presence. The sensation of the "uncanny" overtakes her, as what seems familiar—and so essential to her identity as a writer—suddenly becomes estranged. (The foreign accent of the by-now familiar Voice symbolizes this estrangement.) Pursued by the Voice, Clara finds herself on the threshold between the Imaginary and the Symbolic, seduced by a desire for the Imaginary, at the same time, fearing the dissolution of her identity (that is, the subject as articulated in the Symbolic order).[13]

Clara's disintegration as a subject takes the form of a doubling between herself and Sonia Kraskowa. One day, as Clara enters a bookstore, she recognizes an image of herself on the cover of a book whose author is one Sonia Kraskowa. Furthermore, she finds that the words in the text reproduce her every thought, particularly those that pertain to her writing. The story turns inward self-reflexively, as Kraskowa's work transcribes virtually word-for-word Clara's conversation with the masculine narrator. "Todo lo que yo escribo, está escrito ya," she says, "Todo lo que yo pienso, lo ha pensado antes alguien por mí" [Everything I write is already written. Everything I think has already been thought for me by someone else] (138). The figure of Sonia represents a manifestation of the Imaginary other with whom Clara seeks to merge. Clara essentially becomes Sonia, whose novel *Humo denso* [Dense Smoke] shows the former's life in the process of being written. Soon afterward, Clara fixes her gaze on the swirl of the water in the drain and expresses her desire to travel to the "other" (southern) hemisphere where the water spins in the opposite direction. Her desire to "desremolinar el remolino" [reverse the whirlpool] suggests a process of inversion, of undoing that which has been done (140). Yet, as Rosemary Jackson has shown, one cannot return to undifferentiation without ceasing to exist as a subject, as the very notion of the subject presupposes its articulation within a social and linguistic order.[14] Clara's return to the Imaginary, then, inevitably leads her to a state of madness, of social unintelligibility.

That Clara is an internal narrator within the story told by a masculine narrator is significant, as is the fact that it is he who forces her confrontation with her Imaginary other (Sonia Kraskowa) by presenting her with the complete writings of the latter. The shock of her final recognition in the "other" is what leads directly to her suicide. Yet, the narrator himself is an unstable (not to mention misogynist) subject, whose sense of identity as a man and as a writer is at best precarious: "Jamás había conocido ese momento mágico en que el escritor, poseído por una fuerza milagrosa, se ve compelido a rellenar sin descanso hojas y más hojas, a no concederse tregua, a enfermar, a plasmar sobre el papel los dictados de su mente enfebrecida" [I had never known that magical moment in which the writer, possessed by a miraculous force, is compelled to fill, without a break, page after page, to give himself no respite, to fall ill, to give form on paper to the dictates of his feverish mind] (134). Clara's account of her encounter with the Voice not only arouses his envy, but also precipitates his crisis of subjectivity by forcing him into an awareness of his lack (in the psychoanalytic sense), which contrasts sharply with the "image of a completeness" that he perceives in her.[15] He faces a blank page, transformed into the metaphor of a desire whose satisfaction evades him perpetually: "Impertérrito, amenazante, lanzándome su perpetuo desafío, feminizándose por momentos y espetándome con voz saltarina: 'Anda, atrévete. Estoy aquí. Hunde en mi cuerpo esas maravillosas palabras que me harán daño'" [Undaunted, menacing, hurling at me its perpetual challenge, becoming more feminized by the minute and transfixing me with its restless voice: "Come on, just you dare. I am here. Sink into my body those marvelous words that will hurt me"] (134). Writing, for the narrator, clearly represents a phallic act, one of erotic and linguistic violence against the "feminine," which looms before him as a sign of lack that must be conquered.

Clara's account of her strange doubling with Sonia evokes in him
a sensation of the uncanny, by now so familiar to Fernández Cubas's
readers:

> La historia que Clara acababa de narrarme con tan aparente verismo me
> inquietaba. . . . [m]i amiga había llegado muy lejos en su relato y yo me
> sentía incapaz de contener el creciente nerviosismo que iba adueñán-
> dose de todos mis miembros. Ignoraba aún si el extraño temblor que me
> poseía se debía tan sólo a una seria preocupación por el estado mental
> de mi visitante, o si una rara emoción, surgida de lo más profundo, en-
> traba ahora en funcionamiento de modo inesperado.
>
> [The story that Clara had just told to me with such apparent truthfulness
> disturbed me. . . . [m]y friend had gotten far in her story and I felt myself
> incapable of containing the increasing nervousness that was taking hold
> of all of my limbs. I did not yet know if the strange tremor that possessed
> me was only due to my serious preoccupation with the mental state of
> my visitor, or if a strange emotion, arising out of something deeper, was
> coming into operation in an unexpected way.] (141)

What is so disquieting, yet so familiar, is his repressed desire for the
Imaginary, which can never be attained without following Clara's
same path. Thus, when he sees the reflection of his own lack in
Clara, he precipitates her destruction in a futile attempt to disavow
this lack. Immediately after he hands over Sonia's writings to Clara,
he decides to spend the weekend at the seaside home of his Aunt
Alicia, whom he had not seen in more than ten years. The crossing
of the threshold of his aunt's home and the multitude of memories
that arise in his mind at this moment represent a symbolic return to
childhood, to a maternal space associated with the sea. In the tran-
quil refuge of her abode, he seeks a fantasized pre-Lapsarian space
before the subject's "fall" into division.

Unlike Clara, who undergoes violence and self-mutilation in an
impossible attempt to recapture the Imaginary, the narrator continues to disavow his lack in order to prolong the fiction of the stable
subject. His entire discourse, then, serves to deny lack, to exile into
the unconscious that which threatens the subject. Clara's death permits the narrator to (re)write her story as fiction, casting her into a
plot in which a writer like Clara becomes an innocent and terrified
victim of her overactive imagination. As Cixous observes in her commentary on Freud's work, fiction (re)presents itself as a reserve or
suspension of the uncanny; that is, what might seem uncanny in real

life can become naturalized in the realm of fiction.[16] Thus, through his fiction, the narrator attempts to negate Clara's experience of desire. Significantly, only after Clara's death does the narrator begin to lose his fear of the blank page; that is, her absence allows him to repress his own desire for the Imaginary, once again, and to perpetuate the mirage of harmony between self and other.

Yet just as the narrator resolves to write his novel about Clara, in order to reassert his mastery over symbolic discourse, the repressed returns again, this time in the form of Clara/Sonia's posthumous work *Tornado*. (The whirlwind motion of the tornado, suggestive of circularity/repetition and violence, is symbolic of the unraveling of identities, and reproduces the image of the "remolino" that Clara wishes to "desremolinar.") From the narrator's perspective, the posthumous work of the female protagonist represents nothing less than the return of the dead; that is, death, as the ultimate sign of absence, comes to haunt him while he is still alive. Clara's book *Tornado* turns out to be her version of the novel that the narrator himself had wanted to write. As he reads her narrative, he discovers that it not only reaffirms Clara's experience of the Imaginary, but also casts him into the role of "un hombrecillo ridículo" [a ridiculous little man] tormented by feelings of frustration, confusion, and impotence as a writer (151). The first-person account also tells us of Clara's determination to abandon, once and for all, the "real" world and to pursue her desire for the Imaginary by "putting her dreams into practice" (152). The narrator receives the final blow when he discovers the following dedication in the book, addressed to him: "A ti, a mi (¿mejor?) amigo. Con la firme esperanza de que algún día podamos reírnos ante estas páginas" [To you, my (best?) friend. With the firm hope that some day we can laugh before these pages] (152). Furthermore, in a postscript she reveals that she had won a literary competition during their university years by hiding his book from the jury, an episode that became the narrator's formative experience of failure leading to his writer's block. At this moment, the narrator realizes that Clara has already determined his role in her narrative and that he has fallen into the trap of her "tétrico juego" [gloomy game] (153). As he runs to the sink to splash his face with water, he observes that the water in the drain is swirling in the opposite direction, just as in the southern hemisphere (yet another recurrence of the whirlpool motif). The "other" hemisphere, once again, evokes none other than the Imaginary that the narrator has long repressed; as he confronts the return of the repressed, he

too finds himself on the brink of dissolution as a subject, recogniz-
ing that he is no longer able to disavow his own lack. When he returns to his Aunt Alicia's place that same afternoon, he realizes that
her home no longer provides a refuge for the ego that faces the
threat of fragmentation. The uncanny seems to have invaded even
this space: despite his aunt's expression of surprise upon his entry,
he finds that everything has been prepared for his arrival as if his
visit had been anticipated. At this precise moment, the tale comes
to an abrupt end.

How to make sense of this narrative?[17] My critical task, as I have
defined earlier, is to seek to articulate the relationship between the
psychoanalytic narrative and the process of fictional representation
in the story. Given the highly self-reflexive nature of the tale, we can
say that fiction itself—and the narrator's relationship to it—is the
central subject of Fernández Cubas's tale. The narrator's fiction,
which is the entirety of the story of "En el hemisferio sur," retells
(from a masculine perspective) the same story that Clara has recounted, both in person and in her literature. The narrator, as we
have seen, creates his own fictional discourse in an attempt to repress the uncanny, to keep it under check, lest it reveal itself as a
sign of lack. Yet, by generating fiction—and, no less, one that self-
consciously mirrors his crisis of subjectivity—he reenacts his crisis
through Clara's story and brings to the surface "that which should
have 'remained hidden.' "[18] What comes to the surface is the unconscious of narrative, which ultimately reveals itself as absence, as
death, as the impossible object of representation. The endpoint of
"En el hemisferio sur," which is the *telos* of narrative desire, ironically parallels the narrator's imminent death as a subject. The ending of the tale, then, goes to show, in Cixous's words: "the very
paradox of the writing which stretches its signs in order to 'manifest'
the secret that it 'contains' ";[19] that is, fiction seeks to postpone
death (the secret) even as its repetitive gestures expose the futility
of making this secret (the unrepresentable) disappear.

"En el hemisferio sur" exemplifies one of the most complex ex-
plorations of the relationship between the construction of subjectivity and its fictional representation in Fernández Cubas's early work.
In fact, "En el hemisferio sur" and its companion tales in *Los altillos
de Brumal* (in my view, even more so than the works in her first collection, *Mi hermana Elba*) have set the paradigm for the author's subsequent works, which similarly appropriate a variety of generic
conventions, including the Gothic, the Fantastic, the ghost story,

and the quest narrative, to create a space for the representation of the subject's unconscious, unrepresentable "other."[20] In a number of her most memorable works, the subject's confrontation with the "other" takes the form of a female protagonist's symbolic journey into an unknown past. In "Los altillos de Brumal," the female protagonist Adriana, after her mother's death, travels to their village of origin (Brumal) to recuperate her childhood. The world she (re)-discovers upon her arrival in Brumal is a world anterior to language and syntax, where words and identities are reversed, where the irrational and the inverisimilar reign.[21] Adriana's return to Brumal is simultaneously liberating and destructive for her subjectivity: having lost both speech and memory she is confined to a psychiatric institution, after which she regains her desired identity as the child Anairda. In a more recent short story, "Con Agatha en Estambul," the female protagonist's journey (with her husband) to a foreign land brings her back into contact with a voice from her past and with her literary foremother, Agatha Christie. A series of uncanny accidents and coincidences during her stay in Istanbul leads her to question her sense of reality and even the existence of the city itself, which becomes associated with another world outside chronological time. The narrator's return to Barcelona marks the end of her journey, yet unable to free herself from the voice of her past, which now "formaba parte de mí misma" [formed a part of myself], she chooses to remain in this "other" world of adventure and mystery, "recordando, fabulando" [remembering, inventing].[22] Again and again, repetition, circularity, and (illusory) returns characterize the trajectory of Fernández Cubas's female characters.

Her most recent novel, *El columpio*, presents yet another version of the same quest narrative: that of a female protagonist's search for her origins through a metaphorical journey into the past. The novel opens with the female protagonist's reconstruction of her mother's strange dream in which the latter, still a child, allegedly sees a vision of her (as yet unborn) daughter after falling asleep in the garden. In the dream, the two women are looking at each other with curiosity and perplexity. When she awakens, she finds herself drenched in rain and subsequently falls ill. This dream, invented or otherwise, becomes an emblematic image in the daughter's memory of her now-deceased mother Eloísa, whose narrative evocations have always returned to the same scene: the garden of a house in an abandoned valley of the Pyrenees, where her brothers and cousin live. "Todos los caminos conducían al mismo lugar, a los mismos personajes"

[All roads led to the same place, to the same characters];[23] all memories lead to the same place. Even before the narrator herself decides to travel across the Pyrenees (from France) to meet her mother's estranged relatives, she conceptualizes her mother's old abode, the "Casa de la Torre" [House of the Tower], as a place situated outside of time, like an old photograph of her mother playing with her diabolo as a child.

Like that of Fernández Cubas's other female characters, this narrator's journey across the Pyrenees is also a metaphorical journey back through time, driven by a desire for the maternal fantasy. Given that her bond with her mother (who died prematurely) was precarious even while the latter was still alive, only the act of living the (M)other's memory and her dream of return vicariously will permit the protagonist to (re)capture the ideal of a maternal presence that never was. The protagonist finds herself doubly estranged from the world of her mother's past, of which even the memories are not her own. Her desire is to "revivir otras infancias" [relive other childhoods] through "recuerdos ajenos" [somebody else's memories] (21, 30), imagining that it was her mother's wish for her to "implicarme en un mundo o un pasado que no me pertenecían" [to get me involved in a world or a past that did not belong to me] (24).

From the first moment in which she arrives at her relatives' estate, the narrator observes the enigmatic behavior of her uncles and cousin, who appear to live in a hermetic world of the past, a world perfectly symbolized by the proverbial Gothic space of their "Casa de la Torre":[24] "Una casa grande rematada por un torreón. Allí, en el último ventanuco, debía de hallarse el desván, el cuarto de los juegos" [A big house topped with a turret. There, in the last window, there should be an attic, a playroom] (20–21). As she confronts a world in which everything seems uncertain and deceptive, the sensation of the uncanny overtakes her. Her use of the clause "como si" [as if] throughout her narration, to describe the events and inhabitants in the Casa de la Torre, imbues her entire experience with a sense of irreality, of otherworldliness.[25] Everything in the house, including its inhabitants, seems to her "extraño," "postizo," "falso" [strange, artificial, fake] (24, 25). The first day of her stay, her eyes focus on the water, disappearing down the drain of the bathtub, "describiendo círculos" [tracing circles] (26), suggesting the unraveling of time (and of subjectivity), as in "En el hemisferio sur." (Once again, a seemingly insignificant detail—in this case, the image of the miniature whirlpool—can acquire significance through its repetition in more than one work by the same author.) The world of the "Casa de la Torre," which brings the narrator back to her origins—that is, to a space of fantasized maternal presence— recalls Kristeva's conceptualization of a "monumental temporality" linked to female subjectivity.[26] The child Eloísa, who embodies the maternal fantasy sought by her daughter, is closely identified with two objects, the diabolo and the swing, both characterized by their repetitive, pendular movement. In her hand, the diabolo's circular undulations emblematize the *jouissance* of child's play that defies the laws of the Symbolic; in fact, the diabolo becomes a metonymy for Eloísa, true to her brother Lucas's words that "Eloísa sin su diábolo no es Eloísa" [Eloísa without her diabolo is not Eloísa] (31).

In this world of cyclical temporality—of "repetition and eternity"[27]—the protagonist's identity gradually becomes merged with that of her mother. During an excursion with her male relatives, the protagonist starts swinging on her mother's old swing when she imagines that she hears the child Eloísa's voice from the past. From this moment on, the memory of her mother's voice, which continues to resound in her ears, seduces her and draws her even further into the world of the child Eloísa. The identification between the "voice" and the maternal imaginary is even more explicit in this novel than in the author's other works, as the child Eloísa is embodied in the voice. Like the protagonist of "Los altillos de Brumal," whose confrontation with the Imaginary other culminates in the enclosed space of an attic in her mother's home village, the protagonist of *El columpio* seeks the secret of her mother's—and her own—past in the attic of the tower of Eloísa's childhood home. There, she discovers that the letters written from Paris by her mother to her estranged relatives before her death have never been opened, or, more accurately, it is *as if* they had never been opened. Just as time has frozen for the protagonist in the old, dusty space of the attic ("Los desvanes son como inmensos arcones en los que el tiempo se ha detenido" [Attics are like immense chests in which time has stopped] [70], she says to her uncles), time has long since come to a standstill for Eloísa's brothers and cousin, who have never accepted her departure from *their* world—a world disturbed only by her daughter's return years later. On perusing her mother's letters, what catches the protagonist's eye are the distinctive strokes of her signature, which mirror the circular movement of the child's diabolo: "Una letra de niña envuelta en las oscilaciones de una cuerda de diábolo" [A child's handwriting enveloped in the oscillations of a diabolo string] (60), "como si [mi madre] quisiera dar a entender: 'Nada ha cambiado. Para vosotros ni siquiera he crecido. Sigo siendo la de siempre. Eloísa. Vuestra Eloísa'" [as if she wanted to say: "Nothing has changed. For all of you I haven't even grown. I continue to be the same person. Eloísa. Your Eloísa"] (56). It is in this space of the Imaginary—captured by the metaphor of the attic—where past and present, self and other, mother and daughter, become fused; in the narrator's own words: "pareció como si las dos . . . estuviéramos más unidas que nunca" [it seemed as if the two of us . . . were more united than ever] (64).

For their part, the narrator's male relatives are borderline psychotics who, having rejected the "sociosymbolic contract,"[28] continue to cling to the Imaginary world of the past, that is, to their childhood with Eloísa. The narrator's initial impression of her uncle Tomás, characterized as "algo simple. Un niño grande" [rather simple-minded. A big child] (23), is of a man who has been infantilized; Lucas is "un hombre extraño" [a strange man] (24), whom she glimpses from outside of his window, gesturing and speaking to himself. Lucas, who describes his own mind as "un auténtico desván" [an authentic attic] (65), is writing from memory a cookbook, *Juegos del valle* [Games of the Valley], which bears no semblance of order to anyone other than to himself (65–67). Her cousin Bebo, an artist who once painted the now-faded portrait of Eloísa with her diabolo, rarely ventures out of his room, a peculiarity that Lucas attributes to an "illness," agoraphobia. It is also suggested that Bebo harbored an incestuous desire for Eloísa during their childhood. Their world—and that of the child Eloísa whom they have preserved in their memory—represents an "[a]ll-encompassing and infinite like imaginary space" of "monumental temporality" where *jouissance* reigns[29]: "Ella [Eloísa], sus dos hermanos, su primo. Un universo que empezaba y terminaba ahí. En esa pandilla hermética, autosuficiente, en la que no había lugar para otros. Juegos y más juegos, y siempre los mismos participantes: ellos cuatro" [She, her two brothers, her cousin. A universe that began and ended there. In that hermetic and self-sufficient group, in which there was no place for others. Games and more games, and always the same participants: the four of them] (96). It is from this world that the narrator's aging uncles and cousin seek to expel her, as if to force the recognition that once the subject has left the Imaginary, there can be no return. Having aborted her male relatives' attempt to eject her from their world, the narrator soon discovers that the three men, "unos hom-

bretones infantilizados, unos locos y ociosos" [a bunch of infantilized men, crazy and idle] (177), gather every Friday in their dining
room to relive their childhood habit of "role-playing" together by
imitating each other's words and gestures. These words and gestures, reminiscent of the nonexpressive articulations (rhythms) of
Kristeva's "semiotic" (that is, a reconfiguration of Lacan's Imaginary), represent a denial of symbolic language and of signification.[30]
Having refused the Symbolic, these men have no choice but to preserve their Imaginary fantasy through the ritual of repetition; their
repetitive gestures become their only reality, "lo más real de todo lo
que constituía su vida" [the realest part of what made up their lives]
(119). The narrator, who observes her relatives' weekly ritual from
the other side of the window glass (evocative of Lacan's mirror
phase?), deems them to be completely mad.

Significantly, this is the moment in which the narrator, still outside the dining room window, hears her mother's voice once again,
the same voice that she heard upon mounting Eloísa's old swing
during her first excursion with her relatives. Again, the voice evokes
a sensation of the uncanny in the narrator: seemingly familiar, it also
rings false, as if uttered by an adult impostor impersonating the
child on the swing. Finding herself on the threshold between the
Imaginary and Symbolic, the narrator comes to realize that those
who have already once abandoned the Imaginary cannot reenter
this world with their identities intact, without becoming reduced to
the same state of infantilization and madness as her male relatives.
In her conscious mind, she resolves to abandon the "Casa de la
Torre" and the world it represents; yet the force of desire brings
back the image of her mother Eloísa and her diabolo once again:
while the narrator stands outside in the rain, her mother appears to
her in a vision, transformed into a defiant, menacing presence. This
episode recreates the first scene of the novel in which mother and
daughter stand face to face in the garden of the "Casa de la Torre."
(We must recall that this scene occurs in Eloísa's dream after she
falls asleep on the swing in the rain.) The narrator's vision, then,
represents a reenactment of her primordial desire to recapture the
presence of the Imaginary embodied in the maternal fantasy/phan-
tom. Like the melancholic, whose ego becomes identified with the
loved object that has become lost,[31] the narrator has clung, up to this
moment, to the phantom of her absent mother. In this emblematic
moment, when the boundaries between reality, fantasy and dream
become blurred, Eloísa hurls the strings of her diabolo around the

narrator's neck, nearly asphyxiating her, at which point the sound
of the narrator's own voice frees her from the stranglehold of the
strings—and, symbolically, from her mother's phantom. The image
that her mother leaves behind is no longer that of a menacing phantom, but that of the child Eloísa with a toy in her hand.

Throughout the novel, the narrator is propelled forward by the
contrary forces of desire and horror, embodied in the ambiguity of
the spectral Mother, who is simultaneously the sign of presence and
absence. The subject's desire for the maternal fantasy through a return to the Imaginary inevitably leads to a confrontation with the
horror of lack, that which has been estranged through the process
of repression.[32] Having come face to face with the spectral Mother
at the end of the novel, the protagonist of *El columpio* confronts her
own identity which is on the brink of dissolution: "me encontraba
en el borde mismo de un pozo" [I found myself on the very edge of
a well] (125). During her final flight from the "Casa de la Torre"
and her journey back to the present, the narrator reconstructs the
drama of her subjectivity: the return to the Imaginary, the confrontation with her estranged (M)other and, finally, her return to the
present after freeing herself from her mother's phantom. Like the
swing's movement, she has oscillated between disavowal and recognition of the lack that is at the center of her subjectivity: "Ahora
era yo quien tenía la certeza de haber estado durante aquellos días
balanceándome en un columpio, suspendida en el aire, ingrávida
sobre un inmenso abismo. Hacia atrás, hacia delante..." [Now it was
I who was certain about having spent those days swinging on a swing,
suspended in air, weightless above an immense abyss. Backward,
forward . . .] (134).

Absence, death, and lack are therefore the driving forces of the
protagonist's narration which, in retrospect, reconstructs her symbolic journey from a first-person perspective. Is her narration, then,
yet another form of acting out the experience of loss? In a sense,
through the narrator's identification with her mother and the circularity of the narrative structure itself, the former replicates the journey of the latter, suggesting a repetition of the same cycle from one
generation to the next: "el olvido disfrazó con los años algo que su
mente de adulta se negaba a aceptar, pero que, sin embargo, necesi-
taba repetir compulsivamente" [oblivion covered up with the passing of the years something that her (Eloísa's) adult mind refused to
accept, but that she, nevertheless, needed to repeat compulsively]
(135). Yet, it is the memory of her mother which, in the end, saves

the protagonist from the abyss of the metaphorical "pozo" [well] on whose edge she totters so precariously at the end of the novel. That is, the mother saves her daughter from her own fate of reliving eternally a specter of a past that could be neither remembered nor forgotten. The cycle of repetition-compulsion can be broken only through the act of remembrance, the "working-through" of repressed memories.[33] The "recuerdos ajenos" [somebody else's memories], the estranged memories passed on from mother to daughter, which originally motivated the latter's journey, become transformed into "un hermoso, impreciso recuerdo" [a beautiful, imprecise memory] at the end of the novel (135). By making the journey "back home," a journey that came too late for her mother, the narrator overcomes the specter of the past—the horror of absence—in order to be able to continue her journey in the present. The narrator's thoughts in the final line of the novel: "Nunca . . . volvería a decir: 'Demasiado tarde'" [I would never say again: "Too late"] (137), represent an affirmation of her resolution to live in the present moment, freed from the phantoms of the past.

What is noteworthy in analyzing Fernández Cubas's works from a psychoanalytic perspective is the facility with which they lend themselves to such an approach. Our question, once again, is how the author conceptualizes the relationship between fiction and the psychoanalytic narrative. If, as Jessica Folkart claims, drawing on Peter Brooks, that fiction is about "plotting desire,"[34] what is the function of repetition in Fernández Cubas's narrative of desire? Following Brooks's argument, if narrative desire propels us forward toward the endpoint of (imaginary) satisfaction and plenitude of meaning, repetition is "a kind of remembering, and thus a way of reorganizing a story whose connective links have been obscured and lost."[35] Returning to Freud, narrative acts out, through repetition, that which resists remembrance. In El columpio, repetition finally gives way to remembrance, to an acknowledgment of the impossibility of return to a pre-Lapsarian past before the division of the subject, a past symbolized by the plenitude of the Imaginary Mother.

Not surprisingly, Fernández Cubas's obsession with repetition and remembrance in her fictional works recurs in her recent book of memoirs, Cosas que ya no existen. Like her fictional protagonists, the narrating subject of this autobiographical account (presumably the author herself) embarks on a journey into her past to engage in a process of ever-incomplete remembrance and self-reflection. She seeks to represent, through the repetitive gestures of language, the gaps and absences in her memory, including that which is unspeakable. Her account of the devastating vacuum left in her family after the premature death of her oldest sister, whose image she has erased from her memory until the moment of writing these memoirs, is a token of the power of language to re-present, if not to recuperate fully, that which has been repressed in the unconscious. The sense of estrangement described by the narrator as "la perplejidad" [bewilderment] (261), which overtakes the family members after Ana María's death, plunging them into the empty and relentless ritual of mourning day after day, is reminiscent of the sensation of the uncanny that accompanies the rituals of return reenacted by the protagonists of Fernández Cubas's fiction. (For example, this ritual of mourning evokes the narrator's ritual reenactments of the maternal fantasy in *El columpio*.) In yet another chapter (appropriately entitled "Los regresos" [Returns]) of her memoirs, the author's account of her brief stay in Argentina in 1974, and of her return to that country in 1989 after the end of military dictatorship, suggests the political function of memory, as a way of giving voice to the voiceless, to the victims of political atrocities who have been erased forcibly from existence and from memory. The motif of repetition recurs when describing a sensation of "uncanniness" that overtakes her on revisiting her old haunts in Buenos Aires: what she experiences is a "return" that is not really a return, since time and history (and unmentionable horrors) stand between her and her memories of these places in her past. The problem that confronts the author is how best to render the unrepresentable into words, not having been present to witness the unspeakable, and faced with a society intent on willfully "forgetting" the past. Memory is ever incomplete, as the author pieces together her own past through "retazos de conversaciones de otros tiempos" [fragments of conversations of other times] that she transcribes with difficulty (96) in an attempt to bring to the surface that which has been repressed by national history. Perhaps what ultimately propels the narrative forward, in Fernández Cubas's fiction and autobiography alike, is the impossibility of memory—of recovering the past and of resuturing the fractured subject. The narrating subject's desire for completion, plenitude, and a meaning that continually eludes her, finds expression in symbolic form, in a narrative that "acts out" the repressed through repetition. These repetitive gestures, in the end, can only lead to a consciousness of the impossibility of return, of recuperating that which has been lost. The subject can either acknowledge the loss and live with this knowledge, or continue to deny this loss, reenacting it symbolically through the repetitive acts of language. Fernández Cubas's narrative, then, seeks to represent the unconscious by testing the limits of fiction and of desire, even as the narrating subject struggles to come to terms with the absence that looms behind this representation.

NOTES

1. See Mary Lee Bretz, "Cristina Fernández Cubas and the Recuperation of the Semiotic in *Los altillos de Brumal*," *Anales de la Literatura Española Contemporánea* 13 (1988): 177–88; Kathleen M. Glenn, "Gothic Indecipherability and Doubling in the Fiction of Cristina Fernández Cubas," *Monographic Review/Revista Monográfica* 8 (1992): 125–41; Janet Pérez, "Fernández Cubas, Abjection, and the 'retórica del horror,'" *Explicación de Textos Literarios* 24 (1995–96): 159–71; Lynn K. Talbot, "Journey into the Fantastic: Cristina Fernández Cubas's 'Los altillos de Brumal,'" *Letras Femeninas* 15 (1989): 37–47; Phyllis Zatlin, "Tales from Fernández Cubas: Adventure in the Fantastic," *Monographic Review/Revista Monográfica* 3:1–2 (1987): 107–18.

2. See Kathleen M. Glenn, "Conversación con Cristina Fernández Cubas,"*Anales de la Literatura Española Contemporánea* 18 (1993): 355–63; and Geraldine C. Nichols, "Entrevista a Cristina Fernández Cubas," *España Contemporánea* 6 (1993): 55–71.

3. Sigmund Freud, "The 'Uncanny,'" in vol. 17 of *The Standard Edition of the Complete Psychological Works of Sigmund Freud*, ed. James Strachey (London: Hogarth Press, 1955), 237, 241.

4. Sigmund Freud, "Remembering, Repeating and Working-Through," in vol. 12 of *The Standard Edition of the Complete Psychological Works of Sigmund Freud*, ed. James Strachey (London: Hogarth Press, 1958), 147–56.

5. Cristina Fernández Cubas, *Cosas que ya no existen* (Barcelona: Lumen, 2001), 70. Subsequent references to this work will be cited parenthetically in the text.

6. "To Open the Question," in *Literature and Psychoanalysis: The Question of Reading: Otherwise*, ed. Shoshana Felman (Baltimore: Johns Hopkins University Press, 1982), 10.

7. Zatlin, "Tales from Fernández Cubas," 111.

8. According to Lacan, the constitution of the subject begins in the mirror phase when the child first recognizes itself as an object by seeing an image of itself (*Écrits: A Selection*, trans. Alan Sheridan [New York: Norton, 1977], 1–7). This image, then, becomes a model for its future identifications. In the Imaginary, however, the self only perceives in its image a coherent identity with which it merges and identifies. There is no sense of a separate self until this dyadic unity is ruptured by the child's entry into the Symbolic Order. With its entry into the Symbolic, the self defines itself as separate from the other, and the desire for the Imaginary becomes repressed in the unconscious.

9. Rosemary Jackson, *Fantasy: The Literature of Subversion* (London: Routledge, 1981), 90.

10. *Mi hermana Elba y Los altillos de Brumal* (Barcelona: Tusquets, 1988), 135–36. Subsequent references to "En el hemisferio sur" will be cited parenthetically in the text.

11. Jacques Derrida, *Of Grammatology*, trans. Gayatri Chakravorty Spivak (Baltimore: Johns Hopkins University Press, 1974), 14.

12. Hélène Cixous and Catherine Clément, *The Newly Born Woman*, trans. Betsy Wing (Minneapolis: University of Minnesota Press, 1986), 92–93. "The Voice sings from a time before law, before the Symbolic took one's breath away and reappropriated it into language under its authority of separation. The deepest, the oldest, the loveliest Visitation. Within each woman the first, nameless love is singing" (93).

13. The Voice, which is simultaneously familiar and estranged, is a recurrent motif in Fernández Cubas's works. In her short story "Con Agatha en Estambul," for example, the first-person female narrator is pursued by a voice, which she describes as "al tiempo familiar e irritante, conocida y desconocida" [at the same time familiar and irritating, known and unknown] (*Con Agatha en Estambul* [Barcelona: Tusquets, 1994], 195). The protagonist's confrontation with the Voice occurs, significantly, within the context of her journey to a foreign land, which becomes a symbolic journey back through time: "a tiempos olvidados. Tiempos queridos, tiempos muy lejanos" [to forgotten times. Beloved times, very remote times] (174).

14. Jackson, *Fantasy*, 90–91.

15. Jacques Lacan, *The Four Fundamental Concepts of Psycho-Analysis*, ed. Jacques-Alain Miller, trans. Alan Sheridan (New York: Norton, 1981), 116.

16. Hélène Cixous, "Fiction and Its Phantoms: A Reading of Freud's *Das Unheimliche* (The 'Uncanny')," *New Literary History* 7 (1976): 546; Freud, "The 'Uncanny,'" 251.

17. My approach to this story does not, of course, preclude other interpretations: for example, it would be possible to argue that the narrator is not a separate entity, but another aspect of the schizophrenic double, perhaps Clara's "masculine" side, as Janet Pérez has suggested to me.

18. Cixous, "Fiction and Its Phantoms," 547.

19. Ibid.

20. See Talbot's analysis, which focuses on "the use of the fantastic as a literature of desire" in "Los altillos de Brumal" ("Journey into the Fantastic," 45).

21. See Mary Lee Bretz's analysis of Adriana's pilgrimage back to Brumal as a journey back to the pre-oedipal modality of the "semiotic" as defined by Kristeva ("Cristina Fernández Cubas and the Recuperation of the Semiotic in *Los altillos de Brumal*," *Anales de la Literatura Española Contemporánea* 13 (1988): 184–86).

22. *Con Agatha en Estambul* (Barcelona: Tusquets, 1994), 232, 233.

23. *El columpio* (Barcelona: Tusquets, 1995), 11. All subsequent references to this work will be cited parenthetically in the text.

24. For a discussion of the features of the Gothic in Fernández Cubas's work, see Glenn's "Gothic Indecipherability."

25. For a detailed study of the rhetorical markers that capture the atmosphere of uncertainty in *El columpio* and Fernández Cubas's other works, see Janet Pérez, "Cristina Fernández Cubas: Narrative Unreliability and the Flight from Clarity, or, the Quest for Knowledge in the Fog," *Hispanófila* 122 (January 1998): 29–39.

26. Julia Kristeva, "Women's Time," *Signs* 7 (1981): 16.

27. Ibid.

28. Ibid., 24.

29. Ibid., 16.

30. The situation of the unwelcome outsider who invades a hermetic and Imaginary world created by borderline psychotics is one that recurs in Fernández Cubas's fiction. As Janet Pérez has pointed out to me, the intrusion of the narrator of *El columpio* into her relatives' private world, anterior to sign and syntax, recalls the situation in "La ventana del jardín" [The Garden Window] (published in *Mi hermana Elba*), where the unannounced visit by the story's narrator obliges the reluctant hosts to stage a "representation" to shorten his visit. The scene in which this narrator seeks to communicate with his hosts' son, the infantilized Tomás (even the character's name is identical to that of the narrator's uncle in *El columpio*), from outside of his window, recalls the situation in Fernández Cubas's recent novel. Again, such a repetition evokes an uncanny sense of *déjà vu* in the reader.

31. Sigmund Freud, "Mourning and Melancholia," in vol. 14 of *The Standard Edition of the Complete Psychological Works of Sigmund Freud*, ed. James Strachey (London: Hogarth Press, 1957), 249.

32. Freud, "The 'Uncanny,'" 241.

33. Freud, "Remembering," 147–56.

34. Jessica A. Folkart, "Desire, Doubling, and Difference in Cristina Fernández Cubas's *El ángulo del horror*," *Revista Canadiense de Estudios Hispánicos* 24:2 (Winter 2000): 344.

35. Peter Brooks, *Reading for the Plot: Design and Intention in Narrative* (New York: Vintage Books, 1984), 139.

El año de Gracia and the
Displacement of the Word

Catherine G. Bellver

THE WORD IS POWER. THE POWER OF THE SPOKEN WORD DERIVES FROM ITS dynamic nature, from its identification with movement and event. God is the Word, and humanity but the subsequent and dependent articulation of that Word. Over time, the ephemeral, perishable oral utterance has been supplanted among literate peoples by the fixed, binding written word as the source of power, with the awe for magical potency yielding to a reverence for the might of veracity. The autonomy, immutability, and permanence of written texts lead to the notion that "the book says" is tantamount to "it is true."[1] Until this century, the concept "text" was identified exclusively with writing and carried, especially through the Middle Ages, a strict correlation with divine and secular authority. Recently the term "text" has come to include not only oral discourse but any vehicle of unified articulated meaning. Yet the written word continues to enjoy priority among literate societies and remains at the base of the common concept of text. The notion of the power of the established, self-sufficient written word confers on new literary compositions an inescapable dependency on previously written texts. Texts, we are told, speak to one another in anger, respect, or indifference.[2] Written texts not only furnish material, incentive, or direction for new texts, but in both overt didactic and subtler more unconscious ways, they help inspire, orient, and mold the vision of those who read them. While we think of Paolo and Francesca seduced by the story of Lancelot, Madame Bovary deluded by sentimental novels, or the teenager absorbed by comic books, we all may unconsciously assimilate the written word, making it the architect of our concept of the outside world. To chronicle this absorption of former texts an author must inscribe within his or her original work some nodding acknowledgment of the authority of previous texts over the human

118

psyche, and in doing so exposes his or her dependence on literary heritage.

El año de Gracia [The Year of Grace] (1985), the first novel by the Spanish short story writer Cristina Fernández Cubas, provides a vivid example of the strong imprint books and stories can leave on an impressionable mind. The protagonist sees himself, others, and the world around him from the perspective of the books he has read. Mostly adventure stories, these works nurture in him a longing for excitement, a desire to travel, and a naive sense of confidence. In addition to his early contact with the tales of sailors and pirates, Daniel became familiar with the Bible and proficient in Greek and Latin during his seven years in the seminary. Cloistered from the real world, first by literature and then by the monastery, he is ignorant of the fundamental structures that govern the outside, social world. Armed with both sacred and popular literature, Daniel ingenuously believes he is prepared to confront the adult sphere, but he soon learns that his education is useless and his concept of the world erroneous. Slowly each one of his literary referents is subverted and displaced until almost all possibility for communication dissolves.

From their inheritance, Gracia [Grace] gives her brother a free year away from home, literally "a year of grace." For the twenty-four-year-old inexperienced protagonist, his sister's gift promises him freedom and adventure, the opportunity to pursue that "aire libre, mar, ignoradas y fascinantes sensaciones" [open air, sea, unknown and fascinating sensations] that have always intrigued him.[3] He sets out for Paris where he meets a vivacious photographer and leads a leisurely existence for a few months until he leaves for Saint-Malo. There he meets Captain Jean, the skipper of the *Providence,* whose beard and demeanor instill in him a false sense of trust. An invitation to join the crew provokes in him the delusionary presumption that he is on the verge of reliving the excitement of the seafarers in his adolescent readings. Soon, however, fictional fantasy becomes the brutal reality of murder, danger, and disaster. In the middle of a storm on the high seas, Daniel is shipwrecked and miraculously awakes on an island he later discovers is contaminated by chemical experiments and inhabited only by infected sheep and an equally mangy shepherd named Grock. Gradually his ingenuous illusions of adventure, heroism, and indestructibility are whittled away as experience contradicts each one of his literary models.

El año de Gracia is filled with intertextual references to adventure stories like *Robinson Crusoe, Treasure Island,* and "Sinbad the Sailor" and to archetypes like that of the mythic hero. By flaunting its literary allusions and efforts to emulate other texts, the novel creates a self-conscious referentiality that divides the reader's interest between the text and its referents, calls attention to its artifices, and diverts attention from its potential for mimetic representation of reality. Harold Bloom maintains that in every case a literary text "is not a gathering of signs on a page, but is a psychic battlefield upon which authentic forces struggle for the only victory worth winning, the divinating triumph over oblivion."[4] In *El año de Gracia,* in place of a battle we witness a playful match in which the old and the new banter back and forth until each one cancels out the other. The novel begins with a happy confluence of established narrative threads, but as it progresses and the protagonist struggles to make his life conform to fiction, the narratives serving as points of comparison are subverted by inversion and erasure without being replaced by satisfactory alternatives. As previous literary models are rendered invalid and emerging narrative patterns prove ambivalent, any element of triumph is lost.

Because literature nurtured the protagonist psychologically and molded his expectations, he relates his new experiences to his literary-based vision of the world. Standing before the docks of Saint-Malo, he evokes Henry Morgan, Long John Silver, A. Gordon Pym, and Captain Nemo and associates his feeling "con la ansiedad del pequeño Jim del *Almirante Bembow* ante la inminencia de su primer viaje" [with the excitement of young Jim of the *Admiral Benbow* before his first voyage] (30–31). He mistakes Captain Jean, the ship, and other details for good omens and significant signs. As soon as he touches land, he begins to discover, with a certain disappointment, the discrepancy between fiction and fact: "No era una playa, sino el simple llano del rompiente" [It wasn't a beach, but simply a flat reef] (64). And contrary to what he had read, he finds himself not kissing the earth once safe on land. Incidental divergences such as these announce major contrasts, until all of his exemplary models of confrontation with danger are parodied, subverted, or reversed.

One of the most obvious intertextual references in *El año de Gracia* is to Daniel Defoe's novel. Like Robinson Crusoe, the protagonist of Fernández Cubas's novel runs away to sea, is shipwrecked, and leads a solitary existence on an uninhabited island where he meets a primitive man who becomes his companion. For the modern day, as well as for the eighteenth-century Crusoe, the Bible is instrumental in his survival, but as a technique for manipulation rather than consola-tion. The island he lands on is neither distant nor exotic, and his abbreviated stay includes no series of heroic adventures requiring courage or stamina. Grock may show some similarity (as the novel itself suggests) to the old man in Sinbad's fifth voyage, but within the context of the *Robinson Crusoe* allusions, he must be compared to Friday. Daniel refers to Grock as "mi variable Viernes" [my mercurial Friday] (119), but he soon realizes that "Aquel viejo simple no se parecía en nada al fiel Viernes de la única novela que, ironías de la vida, me había olvidado de evocar ante la visión del 'Providence'" [That simple old man did not resemble at all the faithful Friday of the only novel that, ironically, I had forgotten to evoke when seeing the *Providence*] (124). Rather than a submissive gentle servant, he encounters a volatile and perverse tyrant. By reversing the roles of master and servant, Fernández Cubas subverts the presumed superiority of civilized man. Defoe is often portrayed as the prophet of progress, the defender of the Protestant ethic and Anglo-Saxon ethnicity, and the propagandist for imperialistic commercialism.[5] In Fernández Cubas, any justification of contemporary society yields to scorn, and praise gives way to skepticism. Both Daniel and the civilization that produced him are criticized, the first for his naiveté, and the second for its callousness.

The fragile illusion Daniel had built for himself on the basis of his readings comes tumbling down like a house of cards. The literature in which he steeped himself proves an unreliable guideline for his own behavior and an untrue prediction of new situations. Parody gives way to irony as imitation turns to reversal. Heroism is displaced by perversion, nobility by baseness, and grandeur by banality. Without a valid literary map to assist him, Daniel is deprived of the security of dependable meanings and is consequently obliged to chart new patterns on his own. Having been deceived by the power of the written word, he must look to other spheres to communicate for the sake of survival with the only human being near him.

Those who define language as a "prison-house" or the "law of the father" recognize its constraining force and the influence of its schema. Derrida contends that writing engulfs speech but also notes that "Western metaphysics has systematically privileged voice over writing, on the presumption that *logos,* as the a priori, transcendental power of knowledge and signifier of being is immediately present in speech, whereas writing is displaced, one degree removed as the representation of speech."[6] What is relevant to the present discussion is not the question of priority of either speech or writing, but the authoritarian power of established models over specific representation. In written literature, texts emerge as the preexisting authority and the collective points of reference. Unlike speech, writing always *appears* symbolic, promising meaning by its solidity and apparent autonomy. Literature paradoxically attracts because it is something other than ordinary communication, yet its power and permanence requires us to reduce its strangeness by drawing on a number of conventions to make it into communication.[7] This complex process endows literature with a special mystique and enables it to influence profoundly not only new narrations but thought patterns and even personal behavior. Such conditioning by and authority of the written word is what Fernández Cubas challenges in *El año de Gracia*. In the spirit of postmodernism, she deconstructs standard, preexisting meanings until signs are loosened from their secure grounding. She first rebels against the written word through (re)-writing, displacing its established meaning by the subversive imitation inherent in parody. She then eradicates the written word and exploits the irrational potential of pure sound.

In Fernández Cubas's novel, all formal systems of communication—oral as well as written—fail. As a conventional yet arbitrary system of sounds, language always depends on *"some* level of shared assumption between utterer and receiver."[8] Its arbitrariness is neutralized by the fixedness that allows stable, consistent structures to organize mobile, individual utterances. A common code, context or conduit permits the exchange of messages and the production of communication. In *El año de Gracia* the lack of commonality provided by participation in a common social environment or by the possession of a common vehicle of linguistic communication compels the characters to find points of intersection outside language and social conventions. Phyllis Zatlin has already singled out Fernández Cubas's noteworthy approach to the nonverbal. As she accurately observes, the narrator of the novel, a well-read polyglot, for all his linguistic proficiency is not able to maintain communication as he regresses from knowledge to ignorance in what is, in many ways, an inversion of the myth of the hero.[9] While in her short story "La ventana del jardín" [The Garden Window] the narrator confronts words that sound familiar but take on new meaning, in her novel the "semiotic chaos" in which its narrator finds himself is more severe because Grock's strange mixture of Celtic and English shows no resemblance to anything familiar. With the organized support of literary and oral discourse both undermined, Daniel must regress deep into the primordial roots of language to find a point of minimal exchange, or he must direct himself to other human systems to uncover a way to transcend linguistic communication.

After discovering a Bible that belonged to Grock's mother, Daniel exploits his companion's lost affective bonds to thwart the dominion he holds over him. Every three nights Daniel visits the shepherd's cabin, keeps him company, and reads to him. In exchange, Grock provides him with food and wood. With this "milagroso ardid" [miraculous trick] of reading, Grock's uncontrollable urge to dominate is mitigated; and Daniel can pass from "esclavo a dama de compañía, de náufrago a Sherezade" [slave to lady-in-waiting, from shipwreck to Scheherazade] (137). The power of the word that ends Grock's control over Daniel derives not from the meaning of those sacred words or even from the provocative force of any narrative thread, but rather from the purely verbal nature of the word, from its elemental quality of sound and rhythm devoid of any semantic weight. Daniel himself recognizes that "lo que realmente fascinaba al viejo era el rito en sí mismo, el arte prodigioso de la lectura" [what really fascinated the old man was the rite itself, the wonderful art of reading] (133). Condensed to its primordial essence of acoustic repetition, the word reverts to its magical power of incantation. The potential of words for charm is what helps Daniel captivate and restrain his savage companion, for "the central idea of the magic of charm is to reduce freedom of action, either by compelling a certain course of action or by stopping action altogether."[10] On an extratextual level, the reversion in *El año de Gracia* to the rhythmic, irrational, or "semiotic" dimension of language, as Julia Kristeva calls it, can be considered a continuation of a trend Mary Lee Bretz notices in other works by Fernández Cubas and a part of a broader tendency among many modern women writers to recuperate the alternative feminine discourse repressed by the symbolic order.[11] The association of this prediscursive, prelinguistic semiotic form of language with the maternal is subtly borne out in *El año de Gracia* by the fact that the Bible belongs to Grock's mother. More obvious is the disruption of the sublimated symbolic order. Grock's realm of nonsignification supplants the histories, order, and the apparent clarity of the language and literature that patriarchal discourse had bestowed upon Daniel.

Only through the displacement of the symbolic by the semiotic and the supplantation of verbal communication by psychological communion can the linguistic and intellectual incompatibility be-

tween Grock and Daniel be resolved. The concessions in communication that take place in the novel have ironic social implications
and serious personal consequences for the protagonist, because in
chaos he finds the wholeness that the rational and orderly material
world cannot sustain for him. Besides renouncing the literary referents that helped mold his ingenuous perception of the world, Daniel discovers that the communicative process, the exchange of
messages between addresser and addressee can occur simply
through a psychological contact without a shared system of signs determined by common cultural ties. With his recitations Daniel gives
pleasure to Grock; Grock, in turn, infuses hope in him. This balanced interchange establishes between the two a mutual need and a
symbiotic relationship that transforms each one into the counterpart of the other. In *El año de Gracia,* communication surpasses the
major levels of exchange delineated by linguistic structuralists to include a reciprocity verging on divine communion.[12] Grock unwit-
tingly sacrifices his life for Daniel in a gesture that effects a
comprehensive and ultimate exchange of identities and a spiritual
communication that Daniel will never be able to put into words.
Grock's sublime symbolic exchange, based more on a system of gift-
giving than on equivalent interchanges and predicated upon unilat-
eral sacrifice, transcends the conventional process of linguistic communication the protagonist of the novel anticipated.

Along with this readjustment of his concept of communication
and his loss of faith in his literary inheritance, the protagonist of *El
año de Gracia* must alter his attitude toward writing. He must learn to
transform his interest in the text as a definite written object into an
urgent need to experience the written word as a temporal, ephemeral activity, both because modern society allows no other function
and because personal need can be fulfilled no other way. According
to established archetypes, the returning hero confirms, shares, and
perpetuates his experiences by retelling them to others; however, in
the novel the expected outcome is again displaced. Recognition is
supplanted by indifference and notoriety by silence. Daniel's original manuscript is photocopied and then destroyed for reasons of hygiene by the ecologists who rescue him, and his story itself is
suppressed by the doctors and scientists who are intent on protect-
ing the secrets of the contaminated island. Daniel, for his part, sus-
pects that his guardians question his sanity and refrains from
divulging to them any information about Grock. Repression and
self-restraint, then, cancel Daniel's dream of triumph over anonym-

ity. In his experiences there are further implications for demythifi-
cation not only of the message of established texts but of our
reverence for the physical embodiment of written messages. Western culture has preserved original texts as historical treasures or au-
thoritative evidence, but in *El año de Gracia*, the representatives of
society either disregard or destroy the written word as text, as authority, or permanence. On every level traditional attitudes towards
texts and writing are challenged in *El año de Gracia*.

The destitution that threatened Daniel on the island made him
understand the importance of his spiritual needs. Writing, he discovered, is essential to his survival: "Tenía que escribir . . . mis nece-
sidades iban más allá de comer o dormir. . . . Mi supervivencia no
estaba amenazada por el exterior, sino por mí mismo. Por eso debía
continuar desde mi cabaña el estúpido diario de viaje que, con tanto
engreimiento, había iniciado bajo la mirada sagaz de tío Jean. . . .
Iba a escribir. No podía dejar de hacerlo. La labor de consignar los
principales acontecimientos de la jornada, mis dudas, mi descon-
cierto, se erigía en la única senda para conservar la razón" [I had to
write . . . my needs went beyond eating and sleeping. . . . My survival
was not threatened from the outside but from within myself. This is
why I had to continue, inside my cabin, that stupid travel diary I had
begun with such presumptuousness under Captain John's shrewd
eye. . . . I was going to write. I couldn't keep from doing it. The
chore of noting down the main events of the day, my doubts, my
confusion emerged as the only avenue for keeping my sanity] (81–
83). What began on ship as a misguided belief in his own importance becomes, on the island, a drive for self-expression and basic
communication. Implicitly subscribing to the notion that self-dia-
logue is an incorruptible form of communication, Daniel sees his
diary as a medium for his voice and a place of reception for his
words. Writing, then, provides the juncture necessary for the communication he trusts will give him companionship, sympathy, and
hope. In the absence of a real audience, Daniel invents an accommodating, ideal reader he first addresses as "hypothetical reader"
and slowly defines with greater specificity. "Mi hipotético lector,
nacido sin rostro, habría ido adquiriendo, poco a poco, facciones y
características concretas. Tendría más o menos mi edad, veinticua-
tro, veintisiete, tal vez treinta años; sufría con mis infortunios y se
alegraba ante mis hallazgos" [My hypothetical reader, born without
a face, had gradually acquired concrete features and characteristics.
He was probably more or less my age, twenty-four, twenty-seven, per-

haps thirty years old; my misfortunes caused him grief and he re-
joiced at my discoveries] (139). His imaginary companion gave him
the moral support necessary to sustain his hopes while he waited for
his liberation from isolation. Nurtured on the validity of the written
word, the narrator does not hesitate to embrace writing as an avenue
of truth and to exalt the reader as favorably disposed to that writing.
Daniel's patterning his reader on himself affirms the existential connection suggested in the novel between narration and life and the
literary notion that a text creates its own reader. The concepts of
reader as savior and as mere invention will collide when the latter
idea establishes its reality over what ultimately emerges as a naive
belief in the transcendence of literature.

If the written work is destroyed, as occurs with Daniel's manuscript, the reader residing in it ceases to exist and the life represented in it survives only as memory. *El año de Gracia*, in this
supposition, confirms Todorov's assertion that "Narrative equals
life; absence of narrative, death."[13] On the physical and spiritual levels, storytelling keeps Daniel alive. His meaningless oral recitations
save this modern-day Scheherazade from physical abuse at the
hands of Grock, and his written scribblings defend him from the existential deletion that words, names, and stories prevent. Once he
returns to society and ceases to tell stories, he slips into a stagnant
state of estrangement from which he can escape only by withdrawing
sporadically into memory and the unarticulated word. If narration
is life and the reader is the comforting reconfirmation of that existence, the end of the story equals death in Todorov's terms. Along
with his invented, personal reader, the storyteller himself dies. Daniel is acutely aware that his probable death on the island dashes his
hopes of creating, through writing, the hypothetical reader who
would ratify his self-worth: "Había llegado la hora de emprender la
auténtica, la imprevisible aventura, de la que, desaparecido el rostro
de aquel lejano, imposible y fastidioso lector, no me iba a molestar
en dejar constancia" [The moment had arrived for me to undertake
the real, unpredictable adventure, of which I was not going to
bother to leave any evidence because the face of that distant, impossible and annoying reader had disappeared] (170). With what appears to be his imminent extinction, Daniel is about to lose his
reader, his story, and his very identity.

From Daniel's experiences, the inference emerges that life, as
meaningful existence, is story—movement, progression, and mortal-
ity and that texts endure not as fixed signifieds but only as a contin-

ual, fluid process of writing and rereading "*experienced only in an activity, a production.*"[14] Held in language, Daniel's text exists only in the moment of its generation and the stages of its reconsideration. As already seen, in *El año de Gracia* only when he writes his own story does he sample communication and a sense of self-perpetuity. It is also important to note, as one critic does, that Daniel writes the memoirs of his experiences while they are in progress and at the same time comments upon the process of that writing.[15] The overt intertextuality of the book is a self-conscious, metafictional device that draws attention not only to the literary conventions it inscribes but also to its nature as fictional object. On close examination we discover that the novel is not so much the transcription of Daniel's diary, the extemporaneous recounting of his adventures, as his re-reading of that narration or the story of his story.

Halfway through the book, he writes, "Releí: '*Aunque los mejores años de mi vida transcurrieron de espaldas al mundo...* '" [I reread: "*Although I had spent the best years of my life with my back to the world...*"] (85). The reiteration of the first lines of his narration highlights the dual process of writing and rereading that makes his text into an ongoing process of discovery and evaluation. The illusion of simultaneity is intermittently undermined by the retrospection implicit in phrases like "En aquellos sombríos días yo escribía para mí" [In those dark days I wrote for myself] (99) and "Pero ahora, cuando mi ánimo lleva camino de serenarse definitivamente . . ." [But now, when my spirit finally begins to calm down . . .] (101). This metafictional perspective creates a distance between the action and the narration which, besides contradicting the sense of immediacy of a diary, permits commentary on the naiveté and shortsightedness of its author. Self-directed scorn creates a posture of ironic distance between the narrator and his narration and casts suspicion on the truthfulness of his writings or at least underlines its inadequacy: "Por eso debía continuar desde mi cabaña el estúpido diario de viaje que, con tanto engreimiento, había iniciado bajo la mirada sagaz de tío Juan" [This is why I had to continue, inside my cabin, that stupid travel diary I had begun with such presumptuousness under Captain John's shrewd eye] (82). Writing, then, although the sustaining force of self-identity, proves suspect, vulnerable, and variable when reviewed. The process is valuable, but the product is invalid. Through the process of writing, the naive, presumptuous young man has learned that not heroism, but self-interest motivates human behavior. Any attempt to expose that motivation, Daniel discovers, is barred; his manuscript is sanitized through photocopying and the story it contains is met with restrictive admonitions or incredulous laughter. Any truth his work may contain is prohibited from spreading beyond the private, hidden personal realm where it continues to exist among his private thoughts and is reappraised as interminable reality. Unable to transform itself from Text into Work, Daniel's manuscript awaits in latent expectancy for a new reading that will "incorporate, displace and dismantle" its meaning anew.[16] Only we, its select, confidential readers, can do that, for in the modern society the novel indicts, the freedom to contradict acceptable meanings and prefabricated messages is curbed.

El año de Gracia reveals a world in which the ability of literature to sustain meaning is problematic and meaning itself becomes irrelevant. The discoveries Daniel made on the island are threatening to society and therefore, once silenced, are left unknown. Ignorance brings a bliss indistinguishable from stagnation and indifference. Irony and skepticism dominate the postmodern era. Although emphasizing language as a way to construct new realities and deeming the illusory fictional world more valid than the material realm, the postmodern novelist distrusts the images and thought patterns outlined in established literature and questions the ability of any discourse to fashion valid models or convey significant messages. The paradox of a literature that subverts its own legitimacy, of course, produces a climate of ambivalence and pessimism. In *El año de Gracia* the stale written word is displaced by the magic of the spoken word. Fernández Cubas's fiction regularly displays "a marked logocentrism," an admiration for the effective storyteller and the orally transmitted tale.[17] Her usual emphasis on the act of storytelling over the story itself is carried to its ultimate limit in her novel by the reduction of Daniel's Bible recitations to uncommunicative acoustic repetitions. In her novel as in her short stories, although the voice is admired, writing is identified with authority and power. What intensifies the opposition between oral and written discourse in *El año de Gracia* is that both are in some way restricted, displaced, and depreciated. The voice is deprived of its potential to articulate stories by the linguistic impasse obstructing verbal communication between Grock and Daniel, and writing cannot flourish because the addresser fails to find an accommodating addressee for his words. The cold community of scientists and the fanatic band of ecologists, for differing reasons, are not any better disposed to communicating with Daniel than the coarse shepherd. Since literature proves unable to capture valid meanings and society shows itself unfit to accept truth, the protagonist—as writer and human being—turns away from both in sober complacency. As writer he learns that not the literary works that nurtured his intellect, but language and narration alone can articulate meaning. Yet since his words—both oral and written—are displaced, communication on a collective level ceases.

NOTES

Reprinted with permission from *Studies in Twentieth Century Literature* 16:2 (1992): 221–32.

1. Walter Ong, *Orality and Literacy: The Technologizing of the Word* (London: Methuen, 1982), 79.

2. Julia Kristeva, "Le contexte présupposé," *La révolution du langage poétique* (Paris: Seuil, 1974), 338.

3. Cristina Fernández Cubas, *El año de Gracia* (Barcelona: Tusquets, 1985), 14. Subsequent references to this work will be cited parenthetically in the text.

4. Harold Bloom, *Poetry and Repression. Revisionism from Blake to Stevens* (New Haven: Yale University Press, 1976), 2.

5. J. A. Downie, "Defoe, Imperialism, and the Travel Books Reconsidered," *The Yearbook of English Studies* 13 (1983): 66–83.

6. Hazard Adams and Leroy Searle, eds., "Jacques Derrida," *Critical Theory Since 1965* (Tallahassee: Florida State University Press, 1986), 81.

7. Jonathan Culler, *Structuralist Poetics: Structuralism, Linguistics, and the Study of Literature* (Ithaca: Cornell University Press, 1975), 134.

8. Richard Harland, *Superstructuralism. The Philosophy of Structuralism and Post-Structuralism* (London: Methuen, 1987), 18.

9. Phyllis Zatlin, "Tales from Fernández Cubas: Adventure in the Fantastic," *Monographic Review/Revista Monográfica* 3:1–2 (1987): 114.

10. Northrop Frye, *Spiritus Mundi: Essays on Literature, Myth, and Society* (Bloomington: Indiana University Press, 1976), 124.

11. Mary Lee Bretz, "Cristina Fernández Cubas and the Recuperation of the Semiotic in *Los altillos de Brumal*," *Anales de la Literatura Española Contemporánea* 13:3 (1988): 178.

12. Elmar Holenstein, *Roman Jakobson's Approach to Language* (Bloomington: Indiana University Press, 1976), 188.

13. Tzvetan Todorov, *The Poetics of Prose* (Ithaca: Cornell University Press, 1977), 74.

14. Roland Barthes, "From Work to Text," in *Textual Strategies: Perspectives in Post-Structuralist Criticism*, ed. Josué V. Harari (Ithaca: Cornell University Press, 1979), 75.

15. Zatlin, "Tales from Fernández Cubas," 115.

16. Barthes, "From Work to Text," 75.

17. Ana Rueda, "Cristina Fernández Cubas: Una narrativa de voces extinguidas," *Monographic Review/Revista Monográfica* 4 (1988): 260.

The Seen, the Unseen, and the Obscene in Fernández Cubas's Fiction

Janet Pérez

Numerous critics have noted Fernández Cubas's repeated, systematic use of polyvalent discourse, obfuscation, and self-correction, unwriting, re-writing and similar postmodern techniques that render it difficult for readers as well as the narrative consciousness and/ or protagonist to feel any certainty concerning what has happened, exactly what they have heard, witnessed or experienced, i.e., to distinguish illusion from reality.[1] The real/unreal world she creates has been studied under the guise of ambiguity, the Gothic, or Fernández Cubas's own brand of the Fantastic a la Todorov or silencing and erasure.[2] The author's epistemological investigations and the impact of her discourse of hermeticism and erasure upon what her characters "know" and what readers understand constitute another focus of critical attention.[3] If it be true, as Brian McHale argues,[4] that the epistemological is the dominant of the modern, Fernández Cubas must be considered partly modern and partly postmodern (given postmodern devices, motifs, and techniques already identified in her work). Such a conclusion accords with the position of those theorists of the postmodern who see no clear demarcation between the two categories.

Another critical focus concerning the works of Fernández Cubas involves identity, nearly always unstable, frequently threatened; other foci include language, the world around us, characters' perceptions of the reliability of their own senses, or of those of the narrator. The author's preoccupation with the fluid boundaries of personality and identity's instability produces the merging of characters in "En el hemisferio sur" [In the Southern Hemisphere], "Los altillos de Brumal" [The Attics of Brumal], "Lúnula y Violeta" [Lunula and Violet] and *El columpio* [The Swing]). Identity, closely linked to memory (similarly unreliable and unstable), often identi-

fied with performance, conceals itself by masquerade and decep-
tion, producing a marked theatricality in Fernández Cubas's tales.
Memory returns obsessively to childhood, fixating upon moments of
transition, emblematic rites of passage, or existential crises, which
threaten to disrupt identity. Among devices consistently exploited
by this writer, the conventional topos of the voyage (seen in *El año
de Gracia* [The Year of Grace] and explored by Bellver),[5] places characters in unfamiliar territory, among unknown people with different
customs, values, and/or foreign language—circumstances threatening identity. Variants of the voyage topos appear in "Con Agatha en
Estambul" [With Agatha in Istanbul], *El columpio*, "Los altillos de
Brumal," "Lúnula y Violeta," "La ventana del jardín" [The Garden
Window], "La Flor de España" [The Flower of Spain],[6] "Mundo"
[World], and other stories, depicting strangeness and alienation,
challenging individual adaptation, coping, development, and understanding. Critics' examinations of moments of transition, passage, and existential limit situations from the perspectives of Freud,
Jung, and Lacan are pertinent given numerous abnormal psychic
states among Fernández Cubas's characters: hallucination, delusion,
amnesia, obsession, neurosis, regression, hebephrenia, paranoia,
and schizophrenia, to mention the most obvious.[7] Mechanisms of
repression or "abjection" (in Kristeva's terminology)[8] produce
oblivion, forgetfulness, or apparent ignorance of one's past or surroundings, repeatedly depicted in this writer's tales, with further
consequences for identity. Conversely, sudden discovery or intu-
itions concerning things abjected (repressed or denied, hence usually "unseen") undermines the shifting epistemological—and even
ontological—ground on which a character's unstable identity has
rested (e.g., the enigmatic depression and sudden death of the narrator's elder brother in "El ángulo del horror" [The Angle of Hor-
ror] and the sister's subsequent decline).

Repression and related mechanisms which Kristeva terms "abjection" illuminate causes of flight from reality (via alcoholism, madness, suicide, etc.) among Fernández Cubas's characters. The Abject
corresponds to that stage of development which Jung termed individuation; for Kristeva it apparently falls between subject and object
and thus applies to Eloísa in *El columpio*, fixated at an intermediate
stage between infancy and true adulthood, struggling to escape the
object status to which her male relatives confined her. Kristeva considers the Abject's role in establishing the limits of individual, corpo-
real being (with concomitant ontological implications). In the acts

of revulsion whereby the subject constitutes itself, what is first abjected is the pre-oedipal mother, prefiguring woman's marginal positioning in patriarchal society. Consignment of the feminine to the periphery, Kristeva argues, results in woman's being viewed as saintly or demonic, an aspect of abjection relevant to the enigmatic relationship between Eloísa and her male relatives, and to memory gaps and anomalous perceptions in stories of *El ángulo del horror* (1990) and *Con Agatha en Estambul* (1994).

The child learns to reject the other, that which is "not I," especially products of primal repression: feces, urine, blood, cadavers, festering wounds—objects of taboos, repulsion, and prohibitions. The Abject is repressed, unseen, hidden away (in Fernández Cubas's tales, concealed in attics, trunks, secret drawers, locked rooms, hidden compartments, behind convent walls, in a sealed family mausoleum). The Abject, spectral or invisible, becomes frightening, as in Kristeva.[9] Religious and moral sanctions attach to the prohibited, producing terror and unwillingness to gaze upon the obscene abjected or to acknowledge its existence. Kristeva's examples of things most abjected (cadavers, festering wounds, filth) typically inspire horror or revulsion. Humanity's long history of avoidance of things deemed unclean indicates that "abjection" of the impure or improper acquired early religious sanction (food taboos, moral prohibitions, legal penalties for "obscene" behavior or speech). Other significant taboos include adultery, incest, and avoidance of marriage within certain degrees of blood ties. In one of Eloísa's recollections recounted to her daughter in *El columpio* (1995), Cousin Bebo suggests seeking papal dispensation to marry Eloísa, given their close blood relationship. Decades later, Cousin Bebo uncovers the livid scar around his neck, revealing to the narrator Eloísa's violent punishment of his "taboo" attempt to kiss her.[10]

Visibility and sight possess ontological as well as epistemological implications with consequences for identity. From Plato hence, epistemology has underscored the relationship between seeing and comprehension, the seen belonging to the realm of the understood and understandable, the unseen linked to problems of comprehension. Language reinforces this connection (one does not understand that which one "does not see," e.g., "I don't see what you mean"). The narrator of *El columpio,* barely seeing in the darkened mansion and struggling to understand her enigmatic relatives, experiences repeated desires for light: "me metí en la cama, pero no quise apagar la luz" [I got into bed, but I refused to turn out the light] (47). A few days later she walks to the village to buy stronger lights, "unas bombillas de sesenta, otras de cien" [some 60-watt bulbs, and others of 100] (78). The unseen also negatively impacts the epistemological realm and Fernández Cubas portrays a world wherein what is "seen" is elusive, deceptive, fluctuating, and changeable (as witness narrative reversals, rewriting, contradictions, etc.), while the unseen and obscene (or abjected) occupy positions of obscure power.

The present study examines ambiguous, multivalent, paradoxical, mysterious, and contradictory events both visible and obscure, paranormal experiences, apparitions and enigmatic perceptions, characters and communications seen, unseen, and/or obscene in Fernández Cubas fictions, together with their implications for identity and for understanding. My thesis is simply that Kristeva's concept of the Abject significantly illuminates Fernández Cubas's works. This essay initially examines the presence and functioning of the Abject and related devices in varied tales of Fernández Cubas, then focuses on *El columpio* with passing references to other stories.

In *The Revolution in Poetic Language,* Kristeva (contrary to the stances of many feminist theorists), argues that it is "not the 'woman' in general who is refused all symbolic activity and all social representativity . . . [but] the reproductive woman."[11] This statement is superbly illustrated in *El columpio* as Eloísa's "adoring" male relatives refuse to acknowledge her growth beyond her prepubescent state at ten or eleven years (and Eloísa cannot realize her potential as a sexual woman until after escaping from the valley). Expanding upon Kristeva's statement, the body itself, everything concerning biological reproduction and the physiological (as opposed to humanity's "spiritual" or "clean and proper" side) receives similar treatment in Eloísa's ancestral home. Such topics are taboo, unmentionable, abjected—obscene in the strict, etymological sense of the term, removed from life's stage, invisible (illuminating the refusal of Eloísa's male relatives to acknowledge her physical growth and escape or "see" her as a sexual woman). Enhancing this motif is the accompanying confinement or imprisonment of offenders, nonconformists, transgressors of unspoken taboos in other stories of Fernández Cubas. The narrator's return to Brumal, real or imagined in "Los altillos," involves another journey back in time, to a place of madness, a space of attics and enclosure (motifs recurring with Tomás in "La ventana del jardín," the narrator and her sister Elba in the convent boarding school in "Mi hermana Elba" [My Sister Elba], the maturing girl locked in the convent by her relatives in "Mundo," the narrator in the psychiatric hospital in "Los altillos de Brumal" or the uncles' imprisonment of the narrator of *El columpio*).

Intensification of the platonic mind/body dichotomy, with its medieval counterpart, body/soul, renders physical functions abject or obscene, in the original connotation of offstage or out of sight and the vernacular sense of lewd, filthy, disgusting. Fernández Cubas portrays a special kind of fear, not so much of the unknown as fear resulting from sudden, new perceptions of the familiar, as in the discovery of hidden terror imbedded in the structure of one character's lifelong home ("El ángulo del horror") or another's realization that his petty, vindictive childhood act caused his grandfather's death and sentenced his mother to a life of suffering ("El legado del abuelo" [Grandfather's Legacy]). The latter instance, involving guilt and paradigmatic Freudian repression, demonstrates that Fernández Cubas explores psychic phenomena beyond those identified by Kristeva with the Abject. One observer comments that "objects generating abjection—food, feces, urine, vomit, tears, spit—inscribe the body in those surfaces, hollows, crevices, orifices, which will later become erotogenic zones" (88),[12] illuminating how the threat posed by sexuality provokes flights from reality in Fernández Cubas's works. Kristeva's comments illustrate the etiology and psychogenesis of several forms of psychosis, particularly schizophrenia (possibly the uncles' common malady in *El columpio*):

> There looms, within abjection, one of those violent, dark revolts of being, directed against a threat that seems to emanate from an exorbitant outside or inside, ejected beyond the scope of the possible, the tolerable, the thinkable. It lies there, quite close, but it cannot be assimilated. It beseeches, worries, and fascinates desire. . . . Apprehensive, desire turns aside; sickened, it rejects. A certainty protects it from the shameful. . . . But simultaneously, just the same, that impetus, that spasm, that leap is drawn toward an elsewhere as tempting as it is condemned. Unflaggingly, like an inescapable boomerang, a vortex of summons and repulsion places the one haunted by it literally beside himself.[13]

Kristeva's image of the boomerang (strikingly similar in its trajectory to that of the *diábolo* and *columpio* inseparably associated with Eloísa) shares with the diabolo the capability of being used as a weapon, and Eloísa manipulated this traditional toy of sticks and cord "como si fuera un látigo . . . una fusta, una honda, una ballesta" [as if it were a whip, a riding-crop, a slingshot, a crossbow] (72), bringing down fruit from the trees, and allegedly killing dogs. In one rhetorical anticipation or narrative foreshadowing of the climactic enactment of Eloísa's dream, "la cuerda describía una espiral cerrada, se enrollaba rápidamente en su objetivo, como un reptil al cuello de su víctima" [the cord moved in a tight spiral, rolling itself rapidly around the target, like a snake around the neck of its victim] (72). Like the boomerang or her swing's movement backward and forward, Eloísa's rebelliousness seems simultaneously to intrigue and repel, fascinating Cousin Bebo while provoking rejection by her brothers.[14]

The narrator's uncles, Lucas and Tomás, frequently perceived by the narrator as dichotomous, provoke questioning of their true identities. Nothing in El columpio suggests that the brothers are twins, but the author's repeated use of paired opposites (as in "Lúnula y Violeta") and twins (in "Helicón" [Helicon]) strengthens perceptions of their positioning as a contrasting pair, suggesting that they are mirror images, a notion supported by role reversals when dominant and subordinate positions are exchanged midway in the narrative (relevant here are studies of doubling in tales of Fernández Cubas).[15] Ludic and theatrical aspects of life in the ancestral home harmonize with puerile communal activities culminating in the weekly celebration of "el gran rito" [the great ritual], the male relatives' ritualized "homage" to the supposedly idealized, perpetual girl Eloísa—a role-play wherein all regress to childhood, taking turns at unflattering representations of Eloísa.

Abjection's significant epistemological consequences define what may be seen (legitimately observed and acknowledged), as well as what must remain unseen (silenced and hidden, i.e., that which is abjected and hence obscene), provoking otherwise inexplicable behavior, such as the extreme phobia inspired by twinning in "Helicón." Consequences of the abjected or obscene, while often ontological, also impact the epistemological, resulting in deformations or metamorphoses of perception, as well as the denial and resulting "invisibility" of events or characters previously "seen" by the narrative consciousness and readers. In El columpio, clear perceptions turn murky, fading and disappearing; contrarily, figures materialize out of fog or darkness (a metaphorical "swinging" of perception which expands the symbolic significance of the literal object [columpio/swing]).[16] Obviously symbolic as well are the garden in the Edenic valley and Eloísa's "expulsion from Paradise" via abjection after her "fall." The narrator's literal fall from the swing precipitates her initial encounter with "Eloísa," and first reveals house and garden as an area of intersecting time planes—a space where the past imposes itself upon the present, negating change (as did the Franco regime in postwar Spain).

Encounters with that which has been abjected, previously unseen (as obscene) are problematic: sudden discovery of previous error typically generates fear in Fernández Cubas's tales, as narrators realize the folly of earlier perceptions. "Ausencia" [Absence] portrays a character's panic resulting from sudden amnesia. Occasional epiphanies tend less to resolve than to create dilemmas. Incidents discussed earlier by the family in *El columpio* are denied or distorted; a seemingly transparent world turns opaque, bright sky suddenly threatening, and the narrator's impromptu family reunion becomes a nightmare from which she may not escape alive. In a visual permutation of the *mise en abîme* or "mirroring,"[17] portraits of faces are no longer clearly identifiable; mirrors are darkened or clouded almost beyond reproducing images, "reflecting" a "picture" of people whose character is disputed, whose changing or changed reality is abjected. From seemingly matter-of-fact beginnings with no apparent gap between appearance and reality, the narrator advances into a psychological snake pit where family history belongs to the realm of the obscene and little of what is seen is what it seems.

The narrative point of view, frequently situated in *El columpio* within enveloping darkness, rain, fog, or other conditions that interfere with clear, unobstructed vision, participates in a dialectic of the seen and unseen, as "la francesita" moves from shadows into blinding light or vice versa.[18] What is "seen" appears partially obscured or distorted by improper lighting, e.g., the narrator's first "sight" of her three elderly male relatives who appear in the shadows with their backs to the setting sun which she must face. The situation is repeated with slight variation when she meets them for dinner: "La casa estaba en penumbra, pero distinguí una puerta, coronada por un rosetón, y escuché un rumor apagado. . . . Al principio me costó distinguir sus rostros. Se hallaban en pie, de espaldas al ventanal" [The house was in semi-darkness, but I distinguished a door crowned by a carved garland, and heard a hushed sound. . . . At first it was difficult to make out their faces. They were standing, with their backs to a large window] (28–29). Similarly, the narrator imperfectly "sees" aging photographs and fading letters as in "Mi hermana Elba" or photos in *Hermanas de sangre* [Blood Sisters] (1998) and *Cosas que ya no existen* [Things That No Longer Exist]) (2001). Such objects frequently introduce flashbacks, wherein readers "see" things which may no longer exist, either fictionally or factually. Complicating visual perception in *El columpio* is the dimness of lights, apparently a fetish of the uncles whose low-power bulbs create more shadows than zones of illumination. That the gloom results from conscious choice becomes clear when they reject the brighter bulbs purchased by the narrator. Insufficient light (with attendant epistemological complications) constitutes a recurring motif: "Sobre la consola pendía un cuadro que en la penumbra había pasado por alto. Tampoco la débil luz de las arañas ayudaba ahora gran cosa" [Above the console hung a painting which in the deep shadows I had overlooked. Nor was the weak light from the chandeliers much help] (30). While "la luz mortecina del comedor" [the dying light in the dining room] (36) created twilight and shadows, lighting in the kitchen is worse: "La bombilla que pendía del techo arrojaba una luz más tenue aún que la de las arañas del comedor" [The light bulb hanging from the ceiling cast a light still more tenuous than the dining-room chandeliers] (64–65), concealing more than revealing "la francesita," "amparada en la débil luz de la bombilla" [sheltered by the weak light from the bulb] (73).

Auditory data similarly seem unclear, given the distance of voices and sound distortion: "la bóveda del techo hacía que nuestras voces sonaran algo metálicas, como acompañadas de un pequeño eco" [the dome of the roof made our voices sound somewhat metallic, as though accompanied by a faint echo] (29). Inability to identify voices or distinguish words marks several key scenes, as when the narrator first believes she has heard Eloísa's voice, or is confused by the uncles' changing voices and switching roles while she spies upon the "great ritual" from outside the window. Like muffled sounds, things in gloom or shadows, half-seen or unseen, cannot intrude upon the brothers' collective fantasy: avoidance of the "harsh light of reality" allows the uncles to prolong or perpetuate their fixation with eternal childhood or adolescence. Difficulties of seeing and hearing are compounded by the uncles' surreptitious drugging of their unwelcome guest as well as by time's passing, making it nearly impossible to reconstruct the past given the decades elapsed since certain key events (a motif also in *Hermanas de sangre*, "Mi hermana Elba," and "Con Agatha en Estambul," among others). Fixation upon the past in *El columpio* does not illuminate it: the uncles have ritualized, sanctified, and petrified their official version of Eloísa and their idealized collective childhood.

While the visible is often but imperfectly seen, the unseen figures less frequently, albeit in significant ways: often things are "unseeable" given bad lighting or physical deterioration; reality and truth are metaphorically "unseen" on numerous occasions. The motif of seeing without being seen recurs in *El columpio,* as the narrator, concealed in her mother's room, watches the "performance" of Uncle Lucas; later, she feels herself observed by Uncle Tomás, peering through the keyhole after locking her in her room. In a climactic scene, the narrator—invisible in the dark garden—watches her elderly relatives' performance of the "great ritual." This motif (watching from concealment) reappears in *Hermanas de sangre,* with a variant in "Mi hermana Elba," as the narrator's friend Fátima and her little sister Elba possess the capacity to become invisible, likewise seeing while unseen. Eloísa's spectral apparitions or materializations from invisibility provide yet another example. The unseen and obscene may both be unperceived; the distinction between them is that being unseen can be a transient condition, often the result of improper lighting or concealment.

El columpio incorporates numerous traits identified by critics in the writer's earlier works, especially Gothic and Fantastic aspects, and the rhetoric of uncertainty, ambiguity, doubt, and indecipherability. Fernández Cubas's discourse of obfuscation profoundly affects the epistemological in *El columpio,* whose anonymous narrator, a twenty-five-year-old French woman, decides seven years after her mother's untimely death to fulfill a deathbed promise to visit the maternal childhood home in a remote valley somewhere in the north of Spain—a journey that her mother Eloísa often visualized but repeatedly postponed. "La francesita" travels from cosmopolitan, late-twentieth-century Paris to a tiny, quasi-medieval hamlet: "cuatro casuchas viejas en las que apenas quedaba un par de almas" [four old huts in which scarcely a couple of souls remained] (18), from the known to the unknown (unfamiliar geography, language, culture, and characters), and also moves back in time to an era before her own birth, perhaps a moment beyond time, as implicit in references to the "vetusta Casa de la Torre" [ancient House of the Tower], "fuera del tiempo" [outside of time] (14).

"La francesita" arrives at a wayside bus stop, where no one is awaiting her, and finds it impossible to call: "Los de la Torre nunca han tenido teléfono" [The Tower folks have never had a phone] (18). This constitutes the narrator's first objective indication of her reclusive male relatives' refusal to move beyond the world of their childhood. Next, she is asked to deliver a letter to her uncles and recognizes her own writing on the envelope announcing her arrival. Undelivered messages and unread letters form part of a series of emblems of failed communication which—seen in retrospect—clearly presage the lack of meaningful exchanges between "la francesita" and her uncles, intensifying the isolation(ism) implicit in the remote valley and familial enclosure in the symbolic tower: "un torreón" [a gigantic tower] (20) with obvious phallic connotations, an island within a virtual island, surrounded not by water but by mountains. Significant interior spaces include "el desván, el cuarto de los juegos, el arcón de los tesoros" [the attic, the game room, the treasure chest] (20–21). All but the attic remain locked, like Eloísa's room—all linked to Eloísa's oft-told tales of childhood theatrical improvisations, ritualized performances constituting the uncles' favorite and most symbolic pastime.

Theater and games are conventional metaphors for life, and in addition to "el gran rito" around which the uncles' lives revolve, *El columpio* contains numerous role-playing scenes. Time reveals that the uncles' adoption of the role-playing mode intends to discourage their unwelcome visitor. Isolated locale, the ancient mansion and incommunicado status of the manifestly hostile, reclusive residents—commonplaces of Gothic fiction, as is the endangered female narrator engaged in a quest for explanations—initially receive matter-of-fact treatment, but slowly create a foreboding that advances, recedes, and advances in a swinging motion throughout the narrative. The swing of the title, a real and palpable artifact in the garden of the ancestral home, figures prominently in a key youthful portrait of Eloísa and an extraordinary dream in which the child Eloísa saw herself in the darkened garden with a woman that she recognized as her adult daughter—a prophetic dream, as this sequence is reenacted in the novel's climactic scene. Symbolically, the swing alludes to the narrator's pendular oscillations between logic and disorientation or absurdity, trust and suspicion, confidence and fear, as well as the uncles' "swinging" between illusion and reality, credibility and madness. A powerful visual metaphor of shifting epistemological grounds, the swing encapsulates the novelistic dynamics while simultaneously evoking the old-fashioned locale and ambience of childhood.

As with this author's earlier uses of the voyage topos, the journey imposes beginning and ending parameters and the return trip provides a vaguely circular structure, as happens in *El columpio*: the lim-

ited and repetitive trajectory is subtly underscored by the initial
recounting of the prophetic dream and its real-life enactment just
before the narrator leaves the ancestral home. *El columpio* com-
mences in the manner of fairy tales, retelling a supernatural or magical event long ago and far away: "Un día, mucho antes de que yo
naciera, mi madre soñó conmigo. Ella era una niña aún, tendría
unos diez, quizás once años" [One day, very long ago, before I was
born, my mother dreamed about me. She was still a child, perhaps
ten, maybe eleven years old] (9). And like a fairy tale, *El columpio*
may be read as a transparent allegory (discussed later). The mention
of eleven years is not insignificant, this being the point in time when
the prepubescent Eloísa is forever arrested in the male relatives'
minds, photographs, portraits, and rituals (notwithstanding her
continued maturation before eventually escaping across the Pyrenees to France). Fernández Cubas associates eleven with epiphany:
eleven-year-olds figure in "Mi hermana Elba" at a point of transition
to adolescence, and eleven is the age of the girls in *Hermanas de sangre* at the time of the criminally negligent homicide which marks
their lives—another existential crisis or moment of transition.[19]
Other elements associated with the novel's circular structure appear
at beginning and end: the ramshackle bus stop, the FONDA signs,
the curious blind woman, descriptions of Uncle Tomás, and conjectures about his mental capacity.

Fernández Cubas develops several repetitive themes and variations in this short novel, mostly polarities related to underlying epistemological preoccupations; doubt/belief, seen/unseen, absurdity/
logic, perplexity/certainty, known/unknown, appearance/reality,
darkness/light, visible/invisible. The negative "dark side" of these
polarities prevails as the narrator journeys from belief to doubt and
confusion, experiencing her epiphany (without reaching full comprehension) during the final hours of her stay in the valley. From
the outset, seemingly insignificant episodes set the tone for future
encounters. Her first glimpse of the old bachelors combines the
seen and unseen, with more of the latter: "distinguí tres siluetas en
un orden que se me antojó de recepción" [I made out three silhou-
ettes in an order which struck me as a receiving line] (24). This perception is filtered through obscured vision, paradoxically brought
on by the blinding sun, and (on the epistemological level) "antojo"
[caprice], foreshadowing future misinterpretations. *El columpio* advances the author's inquiry into the nature of knowledge—what we
"know" and how we know it—exploring this timeless conundrum

via her characters' quandaries, doubts, discoveries, and redirection
of their quests. The quest in *El columpio* does not lack perils, but neither does the narrator achieve certainty or final proof. Epistemologi-
cally meaningful imagery of blinding light and darkness (*oscuridad,
tinieblas, penumbra*) [blackness, gloom, shadows] demonstrates that
excess light and poor illumination obstruct seeing equally: the object of focus and the truth remain unseen.

Theatrical motifs abound, first in Eloísa's memories of childhood
games, with everyone acting out different roles, wearing disguises,
and planning a future on the stage: "Iban a ser actores, los mejores
actores del mundo" [they were going to be actors, the world's best]
(21). Theatricality, with its deliberate blurring of boundaries between illusion and reality, compounds the epistemological quandary
posed by difficulties of identifying the visible but scarcely seen. As
part of the novel's metaliterary and self-reflexive quality, characters
are repeatedly termed "personajes" [literary characters], and the
narrator critiques her own performance on more than one occasion. Within this context, the uncles' characterization acquires
added interest. Individual descriptions of these reclusive old bachelors offer few clues to their puzzling reality. Several affirmations of
Cousin Bebo's timidity are enhanced by his metal-rimmed glasses
and reticence: "Era la primera vez que Bebo hablaba, que Bebo *se
atrevía* a hablar" [It was the first time that Bebo spoke, that he *dared*
to speak] (31; italics in text); he is "tan delgado que más parecía un
espíritu" [so thin that he seemed more like a spirit] (25). But Bebo
alone appears genuine in welcoming the narrator and is clearly the
most spontaneous, affable, and communicative; an artist and musi-
cian who lacks confidence in his own ability but also an inventor re-
sponsible for mechanical operations of the estate, he is constructing
cisterns. The narrator's mother recalled Bebo as the author of
scripts that the siblings performed, thus defining to some extent
their roles, notwithstanding his apparent subordination. Uncle
Lucas is perceived as deceptive and the narrator's descriptions of
him repeatedly insinuate the farcical.[20] "La francesita" observes that
Lucas plays many roles: "cómico de la legua" [traveling actor] (65),
gourmet chef, connoisseur, "dueño del valle" [lord of the valley]
(40). Lucas's "performances" witnessed by the narrator result from
his paranoia—perhaps springing from his notion that all the world's
a stage and no actor can be trusted to be what he or she seems.
Lucas fears that rivals will steal ideas from his "mental library" or
exploit the recipes in his unwritten cookbook. Later the narrator

perceives a darker side to Lucas, noting his ill humor, annoyance, and tasteless "joke" concerning Eloísa's "execution" of a stray dog (73). Uncle Tomás initially appears guileless; while Lucas calls him "our supply officer," he slowly emerges as true head of the family. All three strike the narrator as odd, but only Tomás is deemed innocuous, due to her mother's habitual descriptions: "Tomás, pobre, siempre fue algo simple. Un niño grande" [Poor Tomás was always a bit simple-minded. An overgrown child] (23). Eloísa also noted, "Le gusta bromear, confundir. Los que no le conocen le pueden tomar por tonto" [He likes to tease and confuse. Those who don't know him might think him stupid] (23). Lucas calls Tomás "bruto" and "imbécil" [dummy, imbecile] (44) when the latter shoves the swing so abruptly that the narrator falls to the ground, losing consciousness. Nevertheless, she sympathizes with Tomás, seeing him as a simple-minded, hulking giant unable to control his own strength. Readers realize eventually that Tomás drugs the narrator from the beginning, finally preparing a dangerous overdose. After exchanging roles with Lucas midway through the novel, Tomás emerges as not only the manager, but also the most astute. Although Bebo appears distressed by Tomás's decision to ship "la francesita" back to Paris, all three seem in accord that she must not be allowed to interfere with their celebration of "el gran rito" at its appointed hour.

The uncles' description of Eloísa paints a hitherto unseen picture of the narrator's mother: "la princesita" [little princess], adored, spoiled, tyrannical, too childish or infantile for her years, willful and rebellious, defying attempts to control her, "entre angelical y enfurruñada" [midway between angelical and sulking] (30) in Bebo's portrait. "La francesita" initially perceives the voice she takes to be Eloísa's as the shriek of a spoiled, willful, tyrannical child, instinctively rejecting this unpleasant girl so different from the mother she remembers. The narrator's recollections of her mother's repetitive conversations contain nothing to illuminate Eloísa's childhood character, leaving readers to wonder whether Eloísa's memories of her male relatives are more realistic or reliable than theirs of her. Eloísa the woman is a shadow, even more so than the child; all traces of her womanhood have been abjected, erased, and the uncles simply refuse to acknowledge data that contradict their carefully constructed portrait of the child Eloísa. No details enlighten readers concerning the narrator's mother and father, not even the latter's name. Not only do the uncles suppress all information that would require amending their portrait of Eloísa, but also they address the anonymous "francesita" only as "querida niña" [dear child], treating her in a fashion more befitting the eleven-year-old girl in the painting. The trio, led by Tomás, strives to abject her, either by driving her away, or drugging her and confining her to her room, thereby sparing them the need to acknowledge this obscene reminder of Eloísa's role as a sexual and reproductive woman. But "la francesita" refuses to be locked away like Eloísa's letters or her own abjected missive with its obscene news of Eloísa's death.

The image of Eloísa painted by Bebo has totally displaced the "real" model. She is seated in her swing, somewhat annoyed, in the same pose shown in most family photos, with the diabolo and cords seen in the final real-life "staging" of her dream wherein the cord in her hands will nearly strangle the narrator. Significant details of the painting are vanishing—all but unseen: "Es un diábolo—dijo de pronto Bebo señalando la parte más oscura del lienzo—. Está desapareciendo por momentos" [It's a diabolo, Bebo said suddenly, pointing to the darkest area of the canvas. It's disappearing by the minute] (31). The uncles' resultant sense of urgency to restore the painting emblematizes their desire to cling to the idealized, capricious child. They have totally abjected the adult Eloísa who fled as often threatened in childish ire, crossing the mountains to marry a Frenchman and never return. Eloísa the woman and mother is both unseen and obscene, while the highly visible cult of the adored Princess in the Tower dominates life in the Casa de la Torre, perpetuating memories bearing a dubious relationship to the "real" Eloísa. Numerous details suggest that the trio has fabricated an image corresponding to their desire—intuited in the narrator's first impression of the painting, "como si más que un cuadro aquello fuera una instantánea tomada sin su consentimiento, o *como si el autor la hubiera querido precisamente así. Con un mohín de disgusto, de desafío" [as if more than a painting it were a snapshot taken without her permission, or *as if the author had wanted her precisely thus*. With a grimace of disgust and defiance] (31, emphasis mine). The cult of Eloísa—adored, deformed, and petrified—revolves around a reflection of masculine desire unrelated to the woman Eloísa, the mother recalled by the narrator.

The narrator, alone in accepting her mother as an adult, reproductive woman, senses something abnormal in absolute confinement of the remembered Eloísa to the orbit of an eleven-year-old: "era como si mi madre no hubiera muerto, y nunca, a los ojos de los tíos, podría llegar a cumplir cincuenta años" [it was as though

my mother had not died, and could never—in the uncles' eyes—
ever be fifty years old] (50). Repressed sexuality frequently underlies
anomalies of the Gothic, and among numerous Gothic traits in *El
columpio* is the uncles' abjection not only of Eloísa's sexuality, but
also their own. The narrator's analogy (that it was as if her mother
had not died, but could never age) suggests a sort of vampiric, un-
dead state or diabolic possession, implying an inability of Eloísa's
soul to rest so long as the uncles continue to imprison her in the
enchanted portrait. Indeed, diabolic elements attach specifically to
the diabolo: "El diábolo era el amo de Eloísa y ella su adoradora"
[The diabolo was the master of Eloísa and she its worshipper] (71).
So absolute is the uncles' abjection of the sexual woman that they
ignore the narrator's reiterated questions concerning their own
mother (70), thereby "burying" her grandmother in even greater
silence.

Following her first encounter with "Eloísa," the narrator intuits
hostility in the distortions of her mother's voice and the words attributed to her, initially blaming her own imagination (not having
yet discovered the uncles' impersonation): "La voz que me había
parecido escuchar en el columpio seguía resonando en mis oídos
. . . ¿qué oculto resentimiento debía albergar contra mi madre para
hacerle hablar de esa forma, en aquel tono terrible, aunque sólo
fuera con el pensamiento?" [the voice I thought I'd heard on the
swing kept ringing in my ears . . . what hidden resentment must I
harbor against my mother to make her speak in that manner, that
awful tone, even if only in my thoughts?] (47). That hidden resentment—not the narrator's, but the uncles'—surfaces weekly in the
"gran rito" as the uncles avenge Eloísa's abandonment, distorting
her voice, her personality, her will, while they mock her, symbolically
imprisoned in the portrait. It is in the grotesque scene of the "great
ritual" watched by the invisible narrator that the heretofore unseen
truth of the male relatives' real feelings for the abjected, obscene
Eloísa first appears undisguised.

Even earlier, "la francesita" had perceived the uncles' treatment
of her mother as cruel: "¿por qué no contestaban? ¿cómo podían
ser tan crueles?" [why didn't they answer? How could they be so
cruel?] (56). Initial sympathy for the male relatives vanishes in a
flood of tender feelings for her mother: "compadecí a mi madre,
mi pobre madre, inocente como una niña. . . . La indiferencia. El
desprecio. . . . Como si no existieran [sus cartas]. . . . Como si Eloísa,
en fin, al dejar el valle, hubiera arrastrado una condena para el resto

de sus días" [I felt sorry for my mother, my poor mother, innocent as a child. . . . The indifference. The scorn. . . . As if her letters never existed. As if Eloísa, by leaving the valley, were condemned for the rest of her days] (55). Here the narrator's intuitive understanding of the uncles' resentment is fully valid despite her failure to grasp the mechanism of abjection—as is her intuition of their silence as punishment. The male relatives care only for continuing to play their games, perpetuating their control via patriarchal domination. Eloísa's departure disrupted "el gran rito," leaving them no one to control, and rendering her rebellion and abandonment forever unforgivable.

In the initial pages (14–15), the narrator muses that perhaps the reason her mother had never returned to visit, notwithstanding her evident desire to do so, was that she needed her daughter—a strong, autonomous daughter—to accompany and protect her:

> Unicamente tiempo después comprendería que aquellos deseos de protección que tanto me habían irritado eran sólo una verdad a medias, y que mi madre necesitaba de todo mi apoyo para atreverse a desandar el camino y regresar al valle. . . .
> Mamá no podía regresar con las manos vacías, y yo, "la francesita," me había convertido, desde hacía mucho, en la única justificación válida de su existencia, de su deserción.

> [Only later would I understand that those desires of protection that so irritated me were only a half-truth, and that my mother needed all of my support in order to dare to retrace her path and return to the valley. . . .
> Mama could not return empty-handed, and I, "the French girl," had long since become the only valid justification of her existence. Of her desertion.] (15–16)

While the narrator seems not to grasp the full import of the intuited relationship between herself and her mother and the male relatives, the foregoing perception holds the key to complex feelings of the siblings and also to the novelistic subtext, as will now be seen.

Almost as if created by force of desire, a kind of time warp exists in the Casa de la Torre, so that during her *déjà vu* sequence in the attic, the narrator seemingly exists both in the narrative present and two days earlier (57). "La francesita" realizes that she cannot be both observer and observed: she does not belong to the atemporal or supratemporal world of her uncles. They have stopped the clock and turned back the hands to a time when the spoiled and capricious Eloísa was both their princess and their prisoner—the Princess in the Tower—but the narrator can distinguish past from present and identifies the latter with reality. In a flash of intuition, she connects her *desdoblamiento* [*déjà vu* experience] to her mother's dream: "¿No sería eso lo que mi madre había entrevisto en sueños? La imagen de una hija, abatida, triste, perdida en la penumbra de un desván?" [Might that not be what my mother had half seen in her dream? The image of a daughter, exhausted, sad, lost in the dimness of an attic?] (58).

Examining text and context, seen and unseen together suggest the presence of a subtext, unseen, rooted in the intersection of class, gender, culture, politics, and the "generation gap" or time elapsed between Eloísa's generation and her daughter's. The text juxtaposes past and present, "la francesita" and her mother, implicitly contrasting Spanish women's situation "then and now," which is precisely the allegorical reading mentioned earlier. Stopping the clock, another repetitive motif for Fernández Cubas, appears in "El reloj de Bagdad" [The Clock from Baghdad] and "Los altillos," as well as *El columpio*, and the Franco regime—under which Eloísa would have grown up—also turned back the hands of time. The twenty-five-year-old narrator notes that her mother would now be slightly over fifty (thus Eloísa would have left the valley in the 1960s, some twenty-five to thirty years before the novelistic present, set in the 1990s, as visible in growing Europeanization, even in the remote valley). "La francesita," an educated, autonomous woman with her own career, sufficiently "liberated" to travel alone internationally, takes matters into her own hands (however rashly) when she feels her freedom is being curtailed. She appears as an adult, even in Eloísa's dream, in contrast to her mother's confinement to enforced childhood in perpetuity, from the 1940s to the 1960s (until leaving Spain). Readers unfamiliar with the early Franco era can better understand the subtext by placing that time in context: postwar reforms by the dictatorship included legislation making women minors for life—legally permanent wards of their male relatives or husbands, they required male relatives' permission to have a bank account, their own apartment, or travel with their children. Abolishing freedoms granted during the Republic, statutes prohibited employment for married women and discouraged education for females. The uncles' adoration of the virgin child recalls the Madonna/whore dichotomy, the mythologizing of virginity under Franco, and the *encierro* [encloisterment] of girls and women.[21] Females' object status is aptly reflected by Eloísa's portrait and confinement to patriarchally inscribed boundaries (the symbolic swing, with its inherently restricted movement), enclosed and surrounded by prohibitions (the portrait frame). By no accident, swings typically appear in bird cages, and Eloísa is truly a "bird in a gilded cage." Her dream powerfully communicates the message of the subtext, underscoring contrasts between the generations of mother and daughter. Significantly—long before her daughter's birth—Eloísa dreamed of her as an adult, not a perpetual child, more object or doll than person, but an autonomous subject. The misogyny latent in the uncles' confinement of the real-life Eloísa and their obsessive, ritualized deformation of the image and memory of the supposedly adored but disobedient child surfaces in their hostile silences, their mistreatment of her daughter, their unwillingness to grant Eloísa any right to a life of her own. The game motifs and emphasis on childishness foreground the puerile selfishness that limited their sister's role to participant in their games, allowing her only to play the part dictated by their desire.

The perceived subtext illuminates the novel's most enigmatic scene wherein "la francesita" encounters the shade of Eloísa in the darkened, rain-soaked garden and feels the diabolo's lethal cords twine around her neck, choking her, much as their enforced "minoría de edad" [legal status as perpetual minors] strangled Spanish women's maturation. What saves the narrator, rousing Eloísa from a trancelike state, is the daughter's shout, "¡Mamá!" reminding the phantom of her life as a free individual, a sexual and reproductive woman in another time, another place which allows her to bridge the generation gap, throwing off the masculine domination that kept her a child, and saving her daughter. The subtext thus teased out—the autonomy of the daughter's generation contrasted with the lack of freedom of the mother's—is literally unseen within the novel. Not only does Kristeva's theoretical framework explain multiple hermetic aspects of *El columpio*, but it also permits identifying symbiotic and allegorical levels of meaning, delineating a subtext coherent with the text and context of the novel's past and present. Within this frame of reference, the concept of abjection contributes to explaining the male characters' enigmatic behavior, while the categories of seen, unseen, and obscene illuminate the epistemological shadows projected by Fernández Cubas with her rhetoric of obscurity.

NOTES

1. Significant elucidation of Fernández Cubas's postmodernism (among other themes) is provided by John B. Margenot III, "Parody and Self-Consciousness in Cristina Fernández Cubas's *El año de Gracia*," *Siglo XX/Twentieth Century* 11 (1993): 71–87; Kay Pritchett, "Cristina Fernández Cubas's 'Con Agatha en Estambul': Traveling into Mist and Mystery," *Monographic Review/Revista Monográfica* 12 (1996): 247–57; and Robert C. Spires, "Postmodernism/Paralogism: *El ángulo del horror* by Cristina Fernández Cubas," *Journal of Interdisciplinary Literary Studies* 7:2 (1995): 233–45. Her creation of uncertainty and narratorial obfuscation are treated by Kathleen M. Glenn, "Gothic Indecipherability and Doubling in the Fiction of Cristina Fernández Cubas," *Monographic Review/Revista Monográfica* 8 (1992): 125–41; Janet Pérez, "Cristina Fernández Cubas: Narrative Unreliability and the Flight from Clarity, or, the Quest for Knowledge in the Fog," *Hispanófila* 122 (January 1998): 29–39; Luis Suñén, "La realidad y sus sombras: Las obras de Rosa Montero y Cristina Fernández Cubas," *Insula* 446 (June 1984): 5; and Fernando Valls, "De las certezas del amigo a las dudas del héroe. Sobre 'La ventana del jardín' de Cristina Fernández Cubas," *Insula* 568 (April 1994): 18–19.

2. Critics who focus on this writer's blend of reality and fantasy include Kathleen M. Glenn, "Fantastic Doubles in Cristina Fernández Cubas's Tales for Children, *Visions of the Fantastic: Selected Essays from the Fifteenth International Conference on the Fantastic in the Arts*, ed. Allienne R. Becker (Westport, Conn.: Greenwood Press, 1996), 57–62; José Ortega, "La dimensión fantástica en los cuentos de Fernández Cubas," *Monographic Review/Revista Monográfica* 8 (1992): 157–63; Lynn K. Talbot, "Journey into the Fantastic: Cristina Fernández Cubas's 'Los altillos de Brumal,'" *Letras Femeninas* 15 (1989): 37–47; Phyllis Zatlin, "Tales from Fernández Cubas: Adventure in the Fantastic," *Monographic Review/Revista Monográfica* 3:1–2 (1987): 107–18; Ofelia Ferrán, "'Afuera he dejado el mundo.' Strategies of Silence and Silencing in 'Mundo,' by Cristina Fernández Cubas," *Monographic Review/Revista Monográfica* 16 (2000): 174–89; and Ana Rueda, "Cristina Fernández Cubas: Una narrativa de voces extinguidas," *Monographic Review/Revista Monográfica* 4 (1988): 257–67.

3. Critics studying authorial manipulation of the reader's knowledge base include Julie Gleue, "The Epistemological and Ontological Implications in Cristina Fernández Cubas's *El año de Gracia*," *Monographic Review/Revista Monográfica* 8 (1992): 142–56; Janet Pérez, "Narrative Unreliability," 29–39; Kay Pritchett, "Traveling into Mist and Mystery," 247–57; and Fernando Valls, "De las certezas del amigo a las dudas del héroe," 18–19.

4. See Brian McHale, *Postmodernist Fiction* (New York: Methuen, 1987), 3–10.

5. This critic has two relevant studies. See Catherine G. Bellver, "*El año de Gracia* and the Displacement of the Word," *Studies in Twentieth Century Literature* 16:2 (1992): 221–32, and Catherine G. Bellver, "*El año de Gracia*. El viaje como rito de iniciación," *Explicación de Textos Literarios* 22:1 (1993–94): 3–10.

6. The title, "La Flor de España" [The Flower of Spain], points to a pun or double entendre in addition to the literal meaning, i.e., "The Best of Spain," although neither the expatriates who patronize the establishment nor the shop's merchandise represent anything near the best Spain has to offer. A second play on words involves the owner's name, Rosita: Rosie is also the "Flower of Spain."

7. Psychological aspects are examined by Janet Pérez, "Fernández Cubas, Abjection, and the 'retórica del horror,'" *Explicación de Textos Literarios* 24 (1995–96): 159–71; Jessica A. Folkart, *Angles on Otherness in Post-Franco Spain: The Fiction of Cristina Fernández Cubas* (Lewisburg, Pa.: Bucknell University Press, 2002); and Phyllis Zatlin, "Amnesia, Strangulation, Hallucination and Other Mishaps: The Perils of Being Female in Tales of Cristina Fernández Cubas," *Hispania* 79:1 (March 1996): 36–44.

8. See Julia Kristeva, *Powers of Horror. An Essay on Abjection,* trans. Leon S. Roudiez (New York: Columbia University Press, 1982).

9. Ibid., 3.

10. Cristina Fernández Cubas, *El columpio* (Barcelona: Tusquets, 1995), 75–76. Future citations from this novel will be referenced parenthetically in the text.

11. See Julia Kristeva, *The Revolution in Poetic Language,* trans. Margaret Waller (New York: Columbia University Press, 1984), 453.

12. See Elizabeth Gross, "The Body of Signification," in *Abjection, Melancholia and Love,* ed. John Fletcher and Andrew Benjamin (London: Routledge, 1990), 88.

13. Kristeva, *Powers of Horror,* 1.

14. The male relatives' reactions to Eloísa illustrate beautifully Kristeva's description of the mechanism of abjection in the long quotation above in this same paragraph, "a threat that seems to emanate from an exorbitant outside or inside . . . as tempting as it is condemned."

15. The presence of the double has been studied especially by Kathleen M. Glenn, "Fantastic Doubles," 57–62.

16. The image of the whirlpool shares with the boomerang, diabolo, and swing its repetitive motion within the same space, and is associated with "la francesita's" frustrated attempts to understand life in her uncles' dark mansion; epistemological defeats are also represented by imagery of labyrinths and mirrors.

17. Fernández Cubas's narrator-protagonists experience epiphanic moments in which a paradigmatic, symbolic event or scene is witnessed at a distance or in miniature and perceived as replication—a *mise en abîme.* This concept is defined by Lucien Dallenbach, *Le reçit spéculaire* (Paris: Seuil, 1977), subtitled *Essai sur la mise en abîme.* A study of metamorphoses of the form in the *nouveau roman,* the essay examines interior duplication (called "mirroring" by some critics), i.e., the replication of a motif on a smaller scale. The technique assumes several forms in fictions of Fernández Cubas, e.g., in *El columpio* as the anonymous narrator gazes down from the tower attic to "see" her own arrival two days earlier, or her realization (after spying on her uncles) that she is now the spectacle for Uncle Tomás, peering through the keyhole. Similarly, the narrator of "Con Agatha en Estambul" gazes out the plane window at the spectacle of the distant city, imagining the "drama" occurring there. These characters perceive the "picture" as "framed" by windows or less conventional frames (e. g., the epiphanic moment in "La ventana del jardín").

18. The male relatives' refusal to use the narrator's name reflects their wish to "abject" all evidence of Eloísa's maturation and escape from their control; hence, they refer to their niece by an epithet of nationality emphasizing her foreignness, *la francesita* [the French girl].

19. Notwithstanding the perils of [auto]biographical interpretations, it is relevant that Fernández Cubas also cites eleven as her age when she lost her sister (*Cosas que ya no existen*).

20. See descriptions on 24–25, 32, 40–41, and 50–51, where Lucas appears to be rehearsing.

21. For discussion and documentation of the restrictive, repressive conditions for girls and women in Spain during these years, see Carmen Martín Gaite, *Usos amorosos de la postguerra española* (Barcelona: Anagrama, 1987). Martín Gaite graphically illustrates difficulties of growing up feminine under the reactionary fascist regime and the "guidance" of the Sección Femenina of Falange [women's division of the Falangist party]. *Usos amorosos de la postguerra española* is indispensable for understanding the mentality of the narrator's male relatives in *El columpio* because—crazy or not—their treatment of females in their care (under their control) coincides perfectly with treatment of women and girls under the Franco regime.

Looking for Mom in All the Wrong Places: The Mother-Daughter Bond and the Evolution of Identity in *El columpio*

Silvia Bermúdez

FRAMED AS A TRAVEL NARRATIVE WHICH EXPLORES ORIGINS AND THE MA-ternal, the nameless female narrator of *El columpio* [The Swing] embarks on a quest to unravel her mother's family history in order to find the meaning of the uncanny story her mother repeated obsessively when she was still alive: they had met before the daughter was even born. The mother's tale of this supposedly prenatal encounter arises from a dream weighing heavily on our narrator, and the narrator's attempts to assimilate the psychological entrapments of maternal power and the struggle to reclaim a sense of self outside the intersubjective circuit with the mother are the elements that move the story forward. This movement forward requires the narrator-protagonist to go back to the past, to her mother's womb as it were, to solve the dream's riddle. This will not be an easy task, and the difficulty inherent in any process of self-discovery is metaphorically suggested by a journey that implies crossing literal physical borders in the form of the Pyrenees. The complexity of such an enterprise is further emblematized by the fact that three different means of transport are required to get our narrator-protagonist to her final destination: "un expreso, un cercanías y finalmente el autocar" [an express train, a local train, and finally the bus].[1]

It is in working her way backwards to her mother's homeland and childhood stamping grounds that she is confronted with the doubly complex relationship that, as a daughter, she has with her mother—a character named Eloísa, already dead as the narrative begins. The doubling is highlighted in that, within the fantastic mode used by Fernández Cubas to tell the story, the inherently complex, difficult, and even "monstrous" relationship between mother and daughter is further problematized by the haunting notion of this previous,

151

strange, prenatal encounter between the two. Before turning my attention to the relevance of this encounter for an evaluation of the mother-daughter bond, allow me to clarify the use of the word "monstrous" in this context. The term, as such, is used by Marianne Hirsch in the section of a 1981 article dedicated to explaining the tie between mother and daughter from the perspective of feminist psychoanalytic theory.[2] More specifically, the term appears as Hirsch elaborates on Luce Irigaray's personal appeal to her mother for individuation and autonomy in *Et l'une ne bouge pas sans l'autre* [translated as "And the One Doesn't Stir without the Other"].[3]

Taking a cue from Irigaray's powerful and poetic style, Hirsch dramatizes the difficulty of studying this particular familial relationship by arguing that the intellectual enterprise of comprehending the mother-daughter tie implies the need "to plunge into a network of complex ties, to attempt to untangle the strands of a double self, *a continuous multiple being of monstrous proportions* stretched across generations, parts of which try desperately to separate and delineate their own boundaries" (emphasis mine).[4] Hirsch aligns herself with Chodorow's contentions in *The Reproduction of Mothering*: any woman, as a daughter, has a self not completely differentiated from that of her mother. And, while the novel does establish, at one level, this kind of identification, I argue that it is a desire for autonomy that ultimately sustains *El columpio*. For one, it is the protagonist's self-narration that constitutes the novel that we actually get to read. Thus, from the opening pages to the concluding remarks, the daughter struggles to narrate her own story while trying to understand the person her mother was: a girl simply known to her male family members as Eloísa.

In a twist that I dare to call Freudian—though it could also be called Jungian as I explain later in this study—and to corroborate that we are indeed dealing with a complex double self, "a continuous multiple being" impossible to differentiate, Fernández Cubas explains her novel to María del Mar López-Cabrales not as the history of the protagonist-narrator but as the mother's history: "[q]uería contar la historia de la madre, de *aquella madre, simplemente*. . . . La madre de *El columpio*, como personaje—un tanto especial, por otro lado—*no pretende más que representarse a sí misma*" [I simply wanted to tell the history of the mother, of *that mother*. . . . The mother of *El columpio*, as a character—rather special, on the other hand—*seeks nothing more than to represent herself* (emphasis mine)].[5] And while it will be difficult to deny that in telling her story the daughter cannot but recount, at least partially, her mother's tale, it will be more complicated to agree with Fernández Cubas's statement that the mother is actually representing herself, since she is already dead at the beginning of the novel. Moreover, we the readers get to know her only through the narration of her daughter and the comments of the male family members still living in the family's home.

By insisting that the novel tells the story of the mother, Fernández Cubas makes clear that when evaluating mother-daughter relations we are indeed dealing with what appears to be an undifferentiated self. As I mentioned above, Jung is also relevant here because this continuity is articulated as an intermingling by which "every mother contains her daughter and every daughter her mother . . . every woman extends backwards into her mother and forwards into her daughter."[6] Indeed, the lack of differentiation as one of the axes that sustains the novel can be found in that, in a "Purloined Letter" style, El columpio is both the fiction we get to read (the story) and the term used to designate a central object within the fiction, as we shall later see when discussing the actual visit of our protagonist to her mother's familial space.

El columpio, then, is a tale of monstrous proportions because in narrating herself the protagonist is also narrating her mother. And, as Hirsch argues, it is this mirroring that needs to be factored in in any evaluation of female development in fiction. I believe it is evident by now that by quoting (mirroring) the insights of these feminist theorists as they elaborate on each other's reflections, I aim to situate my reading of El columpio at the interstice where psychoanalytical feminist theory and narrative fiction meet. This is not an arbitrary decision but an acceptance of the psychoanalytic terms in which the novel asks to be read. And while Fernández Cubas may have problems with my categorizing of her novel as a feminist text (she stated her disagreement with being considered a feminist writer in an interview with Kathleen Glenn),[7] we cannot but read the novel as a reflection on the significance of motherhood and the ambivalence with which we relate to it. It is not irrelevant, then, and as the author explained to María del Mar López-Cabrales, that the dead mother is the character in which she is most interested.

The most obvious reason, however, for reading the novel in psychoanalytical terms is found in the narrativization of a journey that attempts to explain an uncanny occurrence within the familial mother-daughter bond. Thus it can be argued that by transforming the experiential relation to her mother into narrative, the narrator-protagonist of *El columpio* is involved in a sort of "talking cure" that aims to unveil the reality locked in the riddle's dream. Let us remember that as a therapeutic method, a "talking cure" works by unveiling the actual, "real" significance in the unconscious of the apparent irrelevance of fantasies and dreams. The relevance of the unconscious in the novel in the form of the mother's dream requires that we consider psychoanalytical theories. And, while aware of the ritual of declaring psychoanalysis "dead and buried" as suggested by Slavoj Žižek[8] and of the contentious and difficult relationship it has with feminism, I agree with Diana Fuss's argument that it "constitutes a powerful cultural narrative that continues to shape . . . representations of sexual identity."[9] More recently, Cynthia Marshall has succinctly established its value by arguing that psychoanalysis is "less a vehicle to be abandoned or replaced and more something organic and renewable—an evolving body of ideas that provides techniques for reading."[10]

Let us thus finally turn to the protagonist's actual "talking" in the opening sentences of the novel; let us turn to her first moment of self-narration when she describes the uncanny encounter between mother and daughter:

> Un día, mucho antes de que yo naciera, mi madre soñó conmigo. Ella era una niña aún, tendría unos diez, quizás once años. . . . "Tú eras alta, rubia. Mucho más alta y rubia de lo que eres ahora..." Estábamos las dos frente a frente, mirándonos con curiosidad. . . . *Nunca pudo*, por más que se esforzara, *relatar con exactitud en qué había consistido esa extraña visión*. . . . Tan sólo había algo de lo que estaba absolutamente segura. *Aquella mujer que, burlándose del tiempo, se materializaba inesperadamente en el jardín, era yo, su hija.*

> [One day, long before I was born my mother dreamt of me. She was still a child, was maybe ten, eleven years old. . . . "You were tall and blond. Much taller and blonder than you are now . . ." We were facing each other, looking at each other with curiosity. . . . *She never could*, no matter how hard she tried, *recount what made up that strange vision*. . . . There was only one thing of which she was absolutely certain. *That woman who, mocking time, had materialized unexpectedly in the garden, was I, her daughter.*] (9–10, my emphasis)

To begin with, the *monstrous* proportions of the entanglement between the two are described in temporal terms that appear to echo

Hirsch's notion that this monstrous being "stretches across generations" in more ways than one. Indeed, and in true Fernández Cubas
fashion, the generational crossing is articulated with her characteristic fascination for the strange. Identified both as a dream ("mi
madre soñó conmigo" [my mother dreamt of me]) and as a
"strange vision," we find the daughter trying to explain the temporal riddle locked in the bizarre details of her mother's strange and
inexplicable dream. Also *monstrous* are the difficulties the daughter
will encounter in discovering her own identity, since the narrative of
the emergent self requires her to explain how she originates in a
someone or somewhere that preexists the self. This aspect is dramatized in *El columpio* by the narrative condition in which the protagonist is immersed: her self-narration, an act that points to her desire
to gain legitimacy and authority as a speaker, situates her as a dream,
as a figment of her mother's imagination and unconscious desires.

As the daughter lets us know—"[m]e lo contó una y otra vez"
[she related it to me over and over again] (10)—the mother returned obsessively to the narration of this primal image during her
life as a way to find some source of solace against the lack of companionship offered by the daughter: "fue tal vez la soledad que yo
le ofrecía lo que la volcó en el recuerdo de su infancia" [maybe it
was the loneliness that I offered that threw her into the recollection
of her childhood] (15). It is more than clear that the mother's compulsion to repeat, made evident by the need to retell the same story,
is another way in which the novel works with psychoanalytical notions. Furthermore, the implications of having the mother dead as
our narrator-protagonist embarks on a quest for autonomy and individuation require us to literally consider the mother in *El columpio*
as a phantasm, a spectral apparition that appears to echo Freud's
formulations of associative links between mother and death. But,
while considering these links, we cannot forget that they have been
questioned, most keenly, by Madelon Sprengnether in her aptly
entitled *The Spectral Mother*, where she shows the figure of the mother
as a constitutive absence in Freudian theory and places emphasis on
the importance of maternal power in the mother-child dyad.[11] As
will become apparent later in this essay, maternal power is at the
heart of the "real" significance of the prenatal encounter depicted
by the novel and will have profound consequences in the evolution
of the daughter's identity.

That the daughter is dealing with issues of maternal power is underscored by her desire to understand the repetitious nature of her

mother's story and the need to get rid of the guilt for her lack of tenderness when the mother was alive: "me hubiese mostrado más cariñosa, más comprensiva" [I would have acted more kind, more loving, more understanding] (14). Desire and need are at the heart of what prompts the daughter to tell the story of how currently, at twenty-five years of age and living in Paris, she embarks on a journey back to her mother's homeland and childhood home. The journey will eventually take her to a decrepit manor situated in a lost valley on the other side of the Pyrenees and known to all in the village with the regal name of "La Casa de la Torre" [The House of the Tower] (14). The house is not just a mere location for the events but a double emblem for two different symbolic realms. On the one hand, and as a known symbol of the body in general and the maternal body in particular, the house functions as a womb. It is not surprising, then, that it becomes the *matrix* to which the narrator-protagonist must return to solve the dream's riddle and lay her guilt to rest.

On the other hand, the house also emblematizes the patriarchal social order since at the moment of the narrator's arrival it is inhabited by the three men that shaped her mother's childhood and against whom she rebelled by abandoning the valley and crossing the border: they are her brothers, Tomás and Lucas, and a cousin, Bebo, the man Eloísa originally wanted to marry. The three men live as virtual recluses in a world of their own with no telephone or mail service and with Lucas primarily playing the role of paterfamilias and of "'dueño del valle'" ["lord of the valley"] (40, with quotations in the original). The only external influence barely tolerated inside this all-male enclave is the cleaning service provided twice a month by two village women, both named Raquel: "[l]a irrupción puntual de las raqueles era contemplada por los tíos como una invasión, una fatalidad ineludible de la que cada cual se defendía a su manera" [the punctual irruption of the two Raquels was perceived by the uncles as an invasion, an inescapable fatality against which each one defended himself as best he could] (48). And while the patriarchal order of the house can survive the necessary female disruptions brought by domesticity in the form of the two Raquels, nothing has prepared these men for the disruption brought by the arrival of the narrator, the young woman in search of her mother.

Indeed, the disruptive and disturbing effects of her presence are described in detail as an occasion for laughter:

> me puse a reír e imaginé a los tíos, a esos "solterones tozudos como ellos solos," *invadidos bruscamente en su intimidad*, intentando reponerse

de la sorpresa, *preguntándose qué hacer conmigo, cómo atenderme, de qué hablarme.*

[I started laughing and imagined the uncles, those "stubborn-as-a-mule old bachelors," *abruptly invaded in their privacy,* trying to recover from the surprise, *wondering what to do with me, how to treat me, how to speak to me.*] (27, emphasis mine)

The dramatization of the confusion and commotion created by the invasion of femininity in this all-male order is a striking feature of *El columpio* that needs to be read in light of the challenges proposed by Luce Irigaray to Freudian and Lacanian assumptions on the oedipal complex in *Speculum of the Other Woman.*[12] Moreover, the fact that our narrator is laughing about the alteration she has brought to the functioning of the masculine household needs also to be considered within Irigaray's articulation of women's laughter as "overtaking or exceeding the 'phallic norm.' "[13]

That the "phallic norm" is at play in *El columpio* is apparent when we discover later in the novel that one of the reasons for the three men to close themselves off to the outside world lies in the secret ritual by which the ghost of Eloísa, as she was when she was a girl, is summoned to appear every Friday night: "[e]llos la veían. Eloísa para mis tíos, *estaba* allí. Cada viernes, a las diez de la noche, en el comedor de la Casa de la Torre" [they saw her. Eloísa, for my uncles, *was* there. Every Friday, at ten at night, in the dining room of The House of the Tower] (120). Thus, through the ritual, the mother remains the girl that occupies the ordered place that they have assigned to her in the all-male household. That the uncles can relate to Eloísa only as the girl she was and not as the adult woman and mother of the narrator-protagonist foregrounds the precariousness of feminine subjectivity—that of the unnamed narrator and of the mother before her—framed within a male-dominated society and relying on masculine models as normative. Indeed, the narrator's process of self-discovery is produced within these masculine parameters, as is highlighted in the novel by the fact that the only family she has left after her mother's death is four men: the three uncles and her father, who is an absent figure throughout the novel and is referred to by the men of the family as "el francés" [the Frenchman] (34). Moreover, the uncles' ritual denies what the narrator-protagonist's presence defiantly affirms: that Eloísa became an adult woman and a mother who escaped their control. However, the narrator-protagonist is first "introduced" to her mother in a dining-room portrait that hovers with its towering presence over the three men in the room and where she is forever fixed and framed as their childhood playmate: "sí pude reconocer a mi madre de niña . . . vestida con un traje vaporoso muy parecido al de las fotografías. Tenía una expresión entre angelical y enfurruñada. . . . Una niña a la que acababan de romperle un juguete. Pero el juguete estaba ahí. En el suelo" [I was able to recognize my mother as a child . . . dressed in a diaphanous dress very similar to that of the pictures. She had an expression midway between angelic and sulky. . . . A girl who just had her toy broken. But the toy was there. On the floor] (30–31). Thus, Eloísa greets her daughter in the pictorial representation of a sulking girl, with a defiant face and with a toy lying at her feet: a diabolo, as we subsequently learn (31).

The diabolo, a toy consisting of a wooden spool whirled and tossed on a string tied to two sticks and with obvious metonymical references to the devil, is Eloísa's identifying mark. In fact, the diabolo is Eloísa's distinctive attribute in such a manner that the letters she sent from France to her brothers and cousin in the valley were signed with "unos trazos curiosos que recordaban un lazo, el movimiento de una cinta rematada en los extremos por dos bastas, dos palotes" [odd strokes that recalled a lasso, the movement of a string finished off at the ends by two stakes, two sticks] (56). That Eloísa is called "the queen of the diabolo" (71) and that her mastery and skill with the string are essential to her persona is not irrelevant to the evolution of identity narrated by the novel. In fact, the paradigmatic role of playing with a string in the conceptualization of the child's difference from her/his mother is made by Freud in "Beyond the Pleasure Principle" when discussing the child's playing with a bobbin on a string.[14] The *fort/da* [away/here] dynamics that the mother interprets in the child's actions and utterances are used by Freud to explain how the child differentiates self and (M)other. All of this is central to my reading of *El columpio* as a novel dramatizing some of the premises of psychoanalysis and feminism. And, as I will discuss later, it is the episode involving the narrator-protagonist and her mother as a powerful Eloísa exercising her mastery with the diabolo's string that will mark the culminating moment in which mother and daughter are clearly differentiated.

It is important to keep in mind that Eloísa's playful domains in the valley extend also to the wooded area surrounding the house where a swing, *the swing* of the title of the novel, becomes another space for the Fantastic to appear. Taken to that location by her uncles while on a picnic, the narrator-protagonist discovers the swing and on a whim jumps on it, only to be transformed into her own mother. However, while standing on the wooden swing and suddenly thrown off by the fury of the wind, she hears the voice of a "niña malcriada, caprichosa, tiránica" [spoiled, capricious, tyrannical girl] (44) that sings the telling lyrics that narrate the events that actually happened in her mother's case: "*Me casaré con un francés / Con un francés me casaré / Y nunca, nunca, nunca / Nunca volveré...*" [*I will marry a Frenchman / A Frenchman I will marry / And I will never, never, never / Never will I return . . .*] (44, italics in the original). As we readers know by now, Eloísa, in a story of escape, does leave the manor and the three men behind and finally marries the narrator's father, "the Frenchman." However, the relevance of this moment where *el columpio* appears has to do with the fact that it is here that the ghost of the mother first appears as something that cannot be apprehended by rational thought.

The swing episode is central to the daughter's quest for differentiation and the understanding of the feelings that the memory of her mother evokes. It is only after this instance and the swinging back and forth between the past and the present, between the known and the unknown, that the daughter can actually enunciate one of her darkest emotions: resentment towards her mother. The anxiety that the harboring of such feeling creates is dramatized in that the reality of the event is questioned while the confusion felt is expressed in the form of a query that cannot be answered: "[t]odo había sido una ilusión, no me cabía la menor duda. Sin embargo *¿qué oculto resentimiento debía de albergar yo contra mi madre* para hacerle hablar de esa forma, en aquel tono terrible, aunque sólo fuera con el pensamiento?" [It had all been an illusion, I hadn't the slightest doubt. However, *what hidden resentment must I have harbored against my mother* to make her talk in that manner, with that horrible tone, even if it were only in my thoughts?] (47, emphasis mine). While such a question requires the unveiling of the nature of these repressed feelings by paying attention to how the maternal has been theorized, it also signals an important moment in the subjective development of the protagonist: she recognizes ambivalence towards her mother, "an awareness of the existence of love and hate together."[15] In this sense I argue that this novel appears to side with feminist articulations that understand the recognition of ambivalence as a positive developmental stage by which the child can recognize the mother as a separate person. This recognition is a positive step towards the theorization and understanding of motherhood since the acknowledgment of maternal ambivalence, as expressed in the daughter's question, carries the acknowledgment of maternal subjectivity. More importantly for the evolution of the narrator's identity, the self-awareness implicit in the acknowledgment of maternal subjectivity allows for self-authentication.

MATERNITY AND ITS DISCONTENTS

Dreams, fantasies, slips of the tongue, and jokes, as Freud argued in *The Psychopathology of Everyday Life*, are successful at getting said all that which is otherwise repressed, desired, or feared.[16] Let us briefly elucidate some aspects of Freudian theory to evaluate the scope of Fernández Cubas's revised account of the origins of consciousness. But before turning our attention to Freud, allow me to contextualize *El columpio* within theoretical and fictional narrations of the maternal.[17] In theory, while maternity has long been conceptualized, evaluated, and redefined,[18] it was not until the mid-seventies that the relevance of its evaluation for feminist discourse was brought into the open in the United States by Adrienne Rich's ground-breaking *Of Woman Born: Motherhood as Experience and Institution* (1976).[19] And, while we can say that an evaluation of "the cathexis between mother and daughter, essential, distorted, misused" can no longer be considered "the great unwritten story"[20] within feminist discourses, we can assert that if we take into consideration the extensive attention given to this particular familial relationship in, for example, the literatures of France, Germany, or the United States, the number of contemporary Spanish narratives that have addressed it is relatively small. In fact, Laura Freixas's collection entitled *Madres e hijas* [Mothers and Daughters] makes this argument when introducing the fourteen short stories written by Spanish women authors who publish in Castilian: "the relations between father-son, mother-son, father-daughter are the central theme of innumerable works. . . . On the contrary, the works that depict mothers and daughters are tellingly few, and all are very recent."[21] A clarification is in order here, since we should not forget that the mother-daughter bond is at the core of novels such as Esther Tusquets's *El mismo mar de todos los veranos* [*The Same Sea as Every Summer*] (1978, 1990), Carmen

Martín Gaite's *Lo raro es vivir* [Living Is What's Strange] (1996), and Josefina R. Aldecoa's trilogy, *Historia de una maestra* [The Story of a Teacher] (1990), *Mujeres de negro* [Women Dressed in Black] (1994), and *La fuerza del destino* [The Force of Destiny] (1997), to name a few.[22] While not completely accurate, Freixas's point nonetheless has a certain validity: there is a relative dearth in contemporary Spanish literature with regard to the mother-daughter bond, because the number of texts addressing it is limited in comparison with other literary traditions. Furthermore, and to expand on Freixas's observation, we have to acknowledge that a comprehensive feminist study of such maternal relationships is yet to be undertaken within Hispanic literary and cultural studies. Interestingly enough Freixas's edition, published in 1996 only a year after *El columpio*'s publication, does not mention Fernández Cubas's novel nor is she one of the fourteen women writers included in the collection. Thus, as Janet Pérez suggests, what we need to address is why there is such a reduced number of novels problematizing mother-daughter relations and how is this relative scarcity connected to the still prevalent cultural idealization of the mother figure.[23] It is within this representational frame that I consider *El columpio* to be a paradigmatic text that needs to be evaluated alongside other novels by women authors addressing mother-daughter relations. By so doing, we can offer a more balanced and accurate assessment than the one presented by Freixas in 1996.

Freud's narration of the mother as the first love object of children of both sexes and of the father as the rival with whom they compete is the cornerstone of his formulation of the Oedipus complex, the process through which boys and girls ultimately construct an adult, "normal" gendered identity. Separation, however, occurs gradually and through a complex process of individuation, which in the case of girls is more complicated. As succinctly put by Susan Watkins, "the girl's recognition of her own and her mother's inferior, castrated status provokes a rejection of the mother as love object and the transference of desire to the father."[24] Thus, the relevance of the phallus and the consequent inferiority of female sexuality are what is in store for women in Freud's articulation. It is precisely because of his phallocentrism and the pivotal role granted to the oedipal complex that Freud has been taken to task by feminism, with some of the earliest feminist critiques formulated in the 1920s and 1930s by women psychoanalysts such as Karen Horney and Melanie Klein. Indeed, we must not forget that in her 1928 essay "Early Stages of

the Oedipus Conflict," Klein demotes the penis as privileged signifier and foregrounds the mother's breast and nipples as the central
ones, while Freud's phallocentrism is attacked by Horney in "The
Denial of the Vagina" (1933).[25]

But motherhood in *El columpio* does not follow these feminist foot-
steps since it is framed within a patriarchal system and the contradictions of power/vulnerability assigned to the maternal position.
However, as we have seen in the opening pages of the novel, it is the
dramatization of the encounter between mother and child, without
the apparent presence of the father, that is most telling and positions the novel within a feminist paradigm. The encounter alluded
to in the opening pages is actually narrated towards the end of the
novel and is articulated by the narrator as a terrifying and almost
deadly encounter with the mother. The lengthy description follows:

> Ella estaba allí. De pie, de espaldas a la verja. Vestía el traje blanco de
> organdí y llevaba el cabello recién peinado, en tirabuzones ordenados
> que le caían sobre los hombros. No sé quién avanzó hacia quién, si al-
> guna de las dos siquiera dio un paso. Pero enseguida nos encontramos
> frente a frente. . . . Muy pronto me di cuenta de que su aspecto angelical
> era desmentido por una mirada fuerte, impropia de una niña, y que lo
> que en un principio me había parecido una expresión de enfado no era
> más que una sonrisa desafiante, engreída. Agitaba en la mano una de
> aquellas cuerdas sobre las que ejercía el más absoluto dominio. . . . Lo
> que sucedió a continuación fue al tiempo muy rápido y muy lento, muy
> claro y muy confuso. Un dolor agudo en la garganta, el silbido de un
> látigo agitado con destreza en el aire; un chapoteo, un golpe; mis manos,
> repentinamente vigorosas, luchando por zafarse de un terrible reptil en-
> rollado a mi cuello; la sensación de asfixia, de que los ojos se me salían
> de las órbitas, de que estaba perdiendo el conocimiento... Y mi voz. Un
> quejido ronco. La súplica desesperada de alguien, en el límite de sus
> fuerzas, para quien la razón ha dejado de tener sentido. "¡Mamá! ¡Por
> favor..., mamá!"

> [She was there. Standing up, with her back towards the wrought-iron
> gate. She was wearing the white organdy dress and her just-combed hair
> drooped in orderly ringlets over her shoulders. I do not know who ad-
> vanced towards whom, or if either of us even took a step. But immedi-
> ately we were face to face. . . . I rapidly realized that her angelic
> appearance was negated by a strong gaze, inappropriate for a girl, and
> that what at first seemed to me an expression of anger was nothing more
> than a defiant, conceited smile. In her hand she was fondling one of
> those cords over which she exerted utter control. . . . What happened

next was at the same time very fast and very slow, very clear and very confusing. A sharp pain in my throat, the whistling of a whip skillfully lashed in the air; a splashing, a blow; my hands, suddenly energetic, fighting to free myself of the terrible reptile coiled around my neck, the sense of asphyxia, that my eyes were popping out of their sockets, that I was losing consciousness. . . . And my voice. A hoarse groan. The desperate begging of someone, almost out of strength, for whom logic has ceased to make sense. "Mom!" "Please, mom!"] (123–24)

The power of this passage is not just related to the fact that it confronts us with the Fantastic. Much of its impact derives from the presentation of a feminist psychoanalytic dramatization of the fear experienced in front of the all-powerful mother and how this fear impacts the subjective development of the daughter. By situating our narrator in the face of the imminent danger implicit in a hauntingly spectral encounter with this phallic mother, Fernández Cubas appears to deter the sentimentalization of the mother-daughter relationship found in some feminist articulations. However, by revealing the uncanny in this prenatal encounter, the author also unveils how the otherness revealed by the uncanny is what allows for the daughter's subjective evolution. This liberation works both ways since the disruption of the feminine brought by our narrator to the patriarchal space of "La casa de la Torre" ultimately liberates Eloísa from an eternal, forced childhood. By recovering Eloísa as a mother in the act of calling her "mom," the daughter appears to understand that only as a separate and different being from her, can her mother act as a mother and ultimately "save" her from the fantastic Eloísa and her diabolic whipping cord.

This cord becomes a primary signifier in the novel and through a double "umbilical" and "phallic" metaphor dramatizes not only the intensity and complexity of the mother-daughter bond, but also Fernández Cubas's ambivalence toward the manner in which to represent or understand the figure of the mother. Functioning as a phallic whip, the cord is a symbolic representation of the image of the phallic mother: the object of secret fear and deep desire with the power to "cause or prevent, animate or agitate, signify or deracinate, inspire or terrorize—or deaden."[26] That the mother of the protagonist is represented as a phallic figure in the person of Eloísa with her diabolo indicates the compulsion by psychoanalysis, apparently shared here by Fernández Cubas, to foreclose ambivalence in the psyche. By being represented as having a penis-like cord, Eloísa is beyond "women's castration" and, in that sense and since she is "one" with both a penis and a vagina, she neither embodies nor represents ambivalence. Moreover, the cord as "phallic whip" is also a symbolic representation of the law of the father, the emergence of the father's oedipal interference in the bonding process between the mother and the daughter. Indeed, if according to Freud's conceptualization, the forming of one's identity involves a recognition of, and a struggle with, the agent of the separation between mother and child, this particular episode in the novel can be said to narrate the instance of paternal intervention in the identity-forming process.

However, and because the cord functions also as an umbilical cord, the novel does not eliminate ambivalence. Indeed, here the cord is also an umbilical cord by which mother and daughter are bound in a life/death situation that is one of the basic human conceptual experiences. In fact, it is from this shared commonality— "that *everybody* had one and *everybody* lost one"—that Marcia Ian formulates a phenomenology of the umbilical cord that without becoming essentialized as the phallus has been, can work as the "'objective correlative' for the phantasmic connection human beings can feel or miss."[27] Therefore, it is ultimately from such an experiential stance that the protagonist can forge her own mythic system and worldview. That she achieves her own worldview is made evident by her concluding the novel with the affirmation that she has learned something from her experience in the house of the valley: "[n]unca, estuviera donde estuviera, ocurriese lo que ocurriese, volvería a decir: 'Demasiado tarde'" [never, wherever I was, whatever happened, would I again say: "Too late"] (137).

CONCLUSION

By embarking on a quest for knowledge that ultimately describes the evolution of the narrator's own identity, *El columpio* can be inscribed in the genealogy of the female *bildungsroman*. For one thing, this consideration further emphasizes the paradigmatic role played by the notion of lineage—maternal lineage—in the novel. More importantly, it allows us to understand the narrator's psychically mature condition at the end of the novel as a direct consequence of her having been "touched"—in more senses than one—by the encounter with her mother. Ultimately, the importance granted in *El columpio* to the unconscious and the mother-daughter bond foregrounds the challenges that the novel poses to the oedipal story of cultural and subjective development. For all of these reasons, we can argue that *El columpio* offers the "woman-centered perspective" articulated by Phyllis Zatlin in her reading of *Con Agatha en Estambul* [With Agatha in Istanbul], the collection of short stories published by Fernández Cubas in 1994.[28] By stressing the unconscious, the mother-daughter tie, and a "woman-centered perspective," *El columpio* appears to place itself at the conjunction of literature, psychoanalysis, and feminism. In so doing, it forces us to recognize the ambivalence of our cultural desires and fantasies in relation to mothers.

NOTES

1. Cristina Fernández Cubas, *El columpio* (Barcelona: Tusquets, 1995), 13. Hereafter citations will be referenced parenthetically in the text.
2. Marianne Hirsch, "A Mother's Discourse: Incorporation and Repetition in *La Princesse de Clèves*," *Yale French Studies* 62 (1981): 62–87.
3. Luce Irigaray, "And the One Doesn't Stir without the Other," trans. Hélène Vivienne Wenzel, *Signs: Journal of Women in Society and Culture* 7:1 (1981): 60–67.
4. Hirsch, "A Mother's Discourse," 73.
5. María del Mar López-Cabrales, "Cristina Fernández Cubas: Los horrores de la memoria," *Palabras de mujeres: Escritoras españolas contemporáneas* (Madrid: Narcea, 2000), 170.
6. C. G. Jung and C. Kerényi, "The Psychological Aspects of the Kore," *Essays on a Science of Mythology* (New York: Bollingen, 1963), 162.
7. Kathleen M. Glenn, "Conversación con Cristina Fernández Cubas," *Anales de la Literatura Española Contemporánea* 18 (1993): 360.
8. Slavoj Žižek, *The Metastases of Enjoyment: Six Essays on Woman and Causality* (New York: Verso, 1994), 7.
9. Diana Fuss, *Identification Papers* (New York: Routledge, 1995), 13.
10. Cynthia Marshall, "Psychoanalyzing the Prepsychoanalytic Subject," *PMLA* 117:5 (October 2002): 1207.
11. See Madelon Sprengnether, *The Spectral Mother: Freud, Feminism, and Psychoanalysis* (Ithaca: Cornell University Press, 1990).
12. See Luce Irigaray, *Speculum of the Other Woman*, trans. Gillian C. Gill (Ithaca: Cornell University Press, 1985).
13. See Jan Campbell's cogent explanation of Irigaray's notion in *Arguing with the Phallus: Feminist, Queer, and Postcolonial Theory. A Psychoanalytic Contribution* (London: Zed Books, 2000), 109–10.
14. Sigmund Freud, "Beyond the Pleasure Principle," vol. 18, *The Standard Edition of the Complete Psychological Works of Sigmund Freud*, ed. James Strachey (London: Hogarth Press, 1974; reprint 1986), 14.
15. Campbell, *Arguing with the Phallus*, 35.

16. Sigmund Freud, *The Psychopathology of Everyday Life* (1901), vol. 6, *The Standard Edition of the Complete Psychological Works of Sigmund Freud*, ed. James Strachey (London: Hogarth Press, 1974), 1–279.

17. See Rozsika Parker's *Torn in Two: The Experience of Maternal Ambivalence* (London: Virago, 1995).

18. See, for example, Sara Heller Mendelson and Patricia Crawford's *Women in Early Modern England, 1550–1720* (Oxford: Clarendon Press, 1998) for the spectrum of social and artistic perspectives on the range of early modern maternal roles.

19. Adrienne Rich, *Of Woman Born: Motherhood as Experience and Institution* (New York: Norton, 1976).

20. Ibid., 225.

21. Freixas, *Madres e hijas* (Barcelona: Anagrama, 1996), 14.

22. Tusquets, *El mismo mar de todos los veranos* (Barcelona: Lumen, 1978); Martín Gaite, *Lo raro es vivir* (Barcelona: Anagrama, 1996); Aldecoa, *Historia de una maestra* (Barcelona: Anagrama, 1990), *Mujeres de negro* (Barcelona: Anagrama, 1994), and *La fuerza del destino* (Barcelona: Anagrama, 1997).

23. I thank Janet Pérez for her comments on this point.

24. Watkins, *Twentieth-Century Women Novelists: Feminist Theory into Practice* (New York: Palgrave, 2000), 78.

25. Klein, "Early Stages of the Oedipus Conflict," in *The Writings of Melanie Klein*, vol. 1 (New York: Free Press, 1984): 186–98; Horney, "The Denial of the Vagina," reprinted in *Feminine Psychology*, ed. Howard Kelman (New York: Norton, 1967): 147–61.

26. See Marcia Ian's *Remembering the Phallic Mother: Psychoanalysis, Modernism, and the Fetish* (Ithaca: Cornell University Press, 1993), 8.

27. Ibid., 38, emphasis in the original.

28. Phyllis Zatlin, "Amnesia, Strangulation, Hallucination and Other Mishaps: The Perils of Being Female in Tales of Cristina Fernández Cubas," *Hispania* 79:1 (March 1996): 38.

The Metafictional Metaphor in *El columpio*

John B. Margenot III

Sᴇʟꜰ-ᴄᴏɴꜱᴄɪᴏᴜꜱɴᴇꜱꜱ ɪꜱ ᴀ ᴄʀᴜᴄɪᴀʟ ᴅᴇᴛᴇʀᴍɪɴᴀɴᴛ ɪɴ *ᴇʟ ᴄᴏʟᴜᴍᴘɪᴏ* [ᴛʜᴇ Swing]. This novel reaffirms Cristina Fernández Cubas's ongoing interest in the problematics of composition that emerges in her initial collection of short stories, *Mi hermana Elba* [My Sister Elba]. A cursory reading of this and subsequent works reveals the proliferation of terminology related to fiction and theatricality, such as "representación" [performance][1] and "telón de medio alzar" [half-lifted drop curtain], "espectáculo" [show] and "escenario" [stage].[2] In *Mi hermana Elba*, characters are often writers who surround themselves with the tools of their profession, reread notebooks, keep diaries, and allude to fictional editors. Others even work for publishing houses in *Los altillos de Brumal* [The Attics of Brumal]. This preoccupation with literature comes to fruition in Fernández Cubas's first novel, *El año de Gracia* [The Year of Grace], which openly explores its parodic relationship to inherited subtexts and literary tradition. *El columpio*, however, subtly shifts its focus and scrutinizes the centrality of oral and written discourse as they relate to the creation of texts. Critics such as Janet Pérez and José Ortega have commented briefly on self-consciousness in Fernández Cubas's writing.[3] My extended discussion of the novel explores the narrative strategies that lay bare the fictional artifice, particularly those related to epistolary writing, role-playing, textual actualization and plagiarism, games, and finally the dynamics of power implied in the relationship between author and literary characters.

The title of Fernández Cubas's second novel suggests a plethora of readings. A possible understanding of the noun adumbrates the ludic quality of the work, that is to say, *columpio* signals the potential for the oscillation between fiction and reality. From a different perspective the swing constitutes an emotive link between Eloísa, Lucas, Bebo, and Tomás. Her irreplaceable nature is reaffirmed when Tomás violently pushes the narrator off the childhood swing and injures her knee. Given that the swing belonged to Eloísa, Tomás cannot accept that anyone, intentionally or not, could replace her. For the purpose of the present discussion, however, the *columpio* serves as an adequate metaphor for the narrator's (in)ability to distinguish between reality and appearances. In addition to descriptions of childhood games, such as bicycle riding and the construction of irrigation channels in the garden, readers learn early in the novel that Lucas, Bebo, and Tomás took turns pushing Eloísa on her swing and admired her uncanny expertise with the diabolo.[4] One might even argue the swing functions as a stage for Eloísa's daughter to reenact an event that occurred frequently: "Y de pronto fue como si reviviera una de las fotografías de mi madre. Desde el otro lado. Porque allí estaban ellos, los hermanos y el primo, y yo, de pie sobre un columpio de madera . . . jugaba a irritarlos, a enfadarlos, a hacer valer mi condición de reina absoluta" [And all of a sudden, it was as if I brought one of my mother's photographs back to life. From the other side. Because there they were, brothers and cousin, and I, standing on a wooden swing . . . I played at irritating them, angering them, underscoring my condition as imperious queen] (43–44). Reenactment of a scene between relatives previously captured on film is not simply mimetic; it also explores issues related to power. Eloísa's daughter imitates her mother because doing so facilitates a certain level of control over her uncles.[5] As new "queen," the narrator momentarily acquires a degree of dominance similar to her mother's while she lived in the valley among her siblings and cousin.[6] Furthermore, at the conclusion of the narrator's abbreviated visit, she remarks: "Ahora era yo quien tenía la certeza de haber estado durante aquellos días balanceándome en un columpio, suspendida en el aire, ingrávida sobre un inmenso abismo. Hacia atrás, hacia delante" [Now it was I who was certain of having swayed during those days on a swing, suspended in the air, weightless over an immense abyss. Backward, forward] (134). Finally, somewhat more enlightened about her mother's history, she succeeds in freeing herself from past fictions and returns to Paris. Frequent allusions to the symbolic yet real *columpio* provide multiple readings, the majority of which explore textual strategies.

The opening pages of *El columpio* prepare readers for an acutely self-conscious perusal of the novel. The Cervantine quality of the text immediately inserts readers into what seems palpably real, notwithstanding allusions to the writing process.[7] The initial passages that precede the narrator's trip focus on dreams as part of a writing strategy, and serve to engage the reader. In fact, this section frames the principal elements that receive development throughout the novel. More precisely, the narrator emphasizes the stage metaphor, character development, strategy, and fictionalization. In essence, Eloísa's prophetic dream about her future daughter lends itself to an exploration of the artistic process. While the oneiric motif appears in the first sentence of *El columpio*, the narrator never questions its validity; instead, she stresses the notion of process, the difficulty of accurately conveying what Eloísa tried to tell her on numerous occasions: "Nunca pudo, por más que se esforzara, relatar con exactitud en qué había consistido esa extraña visión" [She never could, no matter how hard she tried, narrate exactly what made up that strange vision] (9).[8] The dream becomes the focal point for repeated conversations between mother and daughter: "Me lo contó una y otra vez . . . como si aún lo encontrara inexplicable, milagroso, absurdo" [She told me about it over and over . . . as if she still found it unexplainable, miraculous, absurd] (10). In fact, whenever they speak of the past, "Todos los caminos conducían al mismo lugar, a los mismos personajes" [All paths led to the same place, to the same characters] (11). The narrator clearly comprehends that her mother's rendition of life in Spain constitutes an "ingenua invención" [naïve invention] (11). That is to say, Eloísa's admittedly difficult and unreliable retelling eventually motivates the nameless daughter to write Lucas, Tomás, and Bebo about her future arrival at their home. Hence, these pages set a tone that encourages readers to approach *El columpio* as fiction about fiction. The inordinate level of playfulness, along with a semantic field related to the fiction-making process—*relatar, contar, hablar, visión, inexplicable, milagroso, escenario, personajes, invención* [*to narrate, to tell, to speak, vision, unexplainable, miraculous, stage, characters, creation*]—reveal the ludic quality of narrative discourse.

Like most self-conscious works, *El columpio* reveals the presence of other written texts, usually in the form of personal, handwritten letters.[9] From the very beginning of the novel, both the narrator and her mother fail miserably in their attempts to establish an epistolary relationship with Lucas, Tomás, and Bebo because the men never respond.[10] At times, fragments of letters work their way into the novel. For example, even though Eloísa's daughter tersely explains the purpose of her trip to Spain—"Y por eso estoy aquí. Para conoceros" [And that's why I'm here. To get to know all of you] (35)—she intimates that oral communication is insufficient, and therefore reads them her inexplicably undelivered letter at the dinner table. By reading the contents of her missive as an academic delivers a paper at a conference, she demonstrates a greater degree of comfort with the written word. In addition, she soon comes to the realization that someone had tampered with the letter: "Aquel sobre había sido manipulado con anterioridad" [That envelope had been tampered with beforehand] (37). The discovery of Eloísa's letters piques her curiosity and enables an informative, yet unauthorized, "reading" of the sibling relationship so frequently evoked during their chats in Paris. Her interest, however, soon turns to indignation on learning that every envelope had been skillfully opened and reglued as if to negate the communicative purpose of its contents: "También aquel sobre había sido pegado por segunda vez" [That envelope too had been glued a second time] (59). Because personal documents are read by unintended parties, resealed, and hidden away in the secret compartments of old coffers, or never reach their destination, *El columpio* reflects ironically on the notion of "private" discourse.[11] Even the narrator's desire to learn more about her mother leads to similar behavior: "En medio de aquella actividad frenética no me paré a pensar que *acababa de sucumbir* a la costumbre local: abrir y cerrar cartas" [In the middle of that frantic activity I didn't stop to think that *I had just yielded* to the local practice: opening and gluing letters] (63, emphasis added). Eloísa's daughter searches for written answers to questions generated by her mother's incomplete oral accounts, and she is only partially successful in her quest. Lucas, Tomás, and Bebo, on the other hand, are clearly up to date on the events surrounding Eloísa and their visiting niece. The narrator conjectures that what at first might be taken as a total disregard for her mother's memory is instead a homage, a peculiar form of fictionalization that keeps alive "el recuerdo de Eloísa cuando aún no había abandonado el valle" [their memory of Eloísa when she had not yet departed from the valley] (61).

On closer scrutiny it becomes clear that this pseudo-epistolary relationship constitutes a veiled commentary on the power of writing.[12] Eloísa's daughter—the narrator—must create a new envelope, glue it, and imitate her mother's handwriting. She therefore becomes the agent that actualizes and destroys all traces of her reading (as had some male relative before her). Letters function as tools to retain power, and this is particularly obvious when the narrator, en route to Paris, reproduces the complete letter from Lucas, Tomás, and Bebo within the novel. Written in a recriminatory tone—"¿Por qué te fuiste así, de repente . . . Es posible que ni siquiera ahora te des cuenta de que podías haber sufrido un accidente" [Why did you leave like that, suddenly . . . It's possible even now you don't realize that you could have had an accident] (131)—the passage suggests an antagonistic relationship, at the very least. Apparently, the uncles suspect that Eloísa's daughter has returned to claim a percentage of the family inheritance and they include a check to guarantee her silence. In addition to wondering how long it took her relatives to craft the letter, she comments that "Aquellas líneas cumplían una astuta función" [Those lines fulfilled an astute purpose] (131). The symbolic power of writing further emerges when the narrator tears this final letter to bits and throws the pieces out the bus window: "Fue como si me desprendiera de otras muchas cartas, de recuerdos ajenos, de un desván con olor a cerrado, de arquillas y baúles, disfraces apolillados y bombillas de quince" [It was as if I divested myself of many other letters, of others' memories, of an unventilated attic, of small chests and trunks, moth-eaten disguises and fifteen-watt light bulbs] (133). In fact, she only feels free after destroying the tempting check. Eloísa's daughter therefore liberates herself from the discourse of others and reaffirms her own voice in *El columpio*.

The narrator often describes her actions in theatrical terms or "performs" for other characters. Upon arriving at her uncles' estate, the visitor observes, "Curiosamente, no me dieron tiempo a excusarme, *a exagerar* la fatiga del viaje" [Curiously, they didn't give me time to excuse myself, *to exaggerate* the weariness from my trip] (25, emphasis added). Her inability to engage in hyperbole through oral discourse adumbrates her lack of control in this situation. In fact, she ludically regrets having squandered a valuable opportunity to present a powerful and confident image upon meeting Tomás, Lucas, and Bebo: "Había actuado como una estúpida al presentarme tan a la ligera" [I had acted like a fool by introducing myself so carelessly] (26). Much like Daniel in *El año de Gracia*, Eloísa's daughter performs to elicit a desired response from her uncles: "Supe lo que debía hacer a continuación . . . admirarme de la belleza de los muebles o explicar lo mucho que mi madre me había hablado de ellos" [I knew what I had to do next . . . marvel at the beauty of the furniture or explain how much my mother had spoken to me about them] (30).[13] As she searches for the correct things to say and to do, the narrator ostensibly attempts to project a strong self-image. While Daniel proves successful in his endeavor, the narrator of *El columpio* is never completely sure just how convincing her performance has been, which augments the level of uncertainty throughout the text. Her reflections on performance emerge, for example, when she meets Bebo and succesfully resists the temptation to reject his unsettling handshake (25). Even when Tomás violently pushes her off Eloísa's childhood swing, badly bruising her knee, she acts as if nothing had happened: " 'No ha sido nada. Cenad tranquilos.' Sin embargo, al empezar a subir las escaleras, me di cuenta de que la rodilla me dolía mucho más de lo que había previsto" ["It was nothing. Eat your dinner without worrying." Nevertheless, upon climbing the stairs, I realized that my knee ached a lot more than I had foreseen] (46). Such attempts at manipulation through fictionalization are only partially fruitful because her presence at the family estate does little, if anything, to alter the uncles' behavior. Yet, she never renounces these strategies; instead, as her suspicions grow to certainty her response becomes increasingly metafictional. For example, upon comprehending that Tomás spies on her through the keyhole of the bedroom door she performs for him: "Me llevé una vez más la copa a los labios, lenta, muy lentamente, como si me hallara sobre un escenario y mi representación fuera dirigida a un único espectador" [I lifted the goblet to my lips one more time, slowly, very slowly, as if I were on a stage and my performance were addressed to a single spectator] (111). As soon as she fakes ingesting the stupefying elixir and turns out the light, Tomás leaves hastily to inform the others. In this instance acting serves to avoid a potentially life-threatening situation.

Other characters likewise appear to perform in clearly theatrical terms. The first time Tomás rides his bicycle around the town square ringing its bell, the narrator comprehends that the rider acted as if he hadn't seen her cooling off by the fountain (20). Similarly when the visiting narrator later runs into Raquel working at the local market, a conversation ensues. Raquel's garrulous responses not only reveal a desire to warn someone else, but are also patently histrionic: "Me pareció que hablaba en voz muy alta, en un tono que no había empleado el día anterior en la casa y que, al hacerlo, miraba con el rabillo del ojo al puesto del pescado, al de los embutidos, a la cajera" [It seemed to me that she spoke in a very loud voice, in a tone that she hadn't used the day before at the house and, when doing so, she looked out of the corner of her eye at the fish stand, at the delicatessen, at the cashier] (77). The narrator's recognition that Raquel addresses a larger group underscores that she puts on a show for others in the market. Furthermore, Lucas's initial appearance is described in terminology associated with drama: "Tuve la sensación de que había algo en él pretendidamente postizo, falso. Tal vez usaba maquillaje. O peluquín. O demasiada agua de colonia" [I sensed that there was something about him intentionally fake, false. Perhaps he wore make-up. Or a toupee. Or too much eau de cologne] (24–25). Comments of this sort serve to establish an extended level of humor and fictiveness throughout the narrative, bringing to mind Robert Scholes's observation that "fabulation puts the highest premium on art and joy."[14] When the narrator abruptly announces her intention to return to Paris the following day, the poker-faced reaction of the uncles seems depressingly distant and uncompromising. She soon understands that they feigned disinterest to surprise her one last time by driving her to the bus station in an antique automobile "en sí mismo todo un espectáculo" [in itself quite a spectacle] (91). The show, however, is just about to begin as the narrator belatedly realizes that her uncles want to ensure her departure. In addition, her irritation acquires theatrical overtones when noticing that several passengers "empezaban a mirarnos sin disimulo" [began to stare at us quite openly] (103). We might accordingly understand Lucas's half-hearted attempt to open a "new" bottle of champagne, even though it is clearly the same one uncorked days before to celebrate her arrival: "Lucas hizo como si la descorchara, pero el tapón salió con suma facilidad" [Lucas acted as if he were uncorking it, but the cork came out very easily] (87). One might simply dismiss this passage as yet another example of the peculiar behavior of these frugal relatives; yet viewed from another perspective such comments highlight the fictional quality of narrative discourse in *El columpio*. To ostensibly suggest that everything in the text is theatrical ultimately questions the limits of writing, and brings into clearer focus the novelistic process.

Not surprisingly, the world is a stage in *El columpio* and several characters, particularly Lucas and the nameless narrator, recognize the function of this metaphor throughout the work. The narration abounds in references to this Shakespearean conceit, and it is therefore worthwhile to examine the intertextual dialogue between the *auto sacramental*[15] and the text. Fernández Cubas apparently removes all allegory associated with religion and instead employs the world-as-stage conceit from a purely technical, literary point of view. It is, for example, noteworthy that the majority of Calderón's characters in *El gran teatro del mundo* [The Great Stage of the World] recognize their function as ludic components in the game of fiction. In Pirandellian fashion, the characters introduce themselves to the author and conspicuously reflect on the varied degrees of success in playing their roles. A case in point is the King, who yields to authorial control: "Polvo somos de tus pies. / Sopla aqueste polvo, pues, / para que representemos" [We are dust upon Thy way / Breathe on that dust, we pray, / That we may begin to perform].[16] Various characters, particularly the Poor Man and the Peasant, are less complacent. In fact, the former complains "¿Aqueste papel me das?" [Alas, is that part for me?] (v. 371) and the latter unhappily states: "Seré en la comedia / el peor representante" [But as to acting I'd say / I shall lack the subtle touch] (vv. 357–58). The Autor, however, emphasizes his omnipotence from the outset by assigning theatrical roles: "Pero yo, Autor soberano, / sé bien qué papel hará / mejor cada uno; así va / repartiéndolos mi mano" [But I that with vision clear / Can see what each one of you / Is best equipped to do / Now cast you within your sphere] (vv. 329–32).

In addition to the disquisitions on the relationship between author and characters, Calderón constructs his play around the ideological conflicts of the period. Valbuena Prat argues in his edition of Calderón's *autos sacramentales* that the Spanish playwright "poses in the work the problem of free will and grace . . . but above all is the essential affirmation of freedom in opposition to complete protestant predestination."[17] Freedom in *El columpio*, however, has little to do with the theological debate underlying Calderón's *auto sacramental*, and Lucas firmly echoes this idea with a parodic twist: "Porque el mundo era un gran teatro y el dinero, ese dios menor, pero dios al cabo, le permitía diseñar el escenario a su único, absoluto e indiscutible albedrío" [Because the world was a great stage and money, that minor god, but god nonetheless, allowed him to fashion the stage according to his sole, absolute and indisputable whim] (39). Lucas's statement falls squarely within Linda Hutcheon's suggestion that parody, understood as repetition with difference, constitutes a major means of modern self-consciousness.[18] As the most powerful businessman in the area, Lucas becomes the "autor soberano" [sovereign author] who openly uses the metafictional metaphor and his wealth to manipulate other characters. The narrator also distances Lucas from the Calderonian subtext by presenting him as an exceptionally bad actor. Even though Eloísa's daughter recognizes that Lucas disguises himself as a "dueño del valle" [lord of the valley] (40), she characterizes him as "posiblemente el peor actor del mundo sobre un escenario, pero un convincente gran señor del valle en sus dominios" [possibly the worst actor in the world on a stage, but a convincing great master of the valley in his domain] (41–42). Paradoxically, the narrator both effaces and supports Lucas's narrative authority. As the reader's uncertainty regarding Lucas emerges, it becomes increasingly difficult—if not totally impossible—to separate fact from fiction in the novel. Thus *El columpio* eschews the spiritual component present in *El gran teatro del mundo* and foregrounds principally its ludic quality.

Since Eloísa, Tomás, Lucas, and Bebo demonstrated a propensity for performance as children, their future plans included becoming the best actors in the world. Bebo, who "escribía para los cuatro" [wrote for the four of them] (21), composed theatrical scripts that they recreated in the mysterious tower of the family estate, and the narrator stresses the playful dimension of this space: "Allí, en el último ventanuco, debía de hallarse el desván, el cuarto de los juegos, el arcón de tesoros" [There, in the highest small window, must be the attic, the playroom, the treasure chest] (20–21). Terms such as treasure chest, playroom, and attic suggest the private yet ludic nature of creation that potentiates the imagination.[19] Early in the novel, the narrator retrieves Eloísa's oral account regarding childhood performance. Apparently, Eloísa had disguised herself as a Christian princess locked away in the tower by Saracen warriors who demanded that she renounce her faith. Role-playing, however, momentarily gives way to reality when she remarks, " 'Por un momento llegué a asustarme de verdad' " ["For a moment I was truly frightened"] (21). Bebo reacts as playwright and saves Eloísa from her captors by modifying the plot of his work. After creating a diversion for Tomás and Lucas, he removes his Moorish robes, hangs a cross around his neck and plays the part of the knightly savior who attempts to rescue his cousin with a kiss. Eloísa, however, rejects the submissive role of women portrayed throughout literary tradition, especially in fairy tales, as helpless creatures that rely on men for their self-realization. At the same time, this scene blends fiction and reality due to Bebo's romantic attachment to his cousin. In short, Bebo the playwright aware of composition as both process and product momentarily takes advantage of Eloísa through literature. The narrator then juxtaposes a passage that signals her particular attitude concerning children's stories. Following her first conversation with Tomás, she reflects: "Enseguida me sentí ridícula. Mi voz había sonado cándida, como la de una heroína de cuento infantil" [I im-

mediately felt silly. My voice sounded naive, like the voice of a heroine from a children's story] (22). The narrative consciousness
recognizes that her behavior falls within an easily identifiable literary model, and this awareness of fictional models together with Eloísa's rebellion against the author (Bebo) not only brings into clearer
focus the issue of narrative discourse as a hegemonic tool but also
foregrounds the relationship between textual composition, character, and author.

As the novel progresses, readers sense that Lucas, Tomás, and
Bebo grow impatient with their role as obliging hosts who at times
seem dutifully to show their niece the grounds and escort her on
excursions throughout the area. That is not to say that dramatic conventions cease to interest them; rather, their principal concern in
fiction culminates every Friday evening when the men "meet" with
Eloísa. When the narrator informs them of her intention to leave
town for Paris the following morning, it is no longer clear whether
their stone-faced reaction is fake or sincere. As the narrator's doubts
grow, she self-consciously concludes that her sojourn was a fabulation: "Y todo lo que, en aquellos días, hubiera podido fabular—la
sensación de reencontrar a mi familia, la ilusión de aliviarles de su
rutina o el cariño que había llegado a sentir por ellos—desaparecía
de golpe. Sin dejar rastro" [And everything that I fabulated during
those days—the sensation of rediscovering my family, the illusion of
easing their routine or the affection I grew to feel for them—
suddenly disappeared. Without leaving a trace] (113). At this moment, the narrator recognizes—in an aptly swinglike reversal of
direction—that she has created an idealized image of her uncles
that does not totally square with the reality of the situation. Just as
she suddenly falls off the swing imitating her mother, the daughter
understands the illusory, fictitious, and essentially vacuous relationship existing between herself and these relatives. No longer befud-
dled, the narrator now capably pulls back from fantasy and
recognizes that Lucas, Tomás, and Bebo have completely surrend-
ered to fiction: "Quién sabe cuántos años llevaban consagrando una
noche a la semana a su juego favorito, el Gran Juego, una fantasía
que, a fuerza de insistencia, había terminado convirtiéndose en un
rito, una obligación ineludible, lo más real de todo lo que constituía
su vida" [Who knows how many years they had spent devoting one
night a week to their favorite game, the Great Game, a fantasy which,
due to their insistence, had become a rite, an inevitable obligation,
more real than anything that constituted their life] (119). Simply

put, this rite by which they fictionalize Eloísa through fantasy acquires central significance and conceals the gnawing reality of her absence in *El columpio*.[20] As the narrator contemplates the "escenario" [stage] (115) from the outside through the garden window,[21] she believes that the uncles look more relaxed and "naturales" [real] (119) than ever. Furthermore, this fantastic rite acquires central importance becoming "lo más real de todo lo que constituía su vida" [more real than anything that constituted their life] (119). The narrator therefore affirms the centrality of fiction in her male relatives' lives. In this sense characters, including the narrating daughter, both create and keep Eloísa "alive" in the novel.

The narrator not only acknowledges the power of the written word in *El columpio* but also understands that oral discourse can transport characters to other illusory, if not oneiric, worlds. Eloísa's apparently incessant retelling of her life created an intriguing cosmos that her daughter attempts to experience and then to express in writing. The strongest case for the transformational quality of speech, however, comes to the fore when Lucas describes for everyone Eloísa's uncanny expertise in the manipulation of the diabolo. The narrator frames Lucas's ability to artfully manipulate and entertain an audience by first comparing him with the town crier at a village fair, then visualizing him as a magician, and finally as ringmaster of a circus who could "con la sola fuerza de la palabra, convocar imágenes, personajes, decorados. O cambiar de escenario" [with the sole power of the word, summon images, characters, settings. Or change the stage] (71–72). Of special importance to the present discussion is the narrator's recognition that her uncle's "performance" transports his listeners to a different locus.[22] Suddenly Lucas's audience perceives that it too forms part of the scene he describes: "Porque de repente fue como si todos nos encontráramos en el campo, junto al río, en la arboleda, siguiendo a pocos pasos a . . . Eloísa" [Because suddenly it was as if we were all in the countryside, next to the river, in the grove, following a few steps behind . . . Eloísa] (72). The clause *como si*, used commonly to express contrary-to-fact situations, clearly adumbrates the fictional quality of events.[23] Curiously, within the narrator's account of Lucas's fictionalization, Eloísa's expertise with the diabolo appears in theatrical terms: "En ocasiones la exhibición era todavía más espectacular" [At times the exhibition was even more spectacular] (72). Furthermore, those who witnessed these events found it hard to believe what they had seen. Lucas adds several ostensibly imaginary layers to his narration, momentarily muddling the distinction between reality and fiction. Yet the framework emerges when Lucas's laughter brings the narrator back "bruscamente a la realidad" [brusquely to reality] (73). Lucas's magical manipulation of Eloísa's daughter augments her antipathy towards him because his powerful narration has deceived and disempowered her. What remains central to the present discussion is the foregrounding of textual strategies. While the narrator resists attempts to control her, she apparently considers it perfectly legitimate to create fictions to achieve her own ends. In fact, the narrator's exploration of her relationship to the other novelistic characters is ultimately based on power and at times reminds readers of Calderón's Autor who boldly states to his characters, "Justicia distributiva / soy, y sé lo que os conviene" [As justice distributive / What suits you best I discern] (vv. 377–78).

It is not surprising that *El columpio* scrutinizes the problematics associated with composition, particularly the relationship between author, text, and reader. This issue becomes most apparent through Lucas, the expert and accomplished chef who meticulously describes the best way to prepare "liebre del valle" [valley hare]. In addition to mentioning other animals worthy of his culinary talents, all within his peculiar understanding of "el arte maravilloso del buen conversar" [the marvelous art of good conversation] (34), the uncle—in his role as cook—never gets beyond the enumeration of the essential ingredients. The adjective *maravilloso* openly suggests the pronounced fictional character of Lucas's discourse, and the narrator pursues the metafictional metaphor as she spies on him through a Venetian blind. Apparently he speaks to himself while pacing back and forth into her view, and she speculates that he rehearses a difficult theatrical role (50–51). She later ascertains that, instead of practicing for the stage, Lucas is rehearsing his book of recipes titled *Juegos del valle* [Valley Games].[24] Furthermore, he envisions an innovative text: "Nunca en el mundo se había escrito un libro como aquél, ni—y ahí radicaba su originalidad—jamás podría leerlo. Obra y autor iban permanentemente unidos, formando un algo indisoluble" [Never in the world had a book like that been written, nor—and that was its originality—could it ever be read. Work and author were permanently united, forming an indissoluble entity] (65). Lucas aspires to create a book resembling an impenetrable archive to which only he may acquire access through a variety of systems that would frustrate any plagiarist's attempts to claim *Juegos del valle* as his own. In an age where the unauthorized appropriation of all kinds of artistic material has become commonplace, Lucas decides to block access to his text.[25] Ironically, the "dueño del valle" [lord of the valley] cannot sleep due to frequent nightmares in which "su libro aparecía impreso, perfectamente encuadernado, pulcramente editado... y firmado por otro" [his book appeared in print, perfectly bound, neatly published . . . and signed by someone else] (66). Accordingly, he defends his text from potential thieves by fashioning "fichas apócrifas" [apocryphal cards] (66) to throw them—and readers—off track, beginning with the very title of his work. In his efforts to thwart the reading process, it becomes patently clear that the word—either in spoken or in written form—functions primarily as a tool of control. As such, Lucas's postmodern cookbook subverts the traditional concept of text as vehicle for openly transmitting knowledge. The "dueño del valle" attempts to ensure his textual authority by locking information away in his mind in a fashion that recalls the hiding of Eloísa's letters in "arcones viejos" [old trunks], even though the narrator finally succeeds in accessing the discourse of her mother. Lucas's efforts to create false leads, detours, and shortcuts to *Juegos del valle* eventually confound and lead him and readers to a labyrinth.[26]

The constant presence of allusions to various forms of games and game-playing throughout *El columpio* serves to liken most adults to children. In the opening pages of the text, Eloísa continuously evokes for her daughter the way she, Tomás, Lucas, and Bebo entertained each other. The narrator's initial contact with her uncles clearly highlights this aspect of the text. As she approaches the town square en route to their house, a bicycle bell rings out: "Alguien estaba dando vueltas a la plaza haciéndolo sonar con insistencia. *Supuse que era un crío,* pero al volverme sólo vi a un hombretón de edad indefinida" [Someone was circling the square ringing it insistently. *I assumed it was a kid,* but as I turned around I only saw a big man of indefinite age] (20, emphasis added). The narrating daughter pursues the metaphor when describing how the cyclist stands on his seat, pulls wheelies and cheers himself on with " 'Bien, bien, bien' " ["Nice, nice, nice"] (20). After zigzagging toward her, he stops childishly, "Con brusquedad" [Abruptly] (22), and introduces himself as Uncle Tomás. During her stay she gradually comprehends that her relatives remain fixated in an almost childlike state: they do nothing to earn a wage. Instead, they live off the wealth accumulated from a lucrative real estate transaction, the "Raquels" keep house for them, and Tomás and Bebo frequently exhibit a pronounced de-

gree of simplicity seldom associated with wealthy, worldly adults. Of
special importance to the present analysis is the amount of creativity
and control associated with "Un universo que empezaba y terminaba ahí. . . . Juegos y más juegos, y siempre los mismos participantes: ellos cuatro" [A universe that began and ended there. . . .
Games and more games, and always the same participants: the four
of them] (96). In one patently self-conscious passage all adults have
been eliminated, expelled, or ignored by the four children. In a
sense they inhabit a paradisiacal world tucked away in the Pyrenees
Mountains.[27] Although Eloísa has died, Tomás, Lucas, and Bebo
demonstrate special admiration for her childhood portrait depicting her with a diabolo, alluding to her exceptional, sometimes excessive and even cruel use of the toy. Despite Eloísa's absence, the
narrator recognizes her enduring importance and conjectures that
her mother's signature is inextricably linked to the diabolo: " 'Nada
ha cambiado. Para vosotros ni siquiera he crecido. Sigo siendo la de
siempre. Eloísa. Vuestra Eloísa' " ["Nothing has changed. For all of
you I haven't even grown up. I remain the same person as always.
Eloísa. Your Eloísa"] (56). Indeed, Lucas underscores the connection when stating that "Eloísa sin su diábolo no es Eloísa" [Eloísa
without her diabolo isn't Eloísa] (31). Clearly the uncles prefer to
live in the past, to remain in an eternally puerile state and to render
homage to her memory. Fictionalization permits childlike characters to eschew the present in El columpio.

As its title suggests, El columpio continuously presents narrative
events from a ludic and shifting perspective. Allusions to works in
progress, for example Lucas's Juegos del valle, highlight the debate
surrounding the dynamics among author, text, and reader, thus
bringing to mind Patricia Waugh's argument in Metafiction that textual composition is foregrounded as the most problematic feature
of a literary work.[28] The narrator frequently addresses strategies concerning the heroic presentation of characters on the world stage
who rebel against narrative models—the fairy tale, oral history,
letter writing—or novelistic devices. The centripetal discourse that
abounds with terminology related to performance and textual
actualization also functions to scrutinize the fictional process. Much
like Daniel in El año de Gracia, the narrator returns home at the
conclusion of the novel with a greater degree of maturity and sophis-
tication acquired through her artistic sensibility. While Daniel com-
pletes his diary, the nameless narrator of El columpio places even
greater emphasis on the acquisition of strategies that frustrate other

characters' wishes to dominate her. Exploration of this process in Fernández Cubas's second novel yields a relentlessly self-conscious text.

NOTES

1. Cristina Fernández Cubas, *Mi hermana Elba y Los altillos de Brumal* (Barcelona: Tusquets, 1988), 36. Subsequent citations will include the page number in parentheses.

2. Cristina Fernández Cubas, *Con Agatha en Estambul* (Barcelona: Tusquets, 1994), 229, 195, 175. Subsequent citations will include the page number in parentheses.

3. Janet Pérez, "Cristina Fernández Cubas: Narrative Unreliability and the Flight from Clarity, or, the Quest for Knowledge in the Fog," *Hispanófila* 122 (January 1998): 29–39; José Ortega, "La dimensión fantástica en los cuentos de Fernández Cubas," *Monographic Review/Revista Monográfica* 8 (1992): 157–63.

4. Cristina Fernández Cubas, *El columpio* (Barcelona: Tusquets, 1995), 14. Subsequent citations will include the page number in parentheses.

5. See Jessica A. Folkart, "Desire, Doubling, and Difference in Cristina Fernández Cubas's *El ángulo del horror*," *Revista Canadiense de Estudios Hispánicos* 24:2 (Winter 2000): 343–62. Folkart concludes that "doubles and differences collide and repel, gazes are imposed and inverted, words and images capriciously twist toward multiple interpretations, all in a kaleidoscopic array of overlays and contradictions that displace the priority of any single angle of vision and subvert the illusion of a unitary, superior subject" (360).

6. Readers witness a similar process in *El año de Gracia*, where Daniel manipulates Grock with periodic readings from Biblical scripture (Cristina Fernández Cubas, *El año de Gracia* [Barcelona: Tusquets, 1985], 137). Subsequent citations will include the page number in parentheses. In Robinsonian fashion, Daniel becomes king of his "dominios" [domain] and lays bare the creative process. It is also noteworthy that the uncles in *El columpio* live apart from everyone else, almost in an insular sense.

7. This aspect of Fernández Cubas's fiction has been noted by Spires who observes that the author's writing, particularly *El ángulo del horror*, "reverses the Cervantine theme of 'la razón de la sinrazón' to 'la sinrazón de la razón'" ["the sanity of insanity" to "the insanity of sanity"] (Robert C. Spires, "Postmodernism/Paralogism: *El ángulo del horror* by Cristina Fernández Cubas," *Journal of Interdisciplinary Literary Studies* 7:2 [1995]: 243).

8. See Kathleen M. Glenn, "Narrative Designs in Cristina Fernández Cubas's 'Mundo,'" *Romance Languages Annual* 9 (1997): 501–4. Glenn comments that "[s]torytelling, in oral as well as in written form, and an interest in problems of communication have been constants of Fernández Cubas's fiction" (504). See also Ana Rueda, "Cristina Fernández Cubas: Una narrativa de voces extinguidas," *Monographic Review/Revista Monográfica* 4 (1988): 257–67, who argues that Fernández Cubas's short fiction "develops agilely, affected—willfully or not—by the fluidity that characterizes oral storytelling" (266).

9. Letters figure in a number of the stories collected in *Mi hermana Elba y Los altillos de Brumal:* "El reloj de Bagdad" [The Clock from Baghdad, 125], "Los altillos de Brumal" (162–63), "La noche de Jezabel" [The Night of Jezebel, 193], "El provocador de imágenes" [The Image Maker, 89–90], and "Mi hermana Elba" (74–75), as well as in *El año de Gracia* (32).

10. See Catherine G. Bellver, "*El año de Gracia* and the Displacement of the Word," *Studies in Twentieth Century Literature* 16:2 (1992): 221–32. Her observation concerning the author's first novel also applies to *El columpio*: "All formal systems of communication fail" (225).

11. See Kathleen M. Glenn, "Conversación con Cristina Fernández Cubas," *Anales de la Literatura Española Contemporánea* 18 (1993): 353–63. In this interview Fernández Cubas comments on the implied receptor of narration: "Naturalmente no escribo para mí misma. El hecho de narrar algo indica, ya de por sí, un deseo de comunicación. Ahora bien, esa presencia del lector, si es que existe, no tiene para mí un rostro ni más características definidas" [Naturally I don't write for myself. The fact of narrating something indicates, in itself, a desire for communication. Nevertheless, that reader's presence, if he exists, doesn't have a face or definite characteristics] (356).

12. For Rueda, all of Fernández Cubas's fiction deals with "how to control representation in order to maintain power" (201).

13. Similarly, Daniel consciously works for an invitation to sail on the *Providence*: "Sólo precisaré que empleé mis argucias a fondo, eché mano de cuatro banalidades de efecto comprobado y acudí, como siempre, a mi infantil ostentación de conocimientos combinada con restos de timidez y una auténtica curiosidad por las características del barco y la utilidad de algunos aparejos" [I'll only add that I exhausted my sophistry, latched on to four well-proven banalities and resorted, as always, to my infantile ostentation of knowledge combined with traces of shyness and genuine curiosity about the features of the boat and the use of some equipment] (31–32).

14. Robert E. Scholes, *Fabulation and Metafiction* (Urbana: University of Illinois Press, 1979), 3.

15. The Spanish Counter-Reformation gave rise to this highly didactic dramatic form concerned with religious themes. The *auto sacramental* uses allegorical characters such as Youth, Power, Virtue, etc. Pedro Calderón de la Barca, one of the most assiduous users of the form, penned eighty *autos sacramentales.*

16. George W. Brandt, trans. *The Great Stage of the World: An Allegorical Auto Sacramental,* by Pedro Calderón de la Barca (Manchester: Manchester University Press, 1976), vv. 296–98. Subsequent citations will include the verse number in parentheses.

17. Ángel Valbuena Prat, ed., prólogo y notas, *Autos Sacramentales I. La cena del Rey Baltasar, El gran teatro del mundo, La vida es sueño,* by Pedro Calderón de la Barca, 6th ed. (Madrid: Espasa-Calpe, 1972), xlix.

18. Linda Hutcheon, *A Theory of Parody: The Teachings of Twentieth-Century Art Forms* (New York: Routledge, 1988), 16.

19. The author acknowledges her attraction for closed spaces and their temporal ramifications (Glenn, "Conversación," 358–59).

20. Fernández Cubas comments that "[l]a literatura es, entre otras muchas cosas, un juego. Un Gran Juego. Pues, por favor, seamos serios y juguemos a fondo" [Literature is, among many other things, a game. A Great Game. Then, please, let's be serious and play for real] (Ibid., 361).

21. The window also serves as a means to infer multiplicity of perspectives in Fernández Cubas's "La ventana del jardín" [The Garden Window] (*Mi hermana Elba*). In addition, both this short story and *El columpio* share numerous similarities: both narrators employ fictional terms to describe events situated in spaces set apart from the other inhabitants. Likewise, neither the male narrator of "La ventana del jardín" nor the female narrator of *El columpio* successfully give advance notification of their arrival. Both narrators suspect that their hosts are faking. Much like Lucas in *El columpio*, José opens a bottle of champagne to celebrate the narrator's unannounced visit. Furthermore, José and Josefina poorly conceal their joy when their friend declares his intention to leave. At times, José's reiterative speech patterns—"Ya sabes, ya sabes" [You know, you know] (*Mi hermana* 43, 44)—resemble those of Uncle Tomás: "Bien, bien, bien" [Nice, nice, nice] (*El columpio* 20, 22, 36).

22. Daniel, in *El año de Gracia*, continuously recognizes the value of performance in achieving his goals. He therefore uses fictional strategies to make friends with students in Paris, to obtain tío Jean's invitation to sail with him and Naguib on the Providence, and to avoid death by impersonating Grock at the end of the novel.

23. See Pérez, "Narrative Unreliability," particularly 33, for an overview of Fernández Cubas's style.

24. Lucas remotely reminds readers of Adriana in "Los altillos de Brumal" who plans to publish a book of recipes based on letters received from the listeners of her popular radio program dedicated to the culinary arts.

25. Fernández Cubas explores the issue from a somewhat different perspective in "El hemisferio sur" [The Southern Hemisphere] where Clara, the author of best-sellers, declares: "Saben que soy una tramposa deleznable, que mis libros no son más que la transcripción exacta de otros... de los de otra mujer" [They know that I am a slippery trickster, that my books are no more than the exact transcription of others . . . of those by another woman] (*Mi hermana Elba y Los altillos de Brumal*, 142).

26. See Antonia Ferriol-Montano, "De la paranoia a la ternura: Ironía y humor en la novela española posmoderna de los años ochenta: Eduardo Mendoza, Cristina Fernández Cubas y Luis Landero," Ph.D. diss., Pennsylvania State University, 1999. Ferriol-Montano observes that the labyrinth in *El año de Gracia* exists in the character's mind and that the accumulation of information serves to further augment confusion (130). Her comments are equally applicable to Lucas's textual strategies in *El columpio*.

27. Hermetic, almost cloisterlike spaces in the text bring to mind Fernández Cubas's observation that closed spaces have always interested her, principally because life stops, detained in "arcones viejos" (Glenn, "Conversación" 358–59). It is also significant that Eloísa's letters are locked away in the secret drawer of her desk (52). It should not be overlooked that Lucas refers to the writing process in a similar fashion: "Han logrado convertir mi cabeza en un auténtico desván" [They have succeeded in turning my head into a real attic] (65).

28. Patricia Waugh, *Metafiction: The Theory and Practice of Self-Conscious Fiction* (London: Methuen, 1984), 22.

Hermanas de sangre: From Published Play to Made-for-Television Movie

Phyllis Zatlin

THE FAME OF CRISTINA FERNÁNDEZ CUBAS IS BASED ON HER SHORT stories and novels. The publication in 1998 of a play, *Hermanas de sangre* [Blood Sisters], therefore may have come as a surprise to anyone who was unaware of the author's active involvement in theater groups during her college years. The work is surprising in other ways as well. Fernández Cubas's narratives are typically marked by ambiguity and unresolved mysteries; *Hermanas de sangre*, while repeating some familiar themes from the author's fictional world, undertakes a probing search of the past to uncover hidden truths. Although written as a play, the work has not yet been staged; nevertheless, it is reaching audiences in Spain through a movie made for television.

The story of *Hermanas de sangre* centers on the reunion of seven women, now in their forties, who attended Catholic boarding school together as children. The basic situation runs the risk of being unoriginal; the reunion of old classmates as a plot device is hardly new in cinema or theater. Two well-known American examples focusing on women are *The Group* (1966, dir. Sidney Lumet), a film based on the novel by Mary McCarthy, and Wendy Wasserstein's 1977 play, *Uncommon Women and Others*. A total list of class-reunion plays and films would doubtless be long indeed. The underlying structure of *Hermanas de sangre* also holds out the potential pitfall of having static, narrative voices take command as the women remember their common past and recount their individual lives.

Fernández Cubas adroitly avoids both of these pitfalls. Her plot is well calculated to keep her audience in suspense; the anticipated subjects for discussion in a reunion quickly are upstaged by a psychological exploration of repressed guilt. Moreover, her text requires ensemble acting, with constant interaction among the characters rather than individual monologues. As a result, the author has created seven splendid women's roles. Given the relative dearth of good vehicles for women actors, particularly middle-aged ones, it is indeed surprising that this script has not yet received a stage production.[1]

Since the advent of the seventh art, innumerable plays have been made into movies. In her book, *Del escenario a la pantalla*, María Asunción Gómez provides extensive lists of Spanish plays transformed into films from 1907 to 1996, both within Spain and abroad.[2] The cinematic adaptation of successful stage plays continues to be common, but it is quite rare for a playscript that was expressly intended for legitimate theater to reach the screen first.[3] In the case of *Hermanas de sangre*, the Catalan film version, *Germanes de sang* (dir. Jesús Garay, filmscript by Maite Carranza and Teresa Vilardell), was first shown on the big screen in February 2002 at a film festival and was first aired on Spanish television on March 8, 2003.[4]

The setting for Fernández Cubas's gripping psychological suspense tale is a private dining room in a fancy restaurant with adjacent garden. The time is the evening of June 21, both the shortest night of the year and the anniversary of the untimely death years before of their classmate Clara. The secret from the past unfolds scene by scene, building in dramatic intensity. The women do relate in snatches what they have done in the intervening thirty-four years, but at center stage is an enhanced home movie from their last day together at school: a day they have all repressed and reluctantly rediscover in its horrifying details.

Because of memories of being boarding students at a convent school, *Hermanas de sangre* readily recalls one of Fernández Cubas's early stories, "Mi hermana Elba" [My Sister Elba].[5] In the first chapter of her recent collection of autobiographical essays, *Cosas que ya no existen* [Things That No Longer Exist], the author establishes that she personally attended a convent school, one not too distant from her home, where she was a day student rather than a boarder.[6] In *Hermanas de sangre* the convent is located some twenty-five miles from the city, a distance that enhances the girls' isolation and hence the potential for a vicious crime in the woods, well out of sight.[7] In the film version, the convent on a high hill can be seen from the restaurant terrace. It is shown twice, near the beginning and again near the end, in panoramic shots that shift in symbolic value from nostalgic to frightening. That visible location, on the outskirts of the city, is closer to the one described in "Mi hermana Elba": "Se trataba de un colegio grande y hermoso, situado a pocos kilómetros de la ciudad donde vivíamos habitualmente y rodeado de bosques frondosos y jardines de ensueño" [It was a large, beautiful building, located a few miles from the city where we usually lived, and surrounded by shady woods and marvelous gardens] (56–57).[8]

Also consistent with "Mi hermana Elba" and Fernández Cubas's memoirs, is the insistence in *Hermanas de sangre* on the girls' age: eleven. The narrator in the short story celebrates her eleventh birthday during the summer when her parents, anticipating their marital separation, decide to send their two daughters to a convent boarding school. In *Cosas que ya no existen*, the author recalls her unjust punishment at the hands of a tyrannical nun at precisely the same age: "Nótese que he dicho niñas de once años. No *de sólo* once años. Cuando alguien tiene once años, los tiene en su totalidad, en bloque, con todo su peso" [Please note that I said girls who were eleven years old. Not *only* eleven years old. When someone is eleven years old, she is that number of years in their totality, as a block, with all their weight] (20). Fernández Cubas makes the point here that no eleven-year-old would say, "I'm only eleven." In *Germanes de sang*, on the other hand, the mature women from their adult perspective attempt to alleviate their guilt by attributing their beating of Clara to their extreme youth.

As Karen Dinicola suggests in the introduction to her translation of the play, childhood memories shared by the characters in *Hermanas de sangre* have universal appeal, at least for women spectators: "having passed through the traditional rites of girlhood (clubs, cliques, rumors, 'best friends,' etc.) has made me better able to appreciate the dynamics of the play's female protagonists."[9]

In *Cosas que ya no existen*, Fernández Cubas dedicates multiple chapters to Ana María, her beloved oldest sister who died from natural causes at the age of twenty-eight when Cristina was sixteen. She relates as well the family's reaction to that death. The author says that both she and her other sisters had repressed their memories of Ana María and that her ability to recall the past becomes hopelessly weak when she tries to evoke Ana María's image: "Y no me cabe otra explicación: yo *la he borrrado*" [I can find no other explanation: I *have erased her*] (214). Fernández Cubas conjectures in *Cosas que ya no existen* that her bereaved family suffered pangs of guilt at her sister's death: "*Ana María* quería decir tragedia, estupor, mente en blanco. Pero *Ana María*, además, nos enfrentaba a una oscura culpabilidad que no tenía tanto que ver con su muerte, como con el hecho de que, a pesar de todo, los demás siguiéramos vivos" [*Ana*

María meant tragedy, numbness, minds gone blank. But *Ana María* also made us confront a dark guilt that had less to do with her death than with the fact that, in spite of it all, the rest of us were still alive] (228–29).

The characters in *Hermanas de sangre* have used the same psychological defense mechanism, with greater reason, for they took an active role in the events that precipitated the death of Clara—attacked by the convent's guard dogs. A major theme of the play, and of its corresponding film version, is the impact on the women's lives of their secret guilt. *Hermanas de sangre* is a realistic work, but even in her tales within the fantastic mode, Fernández Cubas has consistently provided a skillful, if indirect, psychological interpretation for her characters' actions and unconscious desires.[10]

Dinicola notes that Fernández Cubas also draws indirectly in *Hermanas de sangre* on her own experiences at storing memories. The author recalls a three-story childhood home that contained strange rooms, filled with old objects: "Son como baúles de recuerdos que me han atraído siempre" [They are like trunks of memories that have attracted me always].[11] "It's easy to see how these rooms of unused objects may have come to be reborn in *Hermanas de sangre*'s dominant themes of nostalgia, the workings of memory and the mystery of things forgotten. The play even uses the childhood attic as a metaphor for memory when Luisa, in an attempt to avoid dealing with the painful memory of her role in Clara's death says, 'Lo mejor que podemos hacer es ponerle una funda al recuerdo y arrinconarlo otra vez en el desván'" (130).[12] Fernández Cubas earlier highlighted this attic theme in her 1983 story "Los altillos de Brumal" [The Attics of Brumal].[13]

Fernández Cubas indicates in *Cosas que ya no existen* that she had never previously dared write about Ana María, her sister and friend: "Hoy, la primera vez en mi vida que me atrevo a escribir sobre ella. Ana María. Mi hermana mayor. La amiga muerta" [Today, the first time in my life that I dare to write about her. Ana María. My older sister. The dead friend] (217). While that is doubtless true in any overt sense, there are significant links among the memoirs, "Mi hermana Elba," and *Hermanas de sangre* with respect to the repression of memories of a deceased sister/friend. To evoke Ana María's image in various settings, the author has to imagine her smiling, as she did in family photographs (216). Photographic images are also the trigger to memory in the short story and the play. The narrator in "Mi hermana Elba" reads over "aquella letra infantil plagada de errores" [childish writing filled with errors] from her old diary and examines yellowed photographs; she has no recollection of "el instante o los motivos precisos que me impulsaron a desfigurar, posiblemente con un cortaplumas, una reproducción del rostro de mi hermana Elba" [when and why I felt compelled to take something, probably a penknife, and disfigure the likeness of my sister Elba].[14] In *Hermanas de sangre*, Marga, now a television celebrity, invites her classmates to the reunion with an invitation written on the back of a group photo that none of the others remembers having previously seen. During the dinner, she projects the home movie her father and brother had taken at the festivities marking the close of the school year. The unknown photo is a still taken from that movie.

The still photo functions as a flashback to a time of supposedly innocent happiness that was soon to be lost. In the theater, at the outset the audience will not see the photo unless the director chooses to use it on the program or project it in some fashion when the characters first refer to it. In Fernández Cubas's stage directions, the spectators are given their initial view of the photo when Marga freezes the frame while showing the home movie. From the darkened stage, we hear her commenting that all ten classmates are together in the photo. She then freezes another frame that focuses on a pretty blonde: "Estaba feliz. Fijaos bien porque es una de las últimas imágenes que nos quedan de Clara" [She was happy. Look carefully because this is one of the last images that we have of Clara] (54). The author thus sets up a dramatic contrast between the image of smiling faces and the later scene of violence that culminated in Clara's death.

Fernández Cubas's theatrical strategy here is not unrelated to that of Jaime Salom in *La noche de los cien pájaros* [The Night of the Hundred Birds] (1972), a play that similarly deals with a class reunion, a possible crime, and subsequent regret and guilt.[15] Salom, however, is easily able to bring the relatively recent photo to life for the audience. When the protagonist looks at the picture after his wife's death, the cast members form a tableau and thus act out the flashback.[16] In the film version (1975, dir. Rafael Marchent), a home movie was substituted for the photo. As is also true in *Hermanas de sangre*, both play text and film, the audience for the Marchent movie shares the perspective of the characters in viewing the movie.

Dudley Andrew, in his now-classic commentary, has defined three modes of relation between film adaptations and source text: "borrowing, intersection, and fidelity of transformation."[17] Transformation retains the skeletal story and finds cinematic equivalences for the "original's tone, values, imagery, and rhythm."[18] In the transformation process, it is anticipated that the film director will convert a verbal text to the visual language of the new genre. The audience for *Germanes de sang* is thus able to see clearly the group picture on the invitation in one of the first sequences, when Julia receives hers and tears it up. In a later sequence, the picture has been placed on a restaurant table; another close-up is provided when Julia opts to examine it, focusing in particular on a smiling Clara. In the theater, the home movie-within-the-play will be projected on a screen that faces the audience but does not occupy the entire playing space. The home movie-within-the-movie, however, can coincide with the entire screen, thereby merging the audience's point of view with that of the characters.

Jesús Garay in *Germanes de sang* introduces an additional visual element during the opening titles by presenting individual pictures, in black and white, of the eleven-year-olds. Each child actor is juxtaposed with the name of the adult actor who plays the corresponding role. During the final credits, freeze frames taken from sequences in the movie are used to place each adult actor next to her name. The child actors have posed as well for the home movie and the group still. Beyond the movie-within-the-movie, two of them perform in an added flashback scene in which Aurora awakes from her nightmare and she and Julia comfort each other about their guilty secrets from the previous day's horrible events.

Germanes de sang is not the first film version of a Fernández Cubas text. In 1988, Cristina Andreu directed a movie adaptation of "Los altillos de Brumal." The author collaborated with the director in writing the screenplay. In her insightful analysis of *Brumal*, Kathleen Glenn concludes that the film is remarkably similar to the original story, to the point of transferring some passages in their entirety from page to screen. She finds additions to the source to be fully justified and the transition from verbal to visual to be effective: "*Brumal* exemplifies film's capacity to make people, objects, and places immediate and tangible for us, to transform mental impressions into striking visual images, and to use music to express mood."[19] *Brumal*, however, as Fernández Cubas observes, was Andreu's first feature film and was shot on a low budget.[20] *Germanes de sang*, created under more advantageous circumstances, is much more sophisticated and convincing. Although the author did not collaborate on the script for this cinematic adaptation of *Hermanas de sangre*, basically the television movie is an example of fidelity of transformation.

Fernández Cubas's play calls for a cast of nine: seven reunited classmates and two waiters. In listing the cast, the author describes the women in considerable detail, with attention to their appearance and dress. She gives information on their personal lives and careers, as well as providing preliminary clues as to how several of them have been affected by their suppressed feelings of guilt (21–23). Marga, a domineering, self-assured woman, has achieved fame through a television program that purports to seek the truth (called "La verdad al desnudo" [The Naked Truth] in the play and "Certesas" [Certainties] in the movie). Alicia, an attractive and usually kind woman, is a biologist. Toña is a high school teacher who is given to sarcasm. Luisa is married to a wealthy man twenty years her senior, dabbles in interior decorating, and spares no expense in keeping herself looking young and beautiful. Julia, whose work is never specified, drinks too much. Lali, a stay-at-home wife and mother, suffers from headaches, insomnia, and memory lapses and is addicted to prescription drugs. Montse, a successful divorce lawyer, is divorce-prone herself; she is currently embarked on her third marriage. The script of *Germanes de sang* conforms rigorously to these original characters, who are represented with flair by an outstanding cast.[21]

Far less has been written about transformations from stage to screen than from narrative into film. Nevertheless, a number of theorists have tackled the subject. Gómez provides an excellent overview both of the historical relationship between theater and film and of the accompanying theoretical debates. She concludes that, because cinema is itself a narrative genre, film adaptation of plays is in fact more difficult than adaptation of narrative. The latter merely implies transferring a verbal narrative mode to a visual one. "On the other hand, from a structural point of view, turning dramatic action into narrative requires substantial changes that complicate the adaptor's work. A good adaptation does not consist of mechanical reproduction of the play in question. . . . On the contrary, one should take maximum advantage of the wealth of possibilities of the cinematographic medium."[22] Linda Seger, in *The Art of Adaptation*, has provided a practical guide on how that goal may be accomplished. In choosing a play for film adaptation, she recommends finding a realistic context that can be opened up, a story line that can be developed, and cinematic images to give expression to the human themes.[23] Garay's movie illustrates well these recommendations.

Hermanas de sangre is divided into a long first act and a short second act. The principal set is the private dining room. The second act takes place on the adjacent terrace with its view of the starlit sky and the city below. Space in *Germanes de sang* has been opened up to include a variety of exterior and interior locations. In addition to different aspects of the outside of the restaurant and grounds and several rooms inside the building, there are exterior and interior shots of the hospital where Aurora is under care. The camera takes us to the apartments of Julia and Marga. When Marga calls Alicia, there are cross-cut shots between the former's television studio and the latter's home.

Equally predictable in film transformations of plays is the visible presence of additional characters, some of whom may have been mentioned in the dramatic text without appearing on stage. In the play, Marga alludes to a woman secretary who efficiently solves the busy star's problems; in the film, we see Marga interacting with two equally efficient male assistants. Fernández Cubas's text indicates that a wedding reception is also taking place at the restaurant. In *Germanes de sang*, sounds and sights from the festive wedding celebration are juxtaposed, often in dramatic contrast, with the women's reunion. In the play, the audience is to hear, from offstage, a tenor singing at the wedding. In the film, the singer is a noted baritone who has been interviewed by Marga on television and insists upon coming to entertain the women at their reunion. Fernández Cubas has Marga tell the others that Aurora has suffered a stroke and now believes that she is ten-and-a-half years old. Carranza and Vilardell write Aurora into the filmscript. In the opening sequences, at the request of Aurora's distraught husband, Marga goes to visit her old classmate. Following a serious automobile accident, Aurora not only now believes that she is a child but that she must call the police about the murder of Clara. It is Aurora who reminds Marga about the home movie and who serves as the catalyst for the subsequent action. Aurora's expanded role, as well as certain related changes that I shall discuss later, does not, in Andrew's terms, run counter to the "original's tone, values, imagery, and rhythm" but rather represents the kind of development of story line that Seger recommends.

Seger calls for the introduction of cinematic images to express the human themes. At several points, Fernández Cubas's stage directions indicate the sound of barking dogs. Because Clara, after being repeatedly kicked and then abandoned by her classmates, had been mauled to death by the convent's guard dogs, the auditory leitmotif will symbolize the young girl's horrifying death and her classmates' repressed guilt. In Garay's film, no dogs are heard barking in the vicinity of the restaurant. On the other hand, there is a visual leitmotif of red stains against pure white backgrounds: Julia spills nail polish on her lover's shirt; children at the wedding throw strawberries at a couple they catch kissing and stain the man's shirt; at the dinner, Marga is upset by a red splotch she gets on her skirt. The bloodlike red stains, like the guilty memories, mar previous purity and are difficult, if not impossible, to remove.

Other expansions of characters' roles and story lines in *Germanes de sang* are less predictable but may be seen as ways of filling gaps in the theatrical text. In the play, Julia states that she moves frequently. In the film, the audience learns that her whole life is provisional. She cannot bring herself to unpack her boxes and she cannot commit to her relationship with Sergi, a young violinist. In both play and movie, Luisa comes to the reunion but leaves abruptly, claiming that her mother-in-law has just been hospitalized. Because Luisa and Marga have almost identical purses, Luisa inadvertently goes off with Marga's—a purse that contains a hidden tape recorder. When she later returns, several of the other women discover the recorder and play the tape, thereby learning that Luisa has been at a love tryst, not a hospital. In the play, the usually gentle Alicia turns violent and destroys the tape without specific explanation. In the film, we learn that she has just discovered that Luisa's lover is her own husband. The most significant changes to the source text, however, come in the role of Marga.

In "Cristina Fernández Cubas: Narrative Unreliability and the Flight from Clarity, or, the Quest for Knowledge in the Fog," Janet Pérez affirms that the author's tales mystify the reader when the narrator relates "first-person, subjective perceptions" and equally so when the point of view shifts "to the supposedly objective perceptions or conversations of others."[24] Among the multiplicity of reasons why it is impossible to confirm information in the various stories is the lapse of decades between the time when the events occurred and the fictional present.[25] Even though outer masks may be torn away from characters, it is never clear if what lies beneath is a real identity, another mask, or a hallucination.

Contrary to these tales, *Hermanas de sangre* centers on Marga's professional dedication to seeking the naked truth. In the dramatic world, her role is related to that of Oedipus: she feels impelled to investigate step by step the crime from long ago and find out who was guilty of the murder. Ultimately, like Oedipus, the name she uncovers is her own. But Marga is not a tragic hero with a single flaw. In addition to her arrogant pride, she is guilty of being manipulative and deceitful, and, like her classmates, has at least partially suppressed the horrible secret of Clara's death. In the film version, the negative aspects of Marga's role in past events are expanded but build on the elements already present in the source text.

Fernández Cubas makes frequent use of metafictional/metatheatrical devices in her narratives. In "Mi hermana Elba," for example, the narrator's memories are triggered by her old diary, a text-within-the-text, and she recalls her deliberate role-playing as a child and teenager. In *Hermanas de sangre*, the characters also react to texts-within-the-text: the black-and-white home movie of the girls' performance as tarantulas; the notebook, which Lali brings to the reunion, from their secret "Club de las Tarántulas"; a mysterious note, written in childish handwriting and signed "Clara," that is delivered during the reunion and that temporarily makes some of them hope that Clara, in fact, is still alive.

Significantly, several of the women have built their lives on role-playing. Toña finally confesses that she attended the convent school on a scholarship and had been obliged to study hard and do chores for the nuns, including keeping an eye on her classmates; she had always hidden her feelings of inferiority and alienation from the group. Luisa, who has learned to lie with ease, invents and then embellishes the story of her sick mother-in-law as a cover for her adulterous love affair. Marga has created her persona as a seeker of truth but has "enhanced"—that is, manipulated—the home movie to foreground the legs of those stomping on Clara's prone body. Montse quickly adopts her role as lawyer to challenge the validity of the evidence.

When Lionel Abel coined the term "metatheatre," he also defined the concept of the "would-be dramatist," a character who attempts to impose his or her script on others.[26] Marga is a would-be dramatist par excellence, as Toña astutely realizes: "Y que durante gran parte de esta velada ha hecho con nosotras lo que le ha venido en gana. Nada más sencillo. Sólo ella conocía el guión. Pero a partir de un momento, y gracias a la puntual intervención de Julia, Marga ha perdido todos los papeles" [And for a large part of this evening, she's done whatever she wanted with us. Nothing could have been simpler. She alone knew the script. But thanks to Julia's timely intervention a moment ago, Marga's script is out the window] (97–98).

Julia subverts Marga's desired text in two ways. Marga counted on Julia's "objective" reaction to the evidence, and hence her allegiance with Marga, because the latter erroneously believes that Julia left the convent grounds early and was not part of the assault on Clara. After identifying her legs in the movie and thus confessing her role, Julia stuns them with the note signed "Clara" precisely to undo Marga's control: "Pensé que si lograba sorprender a Marga como ella nos había sorprendido a nosotras, si conseguía, tal como habéis adivinado, apartarla de su guión de hierro, podía venirse abajo. Y confesar" [I thought that if I managed to surprise Marga as she surprised us, if I could separate her from her iron script, she might fold and confess] (107). The other characters also not only break away from Marga's script but proceed to impose theirs, including their own search for truth.

In Fernández Cubas's play, Marga is gradually unmasked. Montse skillfully challenges the validity of the evidence, establishing that the home movie and their initial reactions have been manipulated. Lali, whose poor memory and other psychological problems are alleviated by airing the repressed secret, suddenly remembers the whoppers Marga told as a child: that her family had a palatial home in Southern France and that Kirk Douglas's son was in love with her (89). As the women question what Clara had done in violation of the Tarantula code that compelled them to punish her, they trace the cause to stories invented by Marga. They were all upset that they had forgotten their lines and that Clara, in "saving" the show, had upstaged them, but to the pain of their botched performance were added the rumors that Clara had cheated Toña out of the annual writing prize and that she had sabotaged Alicia's collection of worms. It appears that Marga, by examining closely the vague background action in the home movie, discovered a chilling scene of children taking revenge.[27] She had not played a role in the scene herself and apparently had suppressed any memory of her indirect guilt as the person who precipitated the beating. How a weakened Clara fell prey to the dogs is left unclarified. The women experience catharsis, and the play ends with their reconciliation.

Germanes de sang, Garay's film adaptation, includes all of the story line and characterizations cited above but amplifies them. He zooms in on Marga's tendency toward role-playing and deceit from the beginning. She is openly portrayed as a habitual liar. In an early sequence, we see her visiting Aurora; at the reunion, she informs her friends that she could not bring herself to see the ill woman. She tells her cinematography assistant, who has enhanced the old home movie for her that she needs it for her program, but the spectators already know the link between the film and the reunion with her classmates. On occasion she smiles graciously at people who request her autograph, then sneers as she turns away; we see her ordering other people about, then flashing a smile to soften her domineering tone. This "flicker" acting readily reveals Marga's underlying hypocrisy. Her public image contrasts notably with her appearance at home when she looks for the forgotten movie; without professional make-up and hairdo, she is obviously a different person.

In both play and television movie, Marga's penchant for deceit is paralleled by that of Luisa, but *Germanes de sang* reveals the trait with greater emphasis. Fernández Cubas's text alludes to the cosmetic surgery and other treatments that Luisa has undergone to appear younger than her classmates; the role of Luisa will be cast accordingly. In the film, but not the source, she is carrying on an affair with the husband of her childhood friend. She is so accustomed to role-playing and lying that she remains unfazed when it is obvious that Alicia has found out. But her creative bent and acting skills go beyond Marga's. Luisa, too, has visited Aurora and knows that Marga had previously been there. Marga's response to Aurora's obsession with Clara's murder is to declare that Aurora is hopelessly confused. Luisa's solution is to capitalize on her dyed blonde hair to convince Aurora that she is Clara, alive and well.

Playwright José Luis Alonso de Santos has stated that in movies the action is what counts, but in theater what underlies the action may be more important. He observes that spectators leaving a play may ask what did it mean, while movie audiences are more likely to ask what happened.[28] Like light comedy, movies—particularly ones aimed at a popular audience—tend to have closed endings that provide ready answers about what happened. Serious drama, on the other hand, may leave enough matters unresolved to force the spectator to think. At the core of Seger's advice on adapting for the screen is the desirability of having likable protagonists, scenes of reconciliation, and happy endings. To a certain degree, the transformation from *Hermanas de sangre*, the play, to *Germanes de sang*, the movie, goes in the opposite direction of this conventional wisdom.

At the end of Fernández Cubas's play, the other women are prepared to forgive Marga for coercing their confessions with the doctored home movie. Moreover, they are more forgiving with themselves now that they have finally brought the repressed secret to the surface. The audience has every reason to believe that they will never forget Clara and that the memory of her will bring them together for other reunions. The play concludes with a scene of reconciliation among the old classmates, juxtaposed with laughter from the wedding reception.

There is no comparable final scene in the film adaptation, in large part because Marga's role in Clara's death is far greater. In both play and film, several of the women recall a rustling in the leaves that frightened them, thereby causing them to stop the beating and run away. No explanation for the rustling is given in the play. In *Germanes de sang*, the women surmise that Marga was able to enhance the home movie as she did because she had, in fact, witnessed the scene: it must have been she, not her brother, who filmed the final moments, and she must have parted the branches, intending to join her friends before she saw what was happening. Their conjecture leads directly into the substance of Aurora's continuing anguish and desire to call the police.

In both play and movie, Julia did not leave the convent grounds in her father's car. Instead, she stayed in order to go home with Aurora. Thus Julia was with the group that attacked Clara and was witness to Aurora's nightmare. In the play, there is no definitive explanation for how the penned-up dogs were able to attack Clara. In the flashback sequence of *Germanes de sang*, Aurora reveals to Julia that she saw Marga open the pen and unsuccessfully begged her to close it before the dogs got loose. In the present, Marga says in her defense that she let the dogs out to protect her friends; the dogs, not the girls, would be blamed for the assault on Clara.

Although the film version intentionally fills gaps in the play script, moviegoers will leave the theater with questions on why certain things happened and what lies ahead. The underlying reason for Marga's organizing the reunion has changed somewhat. In the play, she seems merely to have a malicious desire to get at the truth, thereby having a laugh at her classmates' expense. In the movie, once she realizes that Aurora's ravings could become a threat, there is an implied effort on her part to convince her classmates of their guilt so that they will say nothing incriminating against her. Marga's self-interest is the catalyst for the evening get-together, but Julia forces a radical revision of the script.

In her 1994 story "Con Agatha en Estambul" [With Agatha in Istanbul], Cristina Fernández Cubas openly revealed her interest in Agatha Christie, both as writer of mysteries and as a person whose psychological motivation for events in her own life might never be known.[29] In *Hermanas de sangre*, she creates her own compelling whodunit with an accompanying rich exploration of the mysteries of the human psyche. This drama represents a new dimension in her work and, even before reaching the stage, enriches her reputation as a multifaceted author. While we await a theatrical premiere of *Hermanas de sangre*, Jesús Garay's excellent film transformation, *Germanes de sang*, will provide television audiences with the opportunity to become better acquainted with one of contemporary Spain's most fascinating writers.

NOTES

1. According to Fernández Cubas, *Hermanas de sangre* was given a staged reading by a university group in Spain shortly after the play was published; a precontract has been signed with the Sociedad General de Autores y Editores for a potential professional production in Barcelona (personal interview, May 29, 2000). Karen Denise Dinicola's English translation, *Blood Sisters*, presented as a masters thesis in translation at Rutgers, The State University of New Jersey, in April 2000 has been circulated to several directors in the United States and in France, the latter through Parisian literary agent Geneviève Ulmann. Professor Steve Hunt, at Converse College in Spartanburg, South Carolina, has scheduled a performance of the text in late spring 2004 as a joint production of his theater department and a community group.

2. María Asunción Gómez, *Del escenario a la pantalla. La adaptación cinematográfica del teatro español* (Chapel Hill: North Carolina Studies in the Romance Languages and Literatures, 2000), 198–217. Gómez concentrates on film adaptations per se. In Spain it has been common for stage plays to be filmed in the theater and then aired on television in their original versions.

Film adaptations of stage plays are, of course, not limited to Spain. Citing from a 1998 article in *Variety*, James Naremore, in the introduction to *Film Adaptation*, indicates that, in addition to the 20 percent of American films the previous year that were adaptations of books, another 20 percent "were derived from plays, sequels, remakes, television shows, and magazine or newspaper articles" (*Film Adaptation*, ed. James Naremore [New Brunswick, N.J.: Rutgers University Press, 2000], 10).

3. In Spain the worlds of theater, cinema, and television are not clearly separated; many playwrights, directors, and actors move freely from one medium to another. It is therefore possible that an author might explore more than one avenue for a particular story idea. In general terms, however, plays have been staged first and adapted as movies later. The only other example I can recall of an unstaged, published play appearing first as a film is José María Rodríguez Méndez's *Flor de Otoño* [Autumn Flower]. Written in 1972 and published in 1974, the play was made

into the 1977 movie *Un hombre llamado "Flor de Otoño"* (dir. Pedro Olea) and then staged in 1982 (dir. Antonio Díaz Zamora). Also exceptional are movies that are later adapted as stage plays. Two examples in Spain of that counter movement are Fermín Cabal's 1992 stage version of Pedro Almodóvar's 1983 movie *Entre tinieblas* [Dark Habits] and Bernardo Sánchez's highly successful stage version of Berlanga and Azcona's 1963 movie *El verdugo* [The Executioner], which was the surprise hit of the 1999–2000 Madrid theater season.

4. A Massa d'Or Production (executive producers Isona Passola and Lluís Ferrando), *Germanes de sang* [Hermanas de sangre] was filmed in Barcelona in June–July 2001 for Televisió de Catalunya and Via Digital. First produced in Catalan, it was then dubbed to Castilian Spanish for broadcast nationally (Fernández Cubas, personal letter August 2001). The schedule for broadcast, however, was in the reverse order: first in Castilian on Via Digital and then in Catalan (personal interview, May 31, 2002). In my essay, on occasion I use the Catalan film title to distinguish the movie version from the original source with its Castilian title. Although I know of no plans to show this particular film in movie theaters, it is not uncommon in Spain for movies to be coproduced by television channels and be shown in both kinds of venues. In his introduction to *Film Adaptation*, Naremore regrets that his anthology includes no "writings about made-for-television adaptations or about the relation between television and theatrical film" (11). In the case of *Germanes de sang*, I believe differences between the two forms would be negligible.

5. "Mi hermana Elba" was first published in 1980 and reprinted in 1988. Page references are to the later edition: *Mi hermana Elba y Los altillos de Brumal* (Barcelona: Tusquets, 1988).

6. *Cosas que ya no existen* (Barcelona: Lumen, 2001), 17–32. Although these autobiographical essays were published after *Hermanas de sangre*, the author states that she began writing them in 1994 (11). Because the two books were in development at about the same time, I find it reasonable to assume that Fernández Cubas's exploration of her own repressed memories of her deceased sister influenced the perceptive psychological analysis of her characters.

7. ALICIA: "Mi hija nunca ha entendido cómo pudimos estudiar internas en un colegio. A cuarenta y tantos kilómetros de aquí" [My daughter has never understood how we could be boarding school students. More than 40 kilometers from here] (*Hermanas de sangre* [Barcelona: Tusquets, 1998], 46). Subsequent references to this work will be cited parenthetically in the text. Unless otherwise indicated, all translations are my own.

8. "My Sister Elba," translated by Phyllis Zatlin, *Student Short Story International* 52 (1993): 47.

9. Dinicola, introduction to *Blood Sisters*, 3.

10. Early studies of Fernández Cubas, including my own, tended to emphasize the elements of the Fantastic and the Gothic in her narrative. It is my position that her third collection of stories, *El ángulo del horror* (Barcelona: Tusquets, 1990), departed from those modes and hence foregrounded her skills at psychological fiction. See my "Beyond the Fantastic: New Tales from Fernández Cubas" in *Hers Ancient and Modern: Women's Writing in Spain and Brazil*, ed. Catherine Davies and Jane Whetnall (Manchester: University of Manchester Spanish and Portuguese Studies, 1997), 73–86.

11. Quoted by Kathleen M. Glenn, "Conversación con Cristina Fernández

Cubas," *Anales de la Literatura Española Contemporánea* 18 (1993): 359. Translation is Dinicola's.

12. Dinicola, introduction to *Blood Sisters*, 4. Here is her translation of the quoted line from the play: "The best thing we can do is throw a tarp over the memory and put it back up in the attic" (*Blood Sisters*, 130).

13. The English title is the one I used in my published translation of this story: "The Attics of Brumal," *Short Story International* 80 (June 1990): 53–75.

14. "Mi hermana Elba," 53–54; "My Sister Elba," 45.

15. Salom's title is derived from the Spanish proverb, "Más vale pájaro en mano que cien volando"; the nearest English equivalent: "A bird in the hand is worth two in the bush." I have not asked Fernández Cubas if she is familiar with the Salom play, but she would have had several opportunities to see it. It was first staged in Salom's native Barcelona in 1973 and toured widely in Catalunya in the early 1970s. In 1982 it was broadcast on Spanish television ("Teatro de TVE," dir. Antonio Chic), featuring a cast of such well-known Catalan actors as Pau Garsaball, Enric Majó, and Rosa M.ª Sardá. Perhaps not coincidentally, the catalyst for the protagonist's infatuation with "the hundred flying birds," his concomitant change of attitude toward his wife, and his desire for her death stem from his attendance at a class reunion that makes him conscious of his lack of material success in life.

16. Salom, *La noche de los cien pájaros/Los delfines* (Madrid: Espasa-Calpe, 1973), 19.

17. Andrew, *Concepts in Film Theory* (Oxford: Oxford University Press, 1984), 98.

18. Ibid., 100. By Andrew's definitions, intersection leaves the original text unassimilated. At the other extreme, borrowings appropriate the form or idea of a prior work and then adapt freely. Andrew focuses on narrative rather than theater; using his definitions, televised stage plays might be considered intersections.

19. Glenn, "Back to Brumal: Fiction and Film," *Romance Languages Annual* 4 (1992): 464.

20. Fernández Cubas, personal interview, May 29, 2000.

21. The cast members, in alphabetical order as they appear in the titles, and the roles they play are: Carme Elías (Luisa), Pepa López (Montse), Rosa Novell (Toña), Vicky Peña (Aurora), Fina Rius (Lali), Mireia Ros (Alicia), Assumpta Serna (Marga), and Emma Vilarasau (Julia). I shall clarify the role of Aurora later in this study.

22. Gómez, *Del escenario a la pantalla*, 51.

23. Seger, *The Art of Adaptation: Turning Fact and Fiction into Film* (New York: Holt, 1992), 42.

24. Pérez, "Cristina Fernández Cubas: Narrative Unreliability and the Flight from Clarity, or, the Quest for Knowledge in the Fog," *Hispanófila* 122 (January 1998): 31.

25. Ibid., 33.

26. Abel, *Metatheatre. A New View of Dramatic Form* (New York: Hill and Wang, 1963).

27. The hidden truth that emerges from staring at the photographic record is reminiscent of *Blow-Up*, Michelangelo Antonioni's 1966 film based on Julio Cortázar's short story, "Las babas del diablo."

28. Alonso de Santos, "De la escritura dramática a la escritura cinematográfica," *Cine y Literatura*, monographic issue of *República de las Letras* 54 (1997): 82.

29. In her tale, Fernández Cubas alludes to the real Agatha Christie's temporary disappearance and sets the action in Christie's favorite hotel in Istanbul, the Pera Palace. This is the title story in *Con Agatha en Estambul* (Barcelona: Tusquets, 1994).

Narrating the Self and the Contingencies of Memory in *Cosas que ya no existen*

David K. Herzberger

CONTEMPORARY LITERATURE OFTEN SEEMS TO EFFACE THE PAST, OR TO evoke it only to show its vulnerability to the contingencies of narration and memory. This does not suggest a diminished preoccupation with the past or with the flow of time in general among writers, but rather a wariness of how time is represented and given meaning. If the past exists as a scattering of vanished events in much contemporary narrative, it is because writers perceive it as patches of oblivion that need to be shaped and filled in. If memory seeks to define these patches from the perspective of the present, it faces an impermeable resistance: matters of ethics, agency, aesthetics, and psychology, to name only a few, coalesce to defy both the desire and need of writers to bring the past into clear focus. Writing the past thus becomes not only a process of remembering with clarity what has grown blurred over time, but of imagining a story with narrative proficiency able to relate what has been remembered.[1]

Storytelling seems often to get in the way of drawing the past into the present, with writers vexed by the slippery referentiality of their texts and readers unable to anchor themselves solidly to the artifice of worlds created and sustained by language. In *Cosas que ya no existen* [Things That No Longer Exist] (2001), Cristina Fernández Cubas's fragmented autobiographical exploration of parts of her youth, the author clearly recognizes the perplexities of writing about the past but eschews the possibility that it is unavailable to her through cognition and narration.[2] This is not to say that she offers an ingenuous recounting of her life, with a dogged insistence on immutable truth and accuracy as she follows the wavering lines of her memory. What is critical to her project, however, is asserted as the engendering tension of her writing: the awareness that parts of her past can be recollected through traces discovered or imagined in the present, countered by the recognition that other parts of her past have disappeared from both consciousness and comprehension and thus defy stories that the author would tell about them. Amid this tension, Fernández Cubas desires to make her life accessible and meaningful by representing it within and as narration.

Cosas que ya no existen thus emerges from the disquietude of loss commingled with the pleasure of recovery, both of which pertain to the composition of the writer's self as it grows from the unfolding of the narrative discourse. The self emerges as a central component of Fernández Cubas's writing not simply as the product of a story in which a first-person narrator (either real or fictional) tells about things from the past in the present. More importantly, the author's manifest desire to explore things that once existed and mattered in her life outside of the present time, is now reconnected to her perception of herself through the creation of a text. As a result, her intention to represent the past creates an ethical bond among her emergent identity, her role as narrator, and references to the real within her discourse.

This bond grows from Fernández Cubas's reflections in the prologue of *Cosas* on the insidious imbrication of the real and the imagined in her previous works of fiction. She had come to believe that the real was intruding upon the imagined to such an extent that the blurring of the two created a passive and torpid mendacity in her writing. The fictive appeared to her not to be fictive, while what the author knew to be sharply factual and salient in real life grew anesthetized as mere content for her storytelling. As she comments in her prologue, which comes to form the cynosure of her narrative intentions in *Cosas*: "Estaba empezando a cansarme de los préstamos que la realidad—mi realidad—concedía a menudo a la ficción—mi ficción—. De disfrazar recuerdos" [I was beginning to grow tired of the borrowings that reality—my reality—often supplied to fiction—my fiction—. Of disguising memories].[3] Faced with a hybridity in her writing that often seemed to betray her intentions, Fernández Cubas sets out in *Cosas* to write a purer form of truth, fettered by the real events of life and sanctioned by her belief in the transparency of her story: "Me propuse así contar únicamente 'la verdad' sobre unos hechos que, curiosamente, tenían mucho que ver con la mentira. No me permití una sola licencia ni el menor aditamento" [I thus proposed to relate only "the truth" about facts which, strangely, had much to do with lying. I did not allow myself the slightest license nor the smallest addition] (12). She labels her work a "libro personal" [personal book] (12) and later a "libro de recuerdos" [book of recollections] (13), thus drawing referential memory to the center of her narrative as impetus for both structure and meaning.

Fernández Cubas's perception of her work links it to the generic traits of autobiography, but not in the traditional sense. While she tells what happened to her in the past in the first person, and while the rendering of details gives to incidents and people portrayed in her work the traditional sense of wholeness associated with autobiography, she eschews perhaps the most critical element of autobiographical narrative: the teleogenic plotting of the story that enables the narrator to move through time from "then" to "now." As a result she conveys no developmental strategy aimed at revealing a self coherently constructed and wholly formed within the text. Still, the purposeful representation of the real (i.e., her desire "to relate only 'the truth'") shapes the narrative from the very beginning and suggests that the self (the "I" of the narrative) will speak itself without the artifice of fiction. Further, Fernández Cubas appears content to allow the language of the text to mirror without mystery or significant encumbrance the narrator's life. In this way, identity may be revealed within a context chosen and occupied by the author/narrator, whose autobiographical signature guarantees the veracity of the life represented.

Fernández Cubas's prologue to *Cosas*, however, serves less as a synopsis of what she plans to do in her narrative than as a meditation on what she has already done. Like most prologues, this one bears the markings of a postscript, written after the narrative is completed as an attempt to define what the author has both intended and achieved. Equally important, it proposes to shape the readers' assumptions and determinations of meaning. The prologue thus prefigures the work from a postnarrative perspective, and is itself prefigured (unlike the main body of the text) by a teleogenic plotting that relates two critical aspects of the author's understanding of her work: 1) her "memory" of her objectives when she began to compose the text, and 2) the transformation of these objectives through her confrontation with writing.

Fernández Cubas explains in the prologue that her initial desire to tell the truth forms part of her recollection of intention. When during the course of writing the prologue she contemplates her text and comments on the outcome of her work, she judges it a failure—a failure rooted not in her attempt to tell something about the past per se but in the ingenuous belief in her ability to recall and mirror the past with referential transparency. And further, a failure that crystallizes not in the author's original desire to speak for herself and thus draw her identity from ambiguity to clarity, but rather in the premise that she could simply reveal a self already there. For in fact, as Fernández Cubas has come to see, it is precisely the act of imagining and constructing the past that defines the self as a corollary and consequence of writing. The past is sutured into a text but not into a whole, thus betraying Fernández Cubas's intention while affirming the contingency, ambiguity, and even deceit of all efforts to write the self as a recollection.

Fernández Cubas's insight (if not epiphany) into the transition from mirroring to constructing grows from her dual role as writer/reader in the prologue. As she gives shape and definition to the past through the act of writing in the main body of the text, she discerns with increasing discomfort that the past (in David Lowenthal's phrase) is indeed a "foreign country."[4] Hence her assuredness turns hesitant, uncertain, and even self-critical. As she writes the prologue (founded largely on the reading of her own narrative) she peels away completely the sheen of mimetic objectivity and questions the adequacy of her discursive and hermeneutic strategy: "El material con el que me enfrentaba se resistía a cualquier clasificación de género. Eran, en apariencia, historias sueltas; retazos de memoria, anécdotas de viajes, fotografías de un álbum caótico que se animaban de repente, respiraban, cobraban vida y, acabada la función, regresaban a su engañosa inmovilidad de tiempo detenido" [The materials that I was dealing with resisted classification by type. They were seemingly random stories; bits of memory, stories about travels, photographs from a chaotic album that suddenly awakened, breathed, gained life and, when the performance ended, returned to their deceitful inertia in time that had stopped] (13–14). In other words, what began as antifiction is transformed not into fiction but into something else. Fernández Cubas is intrigued by the difference of this something else, but cannot lay firm hold of it.

Yet the author remains fully absorbed by her desire to give form and meaning to her reconstruction of time. The vehicles for doing so, however (memory and narration), resist her efforts and spin out of control: "Comprendí entonces que los recuerdos convocados iban más allá del limitado marco que, en mi ingenuidad, les había adjudicado" [I understood then that the memories I had called forth went beyond the limited frame that, in my naiveté, I had af-

forded them] (14). More importantly, she recognizes that the continuity of her discourse turns upon affection rather than action:
"Comprendí también que el orden de sus apariciones no era pro-
ducto del azar o del capricho, ni respondía a deficiencias irremedia-
bles de la memoria. Un viejo reloj de voz cascada se encargaba, con
su tictac defectuoso, de marcar el ritmo. Adelante, atrás, de nuevo
hacia adelante..." [I also understood that the order of their appearance was not the product of happenstance or caprice, nor did it result from irremediable deficiencies of memory. An old clock with a
harsh chime and defective ticktock took charge of marking the
rhythm. Forward, back, forward again . . .] (14). This movement forward and backward in time spawns tiny paroxysms tied less to the
order of her life than to the life of her memory. Fernández Cubas
thus recollects in a way that gives structure but not chronology to
her narrative (except within the fragments of time that form each
story). The continuity that we infer from what appears dispersed and
random stems from a loosely but affectively structured series of
events which enable us to piece together the constructed self.

As I have suggested, Fernández Cubas explains both her writing
and reading of *Cosas* in the prologue, which then serves as a caution-
ary tale for the reader who anticipates encountering in the book
what Fernández Cubas too had once intended for inclusion: the true
and accurate story of the past engendered by her field of memory.
In other words, only four pages into what is announced on the dust
jacket as "el testimonio directo de una vida" [the direct reporting
of a life], we are advised to proceed with care. The questions that
immediately come to mind, of course, relate to authorial intention,
manipulation, and control. For example, what are we able to infer
about the referential validity of the book? Or put another way, is
what Fernández Cubas tells us true? And does it matter? Should we
rely upon what Fernández Cubas writes as author in the prologue or
upon the stories she tells as narrator in the main body of the text?
Are the two distinctly defined parts of the book (prologue and stories) different? Are Fernández Cubas/author and Fernández
Cubas/narrator primarily distinct voices but sometimes blended? To
be sure, the answers do not come easily, in part because of the hy-
brid generic foundation of the narrative, and in part because Fernández Cubas/author/narrator seems perplexed by the reach of her
writing as well as by its limits.

Still, the clues to her thinking are threaded throughout the stories
themselves. At the heart of her narrative lies an ethical (and autobio-

graphical) desire to get things right, but this desire is tempered by her fear that both memory and narration resist her efforts. As she writes the narratives of *Cosas* she explores these countervailing tensions already intimated in the prologue: on the one hand, the intention to be referentially sound as she (re)creates her self in relation to the past; on the other, the realization that to configure her text implies an act of self-endangerment, as memory becomes the shaky ground of her identity.

Fernández Cubas tells fifteen "stories" about her past in *Cosas*, ranging from her trips to South America and Egypt as an adult to her early school years in Barcelona and, later as a teenager, the death of her sister. She varies the tone of her narrative as she recollects the past—sometimes bemused (e.g., her revenge on her sixth-grade teacher for locking her in a closet for misbehaving), other times amazed (e.g., the escape of her friend's sister from a religious cult in Venezuela) or distressed (e.g., the death of her older sister from cancer and the subsequent period of mourning imposed by her mother). The multiplicity of stories and times, however, does not betray the author's compulsion to unity in her narrative. Both her belief in mimetic adequacy and narrative transparency shape the structure of the narrative and enable Fernández Cubas to locate her self in a particular place, sensation, or incident and to scrutinize a time that no longer exists. In effect, she discovers and creates her being by being there, in the past.

As she does this, however, she challenges and even disparages the very methods that enable her to write the past to begin with. In nearly all of her stories the memory design of her writing calls attention to its own logic of incompleteness as the narrator seeks to reconcile memory with experience. It is not a task that comes easily. Indeed, her past is constituted by what she is able to remember, what she convinces herself she remembers, what she has imagined she remembers, and at times what she pretends to remember. What is more, the very awareness of the commingling of these diverse forms of memory not only works its way into her narrative as reflective commentary on the nature of remembering but also as an embodiment of the confounded textuality of memory itself. Her reflections on these matters come to form the underlying meta-discursive content of the form in nearly every one of the stories.

Throughout *Cosas*, Fernández Cubas consistently evokes confusion even as she seeks clarity, and hints at uncertainty when she aspires to truth. This process within her writing is both overt and insidious. For example, when telling one of the stories about her stay in Argentina ("Los regresos") [The Returns], Fernández Cubas recalls her apartment building and many of the residents she came to know there. The story presents several memories over an unspecified period of time (time made ambiguous here more by omission than by imperfect memory), but most importantly, the author confronts the tension between the past captured as a stable source of authenticity and the past confused as an unintended deceit. Fernández Cubas claims that certain sensations of the apartment resonate fully and concisely within her memory ("¡qué fiel resulta la memoria a sabores y olores!") [how accurate memory is for tastes and smells!] (101), but also belies that very memory by recollecting in detail certain features of an apartment that she has never entered. It is not that the detailed description of the apartment lacks precision but rather that her memory of it has been appropriated from a friend: "Sé, lo sabía entonces (probablemente por el señor Ulled), que su vivienda constaba de tres espacios y, aunque nunca estuve en su interior, todavía—falso recuerdo—puedo representármela con cierto detalle. . . . Típico ejemplo de cómo puede crearse un vivo y falso recuerdo. Y ahora me pregunto, ¿cuántas memorias no estarán repletas de falsos recuerdos?" [I know, I knew then (probably from Señor Ulled), that his apartment consisted of three rooms and, though I was never inside it, I can still—a false memory—represent it to myself with a certain amount of detail. . . . Typical example of how a vivid and false memory can be created. And now I ask myself, how many memories may be replete with false recollections?] (99).

Fernández Cubas views her borrowed memory from Señor Ulled with a discerning awareness of its irony, thus enhancing the reliability of her narration by exposing its shortcomings. Further, she places in doubt her relationship with Señor Ulled himself when she first recalls his visit to Barcelona some years later but then realizes that the memory of the visit is not hers at all: "Casi enseguida le vuelvo a ver. De nuevo en el desaparecido Tucumán de la calle Balmes, un par de años después. En realidad yo no estoy allí. Se trata de un recuerdo prestado. Me lo contó Carlos en su momento, pero, por lo que se ve, me caló tan hondo que he terminado por hacerlo mío" [Almost immediately I see him again. Once more at the now closed Tucuman Restaurant on Balmes Street, a few years afterward. In reality, I am not there. It is a borrowed memory. Carlos told it to me at the time, but apparently it struck me so profoundly that I ended up making it mine] (97).

Fernández Cubas's ethical quandary here (imparting the truth about the past while laying bare its amorphousness) is resolved not through shaping the performance of narrative in one way or another to enhance its capacity for realism, or by discovering and regulating the functional modes of memory, but by scrutinizing both time and memory as they relate to the formation of the self. The first-person narrator (author) of *Cosas* understands the contingencies of her project, but she persistently returns to the past as textualized memory bearing the weight of truth (e.g., "La verdad es que, en el momento de escribir estas líneas, tengo que preguntarme una y otra vez si no estaré confundiendo edades o mezclando tiempos. Lo hago únicamente para asegurarme de la veracidad de lo que cuento. Pero sé la respuesta. Era así") [The truth is that, at the time of writing these lines, I must ask myself time and again if I may not be confusing ages and mixing time periods. I ask only to assure myself of the truth of what I am relating. But I know the answer. That's how it was] (224). She knows that she has occasionally plagiarized the memories of others, but promptly sets the record straight, both as an ethical marker of how she views the past and as a practical sanctioning of her own reliability. These concerns then coalesce to define not only her narrative but her life, and therefore, her identity. Fernández Cubas seeks to do justice to the past, and thus to her self, but perceives doing so as fragile and fraught with contradictions. For indeed, her writing in *Cosas* grows from the idea that the accumulation of one's past shapes the self in the present and that the present shapes the meaning of the past.

Recollecting a particular moment in 1962 when she was sixteen years old, Fernández Cubas makes the critical observation concerning this reciprocity: "No me cuesta el menor esfuerzo revivir aquella exaltada tarde que me resisto a calificar de lejana y a la que el tiempo no ha hecho otra cosa que dotar de sentido. Aunque no sea ya el mar lo que aparece ante mis ojos, sino yo, o el recuerdo de lo que yo fui, contemplando el mar" [It takes me little effort to relive that exalted afternoon that I resist labeling as long ago and that time has done nothing other than endow with meaning. Although it is not the sea now that appears before my eyes but rather my self, or the memory of what I was, contemplating the sea] (260). In other words, by locating herself in the track of the past, her present is reoriented by that track while concurrently defining and giving it meaning. Such a process offends against conceptions of unvexed truth and temporal unity, but this is precisely the point. The persistent tension of Fernández Cubas's writing exposes how the elements of time evoked by memory inevitably accrete to fiction—not in the sense that they are lies but rather that they cannot be what they originally were. In the practice of writing, Fernández Cubas actually does nothing to fictionalize her narrative. She retains the right to distinguish between stories that are true and stories that are invented, but the whole of her text belies the distinction as it slowly deliquesces into uncertainty.

It is of course not only memory that confounds Fernández Cubas's desire to draw past and present together, but also the nature of storytelling itself. The author presents a world defined by the stories told about it and embraces the imaginative flight of narrating and reading as vital to the development of her self-identity within these stories. Indeed, the cognitive demand for storytelling is woven throughout the text, from Fernández Cubas's youthful fascination in "Segundo de Bachillerato" [Sixth Grade] with her teacher's "especial habilidad para dejar las frases a medias, para sugerir, insinuar" [special ability to leave sentences hanging, to suggest, to insinuate] (18), to her frustration in "La Muerte cautiva" [Captive Death] with Antonia's constant telling of stories that beguile the children with their apparent transparency soon to be transformed into insidious ambiguity: "La Totó [Antonia] nos embarcaba en sus historias, nos hacía suyas durante horas y horas, y luego en el punto final, se escabullía" [Totó got us involved in her stories, she made us hers for hours and hours, and then at the end, she slipped away] (40).

Fernández Cubas's desire for the sense of an ending in her childhood stories grows from her dual inclination to wrap experience in narration and to constitute her narration with experience—life as story and story as life. But in the practice of writing she finds both to be ontologically slippery. As a teller of tales who seeks to represent the past as material for constructing the self, she comes to embrace the necessity and virtue of contingency rather than rigidity. While writing enables her to traverse the past, to configure it with a desire for completion, she now sees that her writing, "además de un barco, es como un acordeón" [in addition to a ship, is like an accordion] (71). It is constituted by multiple folds that produce an array of sounds as the compressions are tightened and then released. Or in more direct terms, Fernández Cubas knows that she cannot write as if rehearsing the past with a distinct set of structures and procedures always repeatable and thus always the same. Instead, she must balance memory and discourse with truth and fiction, often unable to gain authority over the confounded whole.

When Fernández Cubas sets out to write her own life in *Cosas* she embraces one of the most traditional aspects of storytelling: the distinction between "it was and it was not"—between what occurred and what was invented. She makes the distinction for highly practical reasons rooted in her desire to present the past as a set of serviceable truths. These truths are drawn from memory and cast into language, and then envisioned as a way of revealing the self located in the stories that are told. But as Fernández Cubas eventually understands, the act of remembering and the process of writing, rather than sustaining her intentions, strain resolutely against them. As she writes Fernández Cubas sees the past not as something that she simply went through, later to be memorialized and recorded. To the contrary, the past stands as an absence available through traces in the present, which then must be reconstructed as text and as story. Hence the authorial discomfort that informs her writing from the very beginning gains primacy in the title of her book. While she writes about "cosas que ya no existen" ("things that no longer exist") she also asserts that "Las cosas no dejan de existir mientras quede alguien que las recuerde" [Things do not stop existing as long as there is someone left who remembers them] (242).

Fernández Cubas does not offer her book as a synthesis of these opposing positions, or as support for one side of the conflict or the other, but as an affirmation of how they necessarily coexist in her writing. For in the end, her stories, as with her self, are at once found and constructed. This duality links her writing both to life and to narration and becomes in *Cosas* the content of its form.

NOTES

1. For an overview of recent thinking on how the past is represented in contemporary narrative, particularly in relation to memory, see Peter Middleton and Tim Woods, eds., *Literatures of Memory* (Manchester: Manchester University Press, 2000). For a more general view of time and narrative see Linda Hutcheon, *The Politics of Postmodernism* (London: Routledge, 1989); Andreas Huyssen, *Twilight Memories: Marking Time in a Culture of Amnesia* (New York: Routledge, 1995); and Paul Ricoeur, *Time and Narrative*, trans. Kathleen Blamey and David Pellauer, 3 vols. (Chicago: University of Chicago Press, 1984–1988).

2. Recent work on autobiographical writing has pointed to a number of problems linked to memory, referentiality, and narration. See, for example, Angel Loureiro, *The Ethics of Autobiography* (Nashville, Tenn.: Vanderbilt University Press,

2000); Elizabeth Bruss, *Autobiographical Acts: The Changing Situation of a Literary Genre* (Baltimore: Johns Hopkins University Press, 1976); Paul John Eakin, *Fictions in Autobiography: Studies in the Art of Self-Invention* (Princeton: Princeton University Press, 1985); and James Fernández, *Apology to Apostrophe: Autobiography and the Rhetoric of Self-Representation in Spain* (Durham, N.C.: Duke University Press, 1992).

3. Cristina Fernández Cubas, *Cosas que ya no existen* (Barcelona: Lumen, 2001), 12. Future references to this work are indicated in parentheses in the text.

4. David Lowenthal, *The Past Is a Foreign Country* (Cambridge: Cambridge University Press, 1985).

Bibliography

Works of Cristina Fernández Cubas

El ángulo del horror. Barcelona: Tusquets, 1990.
El año de Gracia. Barcelona: Tusquets, 1985.
El columpio. Barcelona: Tusquets, 1995.
Con Agatha en Estambul. Barcelona: Tusquets, 1994.
Cosas que ya no existen. Barcelona: Lumen, 2001.
Hermanas de sangre. Barcelona: Tusquets, 1998.
Mi hermana Elba y Los altillos de Brumal. 1980 and 1983. Barcelona: Tusquets, 1988.
    Page references are to the 1988 edition.
"Omar, amor." In *Doce relatos de mujeres.* Edited by Ymelda Navajo. Madrid: Alianza,
    1982, 16–20.

English Translations

"The Attics of Brumal." Translated by Phyllis Zatlin. *Short Story International* 80
    (June 1990): 53–75.
"*Blood Sisters.* A Translation to English of Cristina Fernández Cubas's *Hermanas de
    sangre.*" Translated by Karen Denise Dinicola. Masters thesis in translation, Rut-
    gers, The State University of New Jersey, 2002.
"My Sister Elba." Translated by Phyllis Zatlin. *Student Short Story International* 52
    (1993): 45–64.

Films

Brumal. Directed by Cristina Andreu. Screenplay by Cristina Andreu and Cristina
    Fernández Cubas. 1988.
Germanes de sang. Directed by Jesús Garay. Screenplay by Maite Carranza and Teresa
    Vilardell. 2001.
Hermanas de sangre. Directed by Jesús Garay. Screenplay by Maite Carranza and Te-
    resa Vilardell. 2001.

Criticism on Fernández Cubas

Bellver, Catherine G. "*El año de Gracia* and the Displacement of the Word." *Studies
    in Twentieth Century Literature* 16:2 (1992): 221–32.

———. *"El año de Gracia.* El viaje como rito de iniciación." *Explicación de Textos Literarios* 22:1 (1993–94): 3–10.

Bretz, Mary Lee. "Cristina Fernández Cubas and the Recuperation of the Semiotic in *Los altillos de Brumal.*" *Anales de la Literatura Española Contemporánea* 13:3 (1988): 177–88.

Carmona, Vicente, Jeffrey Lamb, Sherry Velasco, and Barbara Zecchi. "Conversando con Mercedes Abad, Cristina Fernández Cubas y Soledad Puértolas: 'Feminismo y literatura no tienen nada que ver.'" *Mester* 20:2 (1991): 157–65.

Ferrán, Ofelia. "'Afuera he dejado el mundo.' Strategies of Silence and Silencing in 'Mundo,' by Cristina Fernández Cubas." *Monographic Review/Revista Monográfica* 16 (2000): 174–89.

Ferriol-Montano, Antonia. "De la paranoia a la ternura: Ironía y humor en la novela española posmoderna de los años ochenta: Eduardo Mendoza, Cristina Fernández Cubas y Luis Landero." Ph.D. diss., Pennsylvania State University, 1999.

Folkart, Jessica A. "Desire, Doubling, and Difference in Cristina Fernández Cubas's *El ángulo del horror.*" *Revista Canadiense de Estudios Hispánicos* 24:2 (Winter 2000): 343–62.

———. *Angles on Otherness in Post-Franco Spain: The Fiction of Cristina Fernández Cubas.* Lewisburg, Pa.: Bucknell University Press, 2002.

Glenn, Kathleen M. "Back to Brumal: Fiction and Film." *Romance Languages Annual* 4 (1992): 460–65.

———. "Gothic Indecipherability and Doubling in the Fiction of Cristina Fernández Cubas." *Monographic Review/Revista Monográfica* 8 (1992): 125–41.

———. "Conversación con Cristina Fernández Cubas." *Anales de la Literatura Española Contemporánea* 18 (1993): 353–63.

———. "Fantastic Doubles in Cristina Fernández Cubas's Tales for Children." In *Visions of the Fantastic: Selected Essays from the Fifteenth International Conference on the Fantastic in the Arts.* Edited by Allienne R. Becker. Westport, Conn.: Greenwood Press, 1996, 57–62.

———. "Narrative Designs in Cristina Fernández Cubas's 'Mundo.'" *Romance Languages Annual* 9 (1997): 501–4.

Gleue, Julie. "The Epistemological and Ontological Implications in Cristina Fernández Cubas's *El año de Gracia.*" *Monographic Review/Revista Monográfica* 8 (1992): 142–56.

Heymann, Jochen, and Montserrat Mullor-Heymann. "Cristina Fernández Cubas." *Retratos de escritorio: Entrevistas a autores españoles.* Frankfurt: Vervuert, 1991, 117–27.

López-Cabrales, María del Mar. "Cristina Fernández Cubas: Los horrores de la memoria." In *Palabras de mujeres: Escritoras españolas contemporáneas.* Madrid: Narcea, 2000, 167–76.

Margenot, John B., III. "Parody and Self-Consciousness in Cristina Fernández Cubas's *El año de Gracia.*" *Siglo XX/Twentieth Century* 11 (1993): 71–87.

Nichols, Geraldine C. "Entrevista a Cristina Fernández Cubas." *España Contemporánea* 6 (1993): 55–71.

Ortega, José. "La dimensión fantástica en los cuentos de Fernández Cubas." *Monographic Review/Revista Monográfica* 8 (1992): 157–63.

Pérez, Janet. "Fernández Cubas, Abjection, and the 'retórica del horror.'" *Explicación de Textos Literarios* 24 (1995–96): 159–71.

———. "Cristina Fernández Cubas: Narrative Unreliability and the Flight from Clarity, or, the Quest for Knowledge in the Fog." *Hispanófila* 122 (January 1998): 29–39.

Pritchett, Kay. "Cristina Fernández Cubas's 'Con Agatha en Estambul': Traveling into Mist and Mystery." *Monographic Review/Revista Monográfica* 12 (1996): 247–57.

Rueda, Ana. "Cristina Fernández Cubas: Una narrativa de voces extinguidas." *Monographic Review/Revista Monográfica* 4 (1988): 257–67.

Spires, Robert C. "Postmodernism/Paralogism: *El ángulo del horror* by Cristina Fernández Cubas." *Journal of Interdisciplinary Literary Studies* 7:2 (1995): 233–45.

Suñén, Luis. "La realidad y sus sombras: Las obras de Rosa Montero y Cristina Fernández Cubas." *Insula* 446 (June 1984): 5.

Talbot, Lynn K. "Journey into the Fantastic: Cristina Fernández Cubas's 'Los altillos de Brumal.'" *Letras Femeninas* 15 (1989): 37–47.

Valls, Fernando. "De las certezas del amigo a las dudas del héroe. Sobre 'La ventana del jardín' de Cristina Fernández Cubas." *Insula* 568 (April 1994): 18–19.

Zatlin, Phyllis. "Tales from Fernández Cubas: Adventure in the Fantastic." *Monographic Review/Revista Monográfica* 3:1–2 (1987): 107–18.

———. "Amnesia, Strangulation, Hallucination and Other Mishaps: The Perils of Being Female in Tales of Cristina Fernández Cubas." *Hispania* 79:1 (March 1996): 36–44.

———. "Beyond the Fantastic: New Tales from Fernández Cubas." In *Hers Ancient and Modern: Women's Writing in Spain and Brazil*. Edited by Catherine Davies and Jane Whetnall. Manchester: University of Manchester Spanish and Portuguese Studies, 1997, 73–86.

OTHER WORKS CITED IN THE ESSAYS

Abel, Lionel. *Metatheatre. A New View of Dramatic Form.* New York: Hill and Wang, 1963.

Adams, Hazard, and Leroy Searle, eds. "Jacques Derrida." *Critical Theory Since 1965.* Tallahasse: Florida State University Press, 1986, 79–136.

Aldecoa, Josefina R. *Historia de una maestra.* Barcelona: Anagrama, 1990.

———. *Mujeres de negro.* Barcelona: Anagrama, 1994.

———. *La fuerza del destino.* Barcelona: Anagrama, 1997.

Alonso de Santos, José Luis. "De la escritura dramática a la escritura cinematográfica." *Cine y Literatura.* Monographic issue incorporating papers from X Ciclo Escritores y Universidad, November 7–December 5, 1995. *República de las Letras* 54 (1997): 77–82.

Anderson, Benedict. *Imagined Communities: Reflections on the Origin and Spread of Nationalism.* 2nd ed. London: Verso, 1991.

Andrew, Dudley. *Concepts in Film Theory.* Oxford: Oxford University Press, 1984.

Armstrong, Karen. *Islam: A Short History.* New York: Modern Library, 2000.

Barthes, Roland. "From Work to Text." In *Textual Strategies: Perspectives in Post-Structuralist Criticism.* Edited by Josué V. Harari. Ithaca: Cornell University Press, 1979, 73–81.

Bauman, Zygmunt. "From Pilgrim to Tourist—or a Short History of Identity." In *Questions of Cultural Identity.* Edited by Stuart Hall and Paul Du Gay. London: Sage, 1996, 18–36.

Becker, Allienne, ed. "Introduction." *Visions of the Fantastic.* Westport, Conn.: Greenwood Press, 1996.

Bloom, Harold. *Poetry and Repression. Revisionism from Blake to Stevens.* New Haven: Yale University Press, 1976.

Brandt, George W., trans. *The Great Stage of the World: An Allegorical Auto Sacramental,* by Pedro Calderón de la Barca. Manchester: Manchester University Press, 1976.

Bretz, Mary Lee. *Encounters Across Borders: The Changing Visions of Spanish Modernism, 1890–1930.* Lewisburg, Pa.: Bucknell University Press, 2001.

Brooker, Peter. *A Concise Glossary of Cultural Theory.* London: Arnold, 1999.

Brooks, Peter. *Reading for the Plot: Design and Intention in Narrative.* New York: Vintage Books, 1984.

———. *Body Work: Objects of Desire in Modern Narrative.* Cambridge: Harvard University Press, 1993.

Bruss, Elizabeth. *Autobiographical Acts: The Changing Situation of a Literary Genre.* Baltimore: Johns Hopkins University Press, 1976.

Butler, Judith. *Gender Trouble: Feminism and the Subversion of Identity.* New York: Routledge, 1990.

———. *Bodies That Matter: On the Discursive Limits of "Sex."* New York: Routledge, 1993.

Campbell, Jan. *Arguing with the Phallus: Feminist, Queer, and Postcolonial Theory. A Psychoanalytic Contribution.* London: Zed Books, 2000.

Cixous, Hélène. "Fiction and Its Phantoms: A Reading of Freud's *Das Unheimliche* (The 'Uncanny')." *New Literary History* 7 (1976): 525–48.

Cixous, Hélène, and Catherine Clément. *The Newly Born Woman.* Translated by Betsy Wing. Minneapolis: University of Minnesota Press, 1986.

Coates, Paul. *The Double and the Other: Identity as Ideology in Post-Romantic Fiction.* New York: St. Martin's Press, 1988.

Crook, Eugene J., ed. *Fearful Symmetry: Doubles and Doubling in Literature and Film. Papers from the Fifth Annual Florida State University Conference on Literature and Film.* Tallahassee: University Presses of Florida, 1982.

Culler, Jonathan. *Structuralist Poetics: Structuralism, Linguistics, and the Study of Literature.* Ithaca: Cornell University Press, 1975.

Dallenbach, Lucien. *Le récit speculaire.* Paris: Seuil, 1977.

Derrida, Jacques. *Of Grammatology.* Translated by Gayatri Chakravorty Spivak. Baltimore: Johns Hopkins University Press, 1974.

Downie, J. A. "Defoe, Imperialism, and the Travel Books Reconsidered." *The Yearbook of English Studies* 13 (1983): 66–83.

Eakin, Paul John. *Fictions in Autobiography: Studies in the Art of Self-Invention.* Princeton: Princeton University Press, 1985.

Felman, Shoshana. "To Open the Question." In *Literature and Psychoanalysis: The Question of Reading: Otherwise.* Edited by Shoshana Felman. Baltimore: Johns Hopkins University Press, 1982, 5–10.

Fernández, James. *Apology to Apostrophe: Autobiography and the Rhetoric of Self-Representation in Spain.* Durham, N.C.: Duke University Press, 1992.

Flood, Gavin. *An Introduction to Hinduism.* Cambridge: Cambridge University Press, 1996.

Freixas, Laura. *Madres e hijas.* Barcelona: Anagrama, 1996.

Freud, Sigmund. "The Relation of the Poet to Day-Dreaming." In *Collected Papers.* Translated under the supervision of Joan Riviere. Edited by Ernest Jones. Vol. 4. London: Hogarth Press and the Institute of Psychoanalysis, 1953, 173–83.

———. "The 'Uncanny.' " In *The Standard Edition of the Complete Psychological Works of Sigmund Freud.* Edited by James Strachey. Vol. 17. London: Hogarth Press, 1955, 217–56.

———. "Mourning and Melancholia." In *The Standard Edition of the Complete Psychological Works of Sigmund Freud.* Edited by James Strachey. Vol. 14. London: Hogarth Press, 1957, 243–58.

———. "Remembering, Repeating and Working-Through." In *The Standard Edition of the Complete Psychological Works of Sigmund Freud.* Edited by James Strachey. Vol. 12. London: Hogarth Press, 1958, 147–56.

———. *The Psychopathology of Everyday Life.* In *The Standard Edition of the Complete Psychological Works of Sigmund Freud.* Edited by James Strachey. Vol. 6. London: Hogarth Press, 1974, 1–279.

———. "Beyond the Pleasure Principle." In *The Standard Edition of the Complete Psychological Works of Sigmund Freud.* Edited by James Strachey. Vol. 18. London: Hogarth Press, 1974; Reprint 1986, 7–64.

Frye, Northrop. *Spiritus Mundi: Essays on Literature, Myth, and Society.* Bloomington: Indiana University Press, 1976.

Fuentes, Carlos. *La muerte de Artemio Cruz.* Mexico, D.F.: Fondo de Cultura Económica, 1962.

Fuss, Diana. *Identification Papers.* New York: Routledge, 1995.

Garber, Marjorie. "The Occidental Tourist: *M. Butterfly* and the Scandal of Transvestism." In *Nationalisms and Sexualities.* Edited by Andrew Parker, Mary Russo, Doris Sommer, and Patricia Yaeger. New York: Routledge, 1992, 121–46.

Girard, René. *Deceit, Desire, and the Novel: Self and Other in Literary Structure.* Translated by Yvonne Freccero. Baltimore: Johns Hopkins University Press, 1965.

Gómez, María Asunción. *Del escenario a la pantalla. La adaptación cinematográfica del teatro español.* Chapel Hill: North Carolina Studies in the Romance Languages and Literatures, 2000.

Graham, Helen, and Jo Labanyi. "Culture and Modernity: The Case of Spain." In

Helen Graham and Jo Labanyi, eds. *Spanish Cultural Studies: An Introduction. The Struggle for Modernity.* Oxford: Oxford University Press, 1995, 1–19.

Gross, Elizabeth. "The Body of Signification." In *Abjection, Melancholia and Love.* Edited by John Fletcher and Andrew Benjamin. London: Routledge, 1990, 80–103.

Hall, Stuart. "Who Needs 'Identity'?" In *Questions of Cultural Identity.* Edited by Stuart Hall and Paul Du Gay. London: Sage, 1996, 1–17.

Harland, Richard. *Superstructuralism. The Philosophy of Structuralism and Post-Structuralism.* London: Methuen, 1987.

Hirsch, Marianne. "A Mother's Discourse: Incorporation and Repetition in *La Princesse de Clèves.*" *Yale French Studies* 62 (1981): 62–87.

Holenstein, Elmar. *Roman Jakobson's Approach to Language.* Bloomington: Indiana University Press, 1976.

Horney, Karen. "The Denial of the Vagina." Reprinted in *Feminine Psychology.* Edited by Howard Kelman. New York: Norton, 1967, 147–61.

"Hotel Pera Palas." www.perapalas.com/English.

Hutcheon, Linda. *A Theory of Parody: The Teachings of Twentieth-Century Art Forms.* New York: Routledge, 1988.

———. *The Politics of Postmodernism.* London: Routledge, 1989.

Huyssen, Andreas. *Twilight Memories: Marking Time in a Culture of Amnesia.* New York: Routledge, 1995.

Ian, Marcia. *Remembering the Phallic Mother: Psychoanalysis, Modernism, and the Fetish.* Ithaca: Cornell University Press, 1993.

Irigaray, Luce. "And the One Doesn't Stir without the Other." Translated by Hélène Vivienne Wenzel. *Signs: Journal of Women in Society and Culture* 7:1 (1981): 60–67.

———. *Speculum of the Other Woman.* Translated by Gillian C. Gill. Ithaca: Cornell University Press, 1985.

Jackson, Rosemary. *Fantasy: The Literature of Subversion.* London: Routledge, 1981.

Jung, C. G., and C. Kerényi. "The Psychological Aspects of the Kore." *Essays on a Science of Mythology.* New York: Bollingen, 1963.

Kaplan, Janet A. *Unexpected Journeys: The Art and Life of Remedios Varo.* New York: Abbeville Press, 1988.

Keppler, Carl F. *The Literature of the Second Self.* Tucson: University of Arizona Press, 1972.

Klein, Melanie. "Early Stages of the Oedipus Conflict." In *The Writings of Melanie Klein.* Vol. 1. New York: Free Press, 1984, 186–98.

Krauss, Wilhelmine. *Das Doppelgängermotiv in der Romantik: Studien zum romantischen Idealismus.* Berlin: E. Ebering, 1930.

Kristeva, Julia. "Le contexte présupposé." *La révolution du langage poétique.* Paris: Seuil, 1974.

———. "Women's Time." *Signs* 7 (1981): 13–35.

———. *Powers of Horror. An Essay on Abjection.* Translated by Leon S. Roudiez. New York: Columbia University Press, 1982.

———. *The Revolution in Poetic Language.* Translated by Margaret Waller. New York: Columbia University Press, 1984.

Labanyi, Jo. "Postmodernism and the Problem of Cultural Identity." In Helen Graham and Jo Labanyi, eds. *Spanish Cultural Studies: An Introduction. The Struggle for Modernity.* Oxford: Oxford University Press, 1995, 396–406.

———. "Narrative in Culture, 1975–1996." In *The Cambridge Companion to Modern Spanish Culture.* Edited by David T. Gies. Cambridge: Cambridge University Press, 1999, 147–62.

———, ed. *Constructing Identity in Contemporary Spain: Theoretical Debates and Cultural Practice.* Oxford: Oxford University Press, 2002.

Lacan, Jacques. *Écrits: A Selection.* Translated by Alan Sheridan. New York: Norton, 1977.

———. *The Four Fundamental Concepts of Psycho-Analysis.* Edited by Jacques-Alain Miller. Translated by Alan Sheridan. New York: Norton, 1981.

Levine, Linda Gould, et al., eds. *Spanish Women Writers: A Bio-Bibliographical Source Book.* Westport, Conn.: Greenwood Press, 1993.

Liddell, H. G., and R. Scott. *Greek-English Lexicon with a Revised Supplement.* Oxford: Clarendon Press, 1996.

Lloyd, Rosemary. "Objects in the Mirror: Gendering the Still Life." *Yearbook of Comparative and General Literature* 49 (2001): 39–55.

Loureiro, Angel. *The Ethics of Autobiography.* Nashville, Tenn.: Vanderbilt University Press, 2000.

Lowenthal, David. *The Past Is a Foreign Country.* Cambridge: Cambridge University Press, 1985.

Lynch, David. *The Image of the City.* Cambridge: MIT Press, 1960.

Marshall, Cynthia. "Psychoanalyzing the Prepsychoanalytic Subject." *PMLA* 117:5 (October 2002): 1207–16.

Martín Gaite, Carmen. *Usos amorosos de la postguerra española.* Barcelona: Anagrama, 1987.

———. *Lo raro es vivir.* Barcelona: Anagrama, 1996.

Matthews, Brander. *The Philosophy of the Short Story.* New York: Longmans, Green, 1901.

May, Charles. *Short Story Theories.* Athens: Ohio University Press, 1976.

McHale, Brian. *Postmodernist Fiction.* New York: Methuen, 1987.

Mendelson, Sara Heller, and Patricia Crawford. *Women in Early Modern England, 1550–1720.* Oxford: Clarendon Press, 1998.

Middleton, Peter, and Tim Woods, eds. *Literatures of Memory.* Manchester: Manchester University Press, 2000.

Minces, Juliette. *The House of Obedience: Women in Arab Society.* 1980. Translated by Michael Pallis. London: Zed Press, 1982.

Miyoshi, Masao. *The Divided Self: A Perspective on the Literature of the Victorians.* New York: New York University Press, 1969.

Montero, Rosa. *Historias de mujeres.* Madrid: Alfaguara, 1995.

Naremore, James, ed. *Film Adaptation*. New Brunswick, N.J.: Rutgers University Press, 2000.

La noche de los cien pájaros. Directed by Rafael Marchent. Screenplay by José Luis Garci and Santiago Moncada. 1975.

O'Connor, Frank. *The Lonely Voice. A Study of the Short Story*. Cleveland, Ohio: World Publishing Co., 1963.

Ong, Walter. *Orality and Literacy: The Technologizing of the Word*. London: Methuen, 1982.

Parker, Andrew, Mary Russo, Doris Sommer, and Patricia Yaeger, eds. *Nationalisms and Sexualities*. New York: Routledge, 1992.

Parker, Rozsika. *Torn in Two: The Experience of Maternal Ambivalence*. London: Virago, 1995.

Prince, Morton. *The Dissociation of a Personality: A Biographical Study in Abnormal Psychology*. New York: Longmans, Green, 1908.

Rank, Otto. *Don Juan: Une étude sur le double*. Paris: Denöel et Steele, 1932.

———. "The Double as Immortal Self." *Beyond Psychology*. New York: Dover Publications, 1958.

———. *The Double: A Psychoanalytic Study*. Translated and edited with an introduction by Harry Tucker, Jr. Chapel Hill: University of North Carolina Press, 1971.

Rich, Adrienne. *Of Woman Born: Motherhood as Experience and Institution*. New York: Norton, 1976.

Richardson, Nathan E. *Postmodern "Paletos": Immigration, Democracy, and Globalization in Spanish Narrative and Film, 1950–2000*. Lewisburg, Pa.: Bucknell University Press, 2002.

Ricoeur, Paul. *Time and Narrative*. Translated by Kathleen Blamey and David Pellauer. 3 Vols. Chicago: University of Chicago Press, 1984–1988.

Rogers, Robert. *A Psychoanalytic Study of the Double in Literature*. Detroit, Mich.: Wayne State University Press, 1970.

Rueda, Ana. *Relatos desde el vacío: Un nuevo espacio crítico para el cuento actual*. Madrid: Orígenes, 1992.

Said, Edward W. *Orientalism*. New York: Vintage, 1979.

"Saint Macarius the Great of Egypt." www.roca.org.

Salom, Jaime. *La noche de los cien pájaros/ Los delfines*. Madrid: Espasa-Calpe, 1973.

Scholes, Robert E. *Fabulation and Metafiction*. Urbana: University of Illinois Press, 1979.

Sedgwick, Eve Kosofsky. *The Coherence of Gothic Conventions*. New York: Methuen, 1986.

Seger, Linda. *The Art of Adaptation: Turning Fact and Fiction into Film*. New York: Holt, 1992.

Smith, Wilfred Cantwell. *On Understanding Islam*. The Hague, Netherlands: Mouton Publishers, 1981.

Spires, Robert C.. *Post-Totalitarian Spanish Fiction*. Columbia: University of Missouri Press, 1996.

Sprengnether, Madelon. *The Spectral Mother: Freud, Feminism, and Psychoanalysis.* Ithaca: Cornell University Press, 1990.

Thigpen, Corbett H., and Hervey M. Cleckley. *The Three Faces of Eve.* New York: McGraw-Hill, 1957.

Todorov, Tzvetan. *The Fantastic: A Structural Approach to a Literary Genre.* Translated by Richard Howard. Ithaca: Cornell University Press, 1975.

———. *The Poetics of Prose.* Ithaca: Cornell University Press, 1977.

Tusquets, Esther. *El mismo mar de todos los veranos.* Barcelona: Lumen, 1978.

———. *El amor es un juego solitario.* Barcelona: Lumen, 1979.

———. *Varada tras el último naufragio.* Barcelona: Lumen, 1980.

———. *La reina de los gatos.* Barcelona: Lumen, 1993.

Tymms, Ralph. *Doubles in Literary Psychology.* Cambridge: Bowes & Bowes, 1949.

Valbuena Prat, Ángel, ed. Edición, prólogo y notas. *Autos Sacramentales I. La cena del Rey Baltasar, El gran teatro del mundo, La vida es sueño.* By Pedro Calderón de la Barca. 6th ed. Madrid: Espasa-Calpe, 1972.

Watkins, Susan. *Twentieth-Century Women Novelists: Feminist Theory into Practice.* New York: Palgrave, 2000.

Waugh, Patricia. *Metafiction: The Theory and Practice of Self-Conscious Fiction.* London: Methuen, 1984.

Wright, Nathalia. "Characters and Types." 1949. In *Critical Essays on Herman Melville's Moby Dick.* Edited by Brian Higgins and Hershel Parker. New York: G.K. Hall, 1992, 310–15.

Žižek, Slavoj. *The Metastases of Enjoyment: Six Essays on Woman and Causality.* New York: Verso, 1994.

Contributors

CATHERINE G. BELLVER, a graduate of the University of California at Berkeley, is Professor of Spanish at the University of Nevada, Las Vegas. Her research focuses on the Generation of 27 and on post–Civil War narrative by women. She has published a book on Juan José Domenchina and another on exile in the poetry of Rafael Alberti. Her most recent book, *Absence and Presence* (Lewisburg: Bucknell University Press, 2001), studies the work of Spanish women poets of the twenties and thirties. Professor Bellver has also written numerous articles, many book contributions, and scores of reviews.

SILVIA BERMÚDEZ is Associate Professor of Iberian and Latin American Studies at the University of California Santa Barbara. She is the author of *Las dinámicas del deseo: subjetividad y lenguaje en la poesía española contemporánea* (1997) and coeditor of the volume entitled *From Stateless Nations to Postnational Spain/De naciones sin estado a la España postnacional* (2002). She has published numerous articles on contemporary Spanish literatures and cultures and Latin American poetic discourses. Forthcoming is her *La esfinge de la escritura: la poesía ética de Blanca Varela* (2005), and she is currently completing *Madre no hay más que una: maternidad y escritura en las narradoras españolas contemporáneas.*

MARYELLEN BIEDER is Professor of Spanish and Adjunct Professor of Comparative Literature at Indiana University, Bloomington. She has written extensively on questions of narrative voice, gender construction, and the subversion of plot conventions in Emilia Pardo Bazán and other Spanish women writers in the late nineteenth and early twentieth centuries. She has also published numerous articles on gender and narrative voice in Carmen de Burgos and Mercè Rodoreda. Her most recent work explores issues of gender, language, and nationality in the narratives of Carme Riera, Cristina Fernández Cubas, Juan Marsé, and Manuel Vázquez Montalbán.

KATHLEEN M. GLENN has published articles on a number of contemporary Spanish writers, including Cristina Fernández Cubas, Carmen Martín Gaite, José María Merino, Carme Riera, and Mercè Rodoreda. She is coeditor of *Spanish Women Writers and the Essay: Gender, Politics, and the Self* (1998), *Moveable Margins: The Narrative Art of Carme Riera* (Bucknell University Press, 1999), *Women's Narrative and Film in Twentieth-Century Spain* (2002), and *Carmen Martín Gaite: Cuento de nunca acabar/Never-Ending Story* (2003).

DAVID K. HERZBERGER is Professor of Spanish and Comparative Literature and head of the Department of Modern and Classical Languages at the University of Connecticut. He is the author of books on Juan Benet and Jesús Fernández Santos, and of *Narrating the Past: Fiction and Historiography in Postwar Spain* (1995). He has also coedited two books on modern Spanish literature. He serves on the editorial board of several journals; his major field of research is the novel and theater of contemporary Spain.

JOHN B. MARGENOT III is Professor of Spanish at Providence College. He is the author of *Zonas y sombras: aproximaciones a Región de Juan Benet* (1991), a Cátedra edition of *Saúl ante Samuel* (1994), and editor of *Juan Benet: A Critical Reappraisal of his Fiction* (1996). He has also published essays on modern Spanish literature in journals such as *Ínsula, Letras Peninsulares, Modern Language Studies, Ojáncano, Romance Notes, Siglo XX/Twentieth Century,* and *Symposium,* among others.

JANET PÉREZ has published some eighty-five articles and chapters in books on women writers in Spanish, Portuguese, Catalan, and Gallego (including women from Mexico, Puerto Rico, and Latina writers in the United States), and has contributed some 130 entries on Spanish women writers to reference works. Fifteen theses and dissertations on Spanish women writers have been completed or are in progress under her direction. Among her fifteen books authored, edited, or coedited are five dealing solely or significantly with Spanish women writers: *Ana María Matute* (1971), *Women Writers of Contemporary Spain* (1988), *Modern and Contemporary Spanish Women Poets* (1996), *Novelistas femeninas de la postguerra española* (ed., 1983), *Dictionary of the Literature of the Iberian Peninsula* (coeditor, 1993), and *Feminist Encyclopedia of Spanish Literature* (coed., 2002).

ANA RUEDA (Ph.D. Vanderbilt) is Professor of Peninsular Spanish Literature at the University of Kentucky. She works on eighteenth-, nineteenth-, and twentieth-century literature, especially genre studies (short story, novel, epistolarity, drama, travel writing); interdisciplinary approaches to literature; and women's writing. *Relatos desde el vacío: Un nuevo espacio crítico para el cuento actual* (1992) explores the short story in Spain from 1970 to 1985. *La agenda negra* (2001), a collection of short stories, is her personal contribution to the genre. *Pigmalión y Galatea: Refracciones modernas de un mito* (1998) provides an interdisciplinary and comparative study of this self-reflexive myth of the artist. *Cartas sin lacrar: La novela epistolar y la España Ilustrada, 1789–1840* (2001) offers the first comprehensive study of a previously forgotten genre.

ELIZABETH SCARLETT was born and raised in Brooklyn, New York. After receiving her doctorate from Harvard University, she joined the faculty of the University of Virginia, and published *Under Construction: The Body in Spanish Novels,* which was selected as a *Choice* Outstanding Academic Book for 1995. Since 1998 she has been on the faculty of the State University of New York at Buffalo, where she is currently Associate Professor. With Howard B. Wescott she edited *Convergencias Hispánicas: Selected Proceedings and Other Essays on Spanish and Latin American Literature, Film, and Linguistics* (2001). She is the author of articles and book chapters on modern through postmodern Spanish literature and culture, with publications that deal with feminist and film theory, Rosalía de Castro, Mercè Rodoreda, Rosa Chacel, Javier Marías, Luis Buñuel, Benito Pérez Galdós, José Cadalso, Camilo José Cela, and Antonio Machado.

AKIKO TSUCHIYA is Associate Professor of Spanish at Washington University in St. Louis and the Peninsular Editor of the *Revista de Estudios Hispánicos.* She is the author of a book on Galdós and has published widely on nineteenth-century Spanish narrative, as well as on women writers of the post-Franco era. She is presently at work on a book manuscript entitled "Marginal Subjectivities: Gender and Deviance in Nineteenth-Century Spain."

NANCY VOSBURG, unlike some of her northern colleagues who might be afflicted by the "desire to be other in another/'s place" during the cruel winter months, feels perfectly at home in DeLand, Florida, where she is Professor of Modern Languages and Literatures at Stetson University. Vosburg teaches courses in Peninsular Literature and Culture, and in the Women and Gender Studies Program. She is the author of several articles on Spanish women writers in exile (Rodoreda, León, O'Neill) and contemporary Castilian and Catalan women writers, and is coeditor of *The Garden Across the Border: Mercè Rodoreda's Fiction* (1993).

PHYLLIS ZATLIN is Professor of Spanish at Rutgers, The State University of New Jersey. Her areas of specialization include contemporary Spanish theater, narrative, and film; translation studies, and crosscultural approaches to theater. She is editor of the translation series ESTRENO Contemporary Spanish Plays and is author of numerous books and scholarly articles. She has translated several short stories by Cristina Fernández Cubas and has published three articles devoted to this author. Her most recent book is *The Novels and Plays of Eduardo Manet: An Adventure in Multiculturalism* (2000). She is currently preparing a book-length study of theatrical translations/transformations.

Index

225